King of
Bollywood

Shah Rukh Khan

and the Seductive World of Indian Cinema

ANUPAMA CHOPRA

NEW YORK BOSTON

Warner Books
Hachette Book Group USA
237 Park Avenue
New York, NY 10017

Visit our Web site at www.HachetteBookGroupUSA.com.

Printed in the United States of America

First Edition: August 2007
10 9 8 7 6 5 4 3 2 1

Library of Congress Cataloging-in-Publication Data
Chopra, Anupama.
King of Bollywood : Shah Rukh Khan and the seductive world of Indian cinema / Anupama Chopra.—1st ed.
p. cm.
Includes index.
ISBN-13: 978-0-446-57858-5
ISBN-10: 0-446-57858-4
1. Khan, Shah Rukh. 2. Motion picture actors and actresses—India—Biography. I. Title.
PN2888.K48C46 2007
791.4302'8092—dc22

[B] 2006033943

For Agni and Zuni,

my sun and my moon,

and

Vinod

Acknowledgments

This book was born in the summer of 2003, when I first spoke to Shah Rukh Khan about writing a book on him. He hesitated and said that he didn't think he deserved it. I persisted and convinced him otherwise. First and foremost, I would like to thank him for his affection and support, his patience with my badgering over the next four years, and his generosity with the only thing he doesn't have: time.

Over the years, many other people helped to give this project a shape. I would like to thank Karan Johar and the crew at Dharma Productions, Fawzan Husain, Rahul Nanda, Joy Datta, Savitha Narayanan, Dinesh Raheja, Jitendra Kothari, Raeshem Nijhon, Rakesh and Preeti Maria, Ram Madhwani, S. Hussain Zaidi, Arun Katiyar, Shankar Aiyar, Sheela Raval, Jitesh Pillai, Kiran Rao, Kishore Lulla, Alice Coehlo at Eros, Faizal Sharif, Krishna Desai, Shankra Pillai, Mihiri Kanjirath, Sujoy Das and Rajesh Sharma at the *India Today* library, and the crew at Vinod Chopra Films.

I would like to especially thank Nasreen Munni Kabir for her support and Leo Mirani for his invaluable help with research.

I would like to thank Suketu Mehta for introducing me to my wonderful agent Anna Ghosh. I would like to thank Anna for her encouragement and unstinting support. She made this possible. I would also like to thank my editors at Warner Books, Devi Pillai and Natalie Kaire.

I would like to thank my husband Vidhu Vinod Chopra for his patience with papers strewn around the bedroom and keyboard sounds at 5 A.M., and for always putting things in perspective with a lewd Punjabi joke.

I would like to thank my parents, Navin and Kamna Chandra, and my sister Tanuja. And finally, I would like to thank my brother Vikram Chandra, who is my first reader and guide.

Contents

Cast of Characters, in Order of Appearance

AMITABH BACHCHAN: Bollywood's most enduring superstar. Through the 1970s and 1980s, he was known as the One Man Industry. At sixty-plus, he continues to be a box office draw.

NASREEN MUNNI KABIR: London-based documentary filmmaker who has, since 1986, made over eighty documentaries on Hindi cinema and written several books on the subject.

DHUNDIRAJ GOVIND PHALKE: India's first feature filmmaker.

MAHESH BHATT: A prominent filmmaker best known for making raw, confessional cinema inspired by his own turbulent life.

JAWAHARLAL NEHRU: India's first prime minister.

PRITHVIRAJ KAPOOR: A statuesquely handsome man from Peshawar who became a leading actor in the 1930s and 1940s. He spawned a dynasty of actors and filmmakers.

DILIP KUMAR: A consummate actor from the 1950s–1960s, famous as the "Tragedy King." His understated acting style influenced a generation of actors, including Amitabh Bachchan.

MEER TAJ MOHAMMAD: Shah Rukh's father.

GHULAM MOHAMMAD GAMMA: Shah Rukh's uncle.

KHAN ABDUL GHAFFAR KHAN: Also called Frontier Gandhi, Khan sustained an Islamic non-violent movement and was closely allied to Mahatma Gandhi. Shah Rukh's father and uncle were followers of Khan.

KANHAIYA LAL POSWAL: Meer's closest friend.

DEV ANAND: An actor-filmmaker who defined style and panache through the 1950s–1970s.

BIMAL ROY: One of Bollywood's greatest directors, who created several definitive films during the 1950s and 1960s.

GURU DUTT: One of India's finest filmmakers, he created hauntingly poetic, angst-ridden dramas of love and longing in an increasingly materialistic world. In 1964, Dutt committed suicide. He was only 39.

MEHBOOB KHAN: Known as the Cecil B. DeMille of India, Khan made *Mother India* in 1957. The watershed film about a peasant woman who single-handedly raises two sons became the first Hindi film to win an Oscar nomination.

RAJ KAPOOR: Prithviraj's eldest son and legendary actor-filmmaker.

K. ASIF: The director of the epic romantic drama *Mughal-e-Azam* (the Great Mughal), considered one of Hindi cinema's watershed films.

SURINDER KAPOOR: One of K. Asif's assistants who befriended Meer in Mumbai. He later became a producer himself.

FATIMA: Shah Rukh's mother.

SHAHNAZ LALA RUKH: Shah Rukh's sister.

MUMTAZ: A leading actress from the 1960s.

RAJESH KHANNA: Considered Hindi cinema's first superstar, Khanna held the nation in thrall in the late 1960s and early 1970s.

JAVED AKHTAR: A renowned writer and poet who, along with partner Salim Khan, was instrumental in creating Amitabh Bachchan's Angry Young Man persona in the 1970s.

AMRITA SINGH: Shah Rukh's friend in Delhi who then moved to Mumbai and became a leading actress in the 1990s.

GABBAR SINGH: The murderous bandit in the film *Sholay* (Embers), widely considered one of the greatest Hindi films of all time.

DHARMENDRA: A robustly handsome man who came from a village in Punjab and established himself as a hero in the 1960s. His two sons are also famous actors.

BROTHER ERIC D'SOUZA: A priest and teacher at Shah Rukh's school who was a seminal influence in his life.

VIVEK KHUSHALANI: Shah Rukh's close friend and a founder-member of their school posse called the C-Gang.

RAMAN SHARMA: Shah Rukh's close friend and a founder-member of their school posse called the C-Gang.

MANI KAUL: A famously esoteric art house director who was one of the earliest to cast Shah Rukh.

BARRY JOHN: The founder-director of the Theater Action Group (TAG) in Delhi, he was Shah Rukh's first and only acting teacher.

BENNY THOMAS: Shah Rukh's friend and co-actor in TAG.

DIVYA SETH: Shah Rukh's friend and co-actor in TAG, who later became a famous television actress.

RITURAJ: TAG's favored leading man, who later became a famous television actor.

SANJOY ROY: Shah Rukh's friend from his theater days in Delhi. Sanjoy was the executive director of the Theater Action Group.

PRADIP KRISHEN: A filmmaker-author who cast Shah Rukh in his first film, *In Which Annie Gives It Those Ones.*

ARUNDHATI ROY: Renowned author and activist who wrote and acted in *Annie.* In 1997, Roy won the Man Booker Prize for her first novel, *The God of Small Things.*

SATYAJIT RAY: Legendary filmmaker who established Indian art house cinema with his seminal first film *Pather Panchali* (Song of the Road, 1955).

MRINAL SEN: A leading figure in the Indian art house movement, Sen is credited with having made the first Hindi non-mainstream film, *Bhuvan Shome* (Mr. Shome), in 1969.

SHYAM BENEGAL: A leading filmmaker in the Indian art house movement.

GOVIND NIHALANI: Benegal's cinematographer, who also became a leading art house director.

GAURI CHIBBA: Shah Rukh's girlfriend and, later, wife.

RAMESH CHIBBA: Gauri's father.

TEJINDER TIWARI: Gauri's uncle.

RAMESH SIPPY: The director of *Sholay*.

COLONEL RAJ KAPOOR: An army man who segued into films and television. He directed the popular television show *Fauji* (Soldier), which starred Shah Rukh as an army man.

LEKH TANDON: A successful film and television director who was among the earliest to cast Shah Rukh in a television serial.

SAVITA CHIBBA: Gauri's mother.

NEERU TIWARI: Gauri's aunt.

VIKRANT CHIBBA: Gauri's brother.

KUNDAN SHAH: Best known for his cult classic *Jaane Bhi Do Yaaro* (Who Pays the Piper), Shah directed Shah Rukh in television serials as well as one film.

SAEED MIRZA: An art house film director.

AZIZ MIRZA: Saeed's brother, who was like a surrogate father to Shah Rukh in Mumbai. He also directed him in television serials and films.

HAROON MIRZA: Aziz's son, who was Shah Rukh's confidant when he first moved to Mumbai.

ASHUTOSH GOWARIKER: An actor who co-starred with Shah Rukh in his earliest films and serials. He switched tracks to direction and made the Oscar-nominated *Lagaan* (Land Tax).

KETAN MEHTA: An art house film director who made *Maya Memsaab*, a remake of *Madame Bovary*, starring Shah Rukh.

AAMIR KHAN: The son of a famous producer, Aamir joined films four years before Shah Rukh and became a huge star.

SALMAN KHAN: A successful but controversy-dogged star, Salman, along with Shah Rukh and Aamir, formed the Khan triumvirate. The three actors enjoyed an unchallenged run at the box office through the 1990s and early 2000s.

ANWAR KHAN: Shah Rukh's secretary/agent. He died in 2000.

VIVECK VASWANI: An actor-producer who befriended and fiercely marketed Shah Rukh in the early 1990s.

RAJIV MEHRA: A director who made two films with Shah Rukh.

RAJ KANWAR: He directed Shah Rukh's Bollywood film debut, *Deewana*, which was an instant success.

RAKESH ROSHAN: A blue-chip filmmaker who directed films with Shah Rukh.

JUHI CHAWLA: A leading actress who played Shah Rukh's love interest in several films. She was also a partner in his production company.

SUBHASH GHAI: A leading filmmaker who made several films with Shah Rukh.

NISHI PREM: A prominent film journalist who was the first to write about Shah Rukh extensively when he moved to Mumbai.

KEITH D'COSTA: A film journalist.

ABBAS MUSTAN: Brothers who directed films in tandem, with one finishing the other's sentences.

YASH CHOPRA: Bollywood's most successful and enduring filmmaker.

B. R. CHOPRA: Yash's elder brother and a leading filmmaker.

ADITYA CHOPRA: Yash's elder son, who was instrumental in transforming their production house into a globally recognized brand.

KARAN JOHAR: A second-generation Bollywood filmmaker who directed some of Shah Rukh's most successful films.

YASH JOHAR: Karan's father and a leading Bollywood producer who died in 2004.

SOORAJ BARJATYA: A third-generation filmmaker who set the family-values tone of the 1990s cinema with his monstrously successful films.

PRAHLAD KAKKAR: One of India's top commercial directors who made several ad films with Shah Rukh.

AISHWARYA RAI: A former Miss World who became an A-list actress.

GULSHAN KUMAR: A prominent entrepreneur who became the Audio King of India but was shot down in an alley by the infamous Mumbai mafia.

ABU SALEM: A mafia don who terrorized Bollywood with extortion threats and murders through the late 1990s.

DAWOOD IBRAHIM KASKAR: Mumbai's most powerful mafia don, who is alleged to have orchestrated the horrific bomb blasts in the city in 1993.

RAKESH MARIA: A leading Mumbai police officer who investigated the bomb-blast case.

MOHAN BHISE: Shah Rukh's security guard.

CHHOTA SHAKEEL: A top player in Dawood's D-Company gang.

SANTOSH SIVAN: A regarded cinematographer-director who worked with Shah Rukh on several films.

HRITHIK ROSHAN: Rakesh Roshan's son, who enjoyed a stratospheric rise to stardom after his blockbuster debut film, *Kaho Naa . . . Pyaar Hai* (Say You Love Me).

SANJAY LEELA BHANSALI: A major Bollywood director known for his opulent, operatic cinematic style.

BHARAT SHAH: A leading financier and distributor of Hindi films, Bharat was also known as Mr. Moneybags.

NAZIM RIZVI: A small-time producer who was arrested along with Bharat Shah for having dealings with the mafia.

King of
Bollywood

Bollywood Dreams

Dreams come true in Dalton. The small, unimposing town in Georgia, mostly known as the carpet capital of the world, is a setting for miracles. Bhavesh Sheth knows that.

Bhavesh, a portly, spectacled man with curly hair and an eager manner, stands out in Dalton. He is among the handful of Indians living there; only 2 percent of the town's 27,912 residents are Asian. Many of these are doctors, but Bhavesh is in the motel business. His father, Ramesh, runs a Super 8 Motel located near the Dalton Convention Center. It is a family business. Ramesh is the general manager and Bhavesh the assistant manager. Their wives also help to manage the two-star, 102-unit motel.

Bhavesh has never lived in India. His father emigrated in the early 1970s, and Bhavesh was born in Canada in 1974. Ramesh went where there was work. Bhavesh grew up in Detroit, Houston, and Tennessee. He visited India with his parents when money and time permitted. But in 1999, in accordance with his parents' wishes, Bhavesh had an arranged marriage with Tejal, a girl born and brought up in Gujarat.

Like millions of Indians across the world, Bhavesh connected with India through Hindi films. His parents watched them regularly, usually on video. The grainy pirated prints couldn't take away from the power of these fantasies. Each time Amitabh Bachchan died artfully on-screen, Bhavesh, only nine, wept copious tears. Ramesh assured him that India's most enduring superstar was only "faking it." As he grew older, Bhavesh continued to watch Hindi films avidly. Tejal was also a fan. Their son Kishan, born in 2002, was seduced by song-and-dance before he could talk. So when Temptation 2004, a Bollywood rock concert performed by some of Mumbai's leading actors, came to the Gwinnett Center in Atlanta, there was little choice. Bhavesh cashed in his birthday and marriage anniversary gifts and bought tickets at $150 each. By the time he called, the best seats at $200 were already sold out.

Temptation was a typically Bollywood blend of actors lip-synching popular songs and dance performances interspersed with comedy routines and fan interactions. It featured six leading stars, each enacting a different temptation. The biggest draw was superstar Shah Rukh Khan. The two-month-long tour was sold out in sixteen cities across Europe, the United Kingdom, the United States, and Canada. Each venue, with seating ranging from 7,000 to 20,000, was packed. The most expensive tickets were between $300 and $400, but the steep prices did not deter fans. In Toronto, so many people were turned away from the gargantuan Air Canada Centre, which seats 19,800, that a second show had to be organized three days later. In London, two shows were done back to back. In Antwerp, the hall was packed with immigrants. These were

Indians who had immigrated to Holland via its erstwhile colony Suriname, where Indians were shipped between 1873 and 1916 as indentured labor. Being several generations removed from India had not diminished their passion for Bollywood.

It was, as filmmaker Nasreen Munni Kabir documented in her film *The Outer World of Shah Rukh Khan*, Elvis-level hysteria. Fans speaking in thick American accents kept vigil in hotel lobbies at 2 A.M. to catch a glimpse of their favorite star. At the shows, weeping girls screamed, "We love you, Shah Rukh Khan!" Local organizers said they were refusing $2,000 offers for backstage passes. *Time* magazine's Asian edition, which featured Shah Rukh on the cover of the *Asia's Heroes* special issue the following month, reported that Shah Rukh's bodyguard, a burly bald man with two teenage daughters, had so many offers of sex in exchange for access that it had become "disturbing" for him.

On September 3, 13,000 people filled the cavernous arena at Gwinnett Center to capacity. Bhavesh, Tejal, Kishan, and Bhavesh's brother Rupesh drove in from Dalton. Bhavesh was carrying a printout from Yahoo! Maps in his pocket. When Tejal asked him why he was holding on to the piece of paper, Bhavesh replied, "You never know. I might go onstage and meet Shah Rukh Khan. Then I'll get an autograph for Kishan." A week before the concert, Bhavesh had told Tejal that he had a dream that he was dancing onstage with Shah Rukh. Tejal had laughed and remarked that there was no way that was going to happen.

They were seated twelve rows away from the stage. As part of the act, Shah Rukh selected two audience members to do a routine with him. A girl who had won a raffle contest was called first. Then Shah Rukh announced that he was looking for a man who could dance. Something came over Bhavesh.

He told Tejal that he had a crazy idea that was likely to embarrass her. Tejal, by then giddy with the glamour, said she didn't care. So Bhavesh, who weighs 200 pounds and is five foot nine inches tall, stood on his seat and started to do the *Bhangra*, a robust North Indian dance. Shah Rukh pointed at him and said, "You, over there, come onstage."

The realization that he was actually going to dance on a stage with Shah Rukh Khan didn't sink in immediately. Bhavesh stood still on his chair, confused. Was Shah Rukh calling to him or someone else? Tejal yelled, "Go before they call someone else!" Bhavesh ran. His legs were moving, but his mind wasn't fully alert. He was in shock. Bhavesh clambered up onstage, panting, holding his heart, overcome by the intensity of emotions rushing through him. Tejal thought he was going to start crying.

When Shah Rukh handed him the mike, Bhavesh said, "I had a dream seven days ago that I would dance in Atlanta with Shah Rukh Khan. I swear to God. My wife wouldn't believe me. She said, 'You're crazy, Bhavesh.' I said, 'Goddamnit, it's going to happen.'" Shah Rukh listened with the indulgent smile of a much-loved deity and replied, "I'm very touched, but as a guy you should be dreaming of naked women." Then Bhavesh mumbled, "I must do this; don't get insulted." And in the ultimate Indian gesture of reverence and respect, one reserved for family elders and men of God, Bhavesh bent down and touched Shah Rukh Khan's feet.

Bhavesh spent almost thirty minutes onstage with Shah Rukh. They performed a popular dance routine from the film *Devdas* together. Shah Rukh asked if there was anything in particular Bhavesh wanted. Tejal's birthday was coming up so Bhavesh requested that Shah Rukh wish her a Happy Birthday. Bhavesh also got him to sign the map for Kishan, who was sleeping by then. As the grand finale, Shah Rukh gifted Bhavesh with an autographed bottle of Johnnie Walker Black Label whiskey and a round-trip ticket to any destination in the world.

Those moments at Gwinnett Center marked Bhavesh. He became "the man who danced with Shah Rukh Khan." Bhavesh felt that he had been touched in a special way. "It is one of the biggest highlights of my life," Bhavesh said, "right after the birth of my son and my marriage."

Indians suffer from a particularly virulent case of movie madness. India is the largest film producer in the world, making 800-odd movies a year. Of these, nearly 200 come from Mumbai, formerly known as Bombay. They range from shoddy quickies made on threadbare budgets in twenty days to epics that feature as many stars as costume changes.

In a country mired in poverty, crowds, and oppressive heat, each day some 15 million people troop into over 12,500 cinemas to watch a movie. The demand for tickets outstrips the supply to the point that scalpers, or "black market" men, are as ubiquitous at theaters as popcorn. They shuffle near the theater entrance, muttering the increased price of the much-wanted ticket. The venue itself can differ dramatically. Large cities such as Mumbai and Delhi have ultra-plush multiplexes where uniformed servers bring caramelized popcorn to velvet seats. Villages make do with stiflingly hot tent cinemas where the audience sits on the floor and the projectionist manually rewinds the film. But the movie will nearly always be the same: an extravaganza of song and dance, in which romance, melodrama, comedy, tragedy, and action are blended, sometimes skillfully and as often clumsily, to create a unique *masala* mix.

The audience's involvement with the frames flickering

on-screen is passionate, noisy, and sometimes aggressive. So viewers will applaud loudly when a star makes his first entry or when a line of dialogue is particularly pleasing. They will sing along with songs and sometimes even throw coins at the screen and dance in the aisles. A successful film in India is one that has a "repeat audience," that is an audience who watches the same film many times. Some blockbusters have run consecutively for five, even ten years. Spectators are not looking for realism in the Western sense of the word. Instead they want spectacle—a larger-than-life drama.

Classical Indian aestheticians advocated the mixing of *bhavas,* or emotional states, in drama. The Hindi film unapologetically mixes genres, locations, style, and tone. In Bollywood anything is possible. So the sweaty tension of a murder mystery might be broken by a fantasy sequence in which the hero or heroine dreams of gamboling on Swiss hilltops. A separate comedy track can interrupt the main plot at random intervals. The hero can, without extensive effort or injury, fight ten men and emerge victorious. The heroine will wear trendy mini-skirts and perform a seductive dance number but remain a virgin till the end titles roll. Characters and homes are impeccably groomed. Even those meant to be poor exude a carefully constructed frayed glamour. There are only two rules: There must be love and there must be songs.

Songs are the living heart of popular Hindi film. Music has traditionally been part of the Indian narrative. The great Indian epics, the *Mahabharata* and the *Ramayana*, were written in verse. *Mirch Kattika*, a 3,000-year-old Sanskrit play, had narrative interspersed with songs. Bollywood form originates in theater: the high classical traditions, Urdu-Parsi theater, and folk forms such as street theater, all of which use music and song as part of the dramatic experience. Music in cinema is a logical progression.

In the 1930s and 1940s, it wasn't unusual for films to have as many as forty songs. *Indrasabha* or *The Court of God Indra*, made in 1932, had seventy-one songs. But by the 1950s songs had dropped down to less than ten per film. Most Bollywood films average six. These songs permeate and punctuate South Asian lives around the globe. They are played at weddings, parties, nightclubs, religious ceremonies. A popular Indian way to "do time pass," or kill time, is to play *Antakshari*, a game that involves singing film songs. Until the 1970s, practically the only pop music tradition that existed was film music. In India, film stars are also rock stars.

Bollywood plots are overwrought but uncomplicated. Hindi films are largely morality plays with actors inhabiting archetypes. The earliest Indian films were mythological; India's first filmmaker, Dhundiraj Govind Phalke, who made *Raja Harishchandra* in 1913, came from a family of priests. The traditional Hindi film hero is invariably an avatar of Lord Ram, who in the *Ramayana* is referred to as *maryada purushottam*, the Upholder of Honor. That is, he is handsome (usually light-complexioned), upright, and without blemishes. While the hero is virtuous, the villain is immoral, and good always conquers evil. The story might include a passionate rain song (in which the leads, usually in wet, clinging clothes, are amorous) or dastardly acts of wickedness, but invariably the narrative affirms the status quo. It is wholesome entertainment in which family values and the heroine's virtue stay intact. Hindi films present life not as it is but as it should be, which perhaps explains why they travel so well. Non-Indians, in countries as diverse as Peru, Indonesia, Greece, and Ethiopia, can connect with the songs, spectacle, and unbridled optimism. For an estimated annual audience of 3.6 billion worldwide, Hindi cinema is a necessary comfort and a collective expression of hope.

But Bollywood isn't just a style of filmmaking. It is also a culture and a religion. Hindi films dictate dress codes, language, rituals, and aspirations for both the Silicon Valley software engineer and the villager in India's most backward state, Bihar. Technology has helped to spread the Bollywood cult. DVD, satellite, and the Internet have cultivated fans even in countries where Hindi films are not distributed.

In South Korea, a curious ritual plays out weekly. A group calling themselves the Bollywood Lovers Club gathers to watch Hindi movies, which they themselves have painstakingly subtitled in Korean. They watch, in the club leader Kwanghyun Jung's words, in "Indian style." That is, they "make noise, laugh, and abuse the villain." The club also runs Bollywood dance classes. Some of the 7,000-odd members wear Shah Rukh Khan T-shirts and drink coffee from cups with his photograph on them. Only one Indian movie has ever been released in South Korea—a Tamil language film called *Muthu: The Dancing Maharaja*, in 1998.

In a paper called *Indian Films and Nigerian Lovers: Media and the Creation of Parallel Modernities*, anthropologist Brian Larkin writes about the influence of Bollywood in northern Nigeria, where Lebanese exhibitors started importing Indian films in the 1950s. Larkin writes: "To this day, stickers of Indian films and stars decorate the taxis and buses of the north, posters of Indian films adorn the walls of tailors' shops and mechanics' garages, and love songs from Indian film are borrowed by religious singers who change the words to sing praises of Prophet Mohammed. For over thirty years, Indian films, their stars and fashions, music and stories have been a dominant part of everyday culture in northern Nigeria." The Germans are more recent converts. The first Bollywood film to have a major theatrical release was *Kabhi Khushi Kabhie Gham* (Sometimes Happiness, Sometimes Sorrow) in 2003. In Germany, DVDs of dubbed Hindi films are sold with the tag line *Bollywood macht glücklich!* Bollywood makes you happy!

In Pakistan, Bollywood has had the added frisson of being contraband. In 1965, after the second Indo-Pak war, the Pakistani government banned the import and screening of Indian films. But Bollywood is everywhere. Pirated DVDs of the latest films are available on the day of release. The press, both English and vernacular, carries reviews of these films. Even though Radio Pakistan does not play Hindi film songs, fans are up to date on the latest hit numbers, dances, fashions, and gossip. On the streets of Karachi and Lahore, Shah Rukh looms large from billboards, selling international products. His ancestral home in Peshawar is a tourist destination. Filmmaker Mahesh Bhatt once remarked that one of the reasons Pakistan will never go to war with India is because Shah Rukh lives there.

The name Bollywood, which combines Bombay with Hollywood, has long been a controversial construct. *New York Times* language guru William Safire traces it to crime fiction writer H. R. F. Keating, who first used it in 1976. The culturally disparaging name suggested that the Hindi film industry was a derivative of the American film industry—the Third World clone of its infinitely more powerful, artistic, and glamorous Western counterpart. Hindi film actors and filmmakers have persistently objected to it, but Bollywood was picked up and popularized by the Indian film press. The coinage passed into popular usage (in 2001, it was included in the fifth edition of the *Oxford English Dictionary*) and became, over the years, a global brand. Like Yoga or the Taj Mahal, Bollywood is shorthand for India.

There are many Indias. The country is the seventh-largest globally in terms of size, with the second-largest population. It has twenty-three officially recognized languages and 2,000-odd dialects. It is home to multitudes of religions and has the third-largest Muslim population in the world, after Indonesia and Pakistan. India is a nation of extremes where affluence, progress, and education are matched by poverty, backwardness, and illiteracy. Disparate centuries exist side by side. In Mumbai, the largest slum in Asia is separated only by a ten-minute car ride from a five-star hotel where Louis Vuitton bags are showcased in the lobby and meals cost several hundred dollars. Both are valid Indian realities. In his book *From Midnight to the Millennium*, author Shashi Tharoor asks, "What makes so many people one people?"

One answer is Bollywood. Hindi films function as a global glue, binding together Indians across gender, geography, religion, and age. This includes the estimated 20 million non-resident Indians scattered across 110 countries. For them, Hindi movies are an umbilical cord to the motherland. Second- and third-generation immigrants watch Hindi movies with subtitles because they can no longer speak the language. Bollywood is a primary and sometimes solitary link to an exotic ancestral homeland that they have heard of but perhaps never visited. In cities like New York and London, they flock to nightclubs for *Desi* nights, where Indian DJs play Bollywood remixes. In fact, Bollywood is no longer the shabby, slightly embarrassing country cousin that the parents insist on bringing home. Hindi films are trendy. So is India.

Shah Rukh Khan is the face of a glittering new India. He is a modern-day god. On streets in India, his posters are sold alongside those of religious deities. Shrines have been erected in his name. For Indians and the varied non-Indian lovers of popular Hindi cinema, Shah Rukh is bigger than Tom Cruise and Brad Pitt combined. Over fifteen years and fifty films, he has straddled Bollywood like a colossus. In the *paan*-stained studios of Mumbai, Shah Rukh's story, how a middle-class Muslim boy from Delhi became one of the biggest movie stars in the biggest film industry in the world, is legend. So when he flicks away cigarette butts people pick them up as souvenirs. The media, in tones that aren't ironical or mocking, refer to him as King Khan.

Shah Rukh's home, a sprawling heritage bungalow in suburban Mumbai, has long been a tourist magnet. Buses carrying vacationers routinely stop in front of the gate. On Sunday evenings, when Mumbai, a frenetic city of 18 million people, pauses for breath, men and women gather for a *darshan* (sighting). Sometimes, when he is at home, Shah Rukh Khan steps out on the terrace and waves at his devotees.

But Shah Rukh's life is more than just a dramatic show-biz success story. He is a Muslim superstar in a Hindu-majority country and his life reflects the fundamental paradoxes of a post-liberalization nation attempting to thrive in a globalized world. His story provides a ringside view into the forces shaping Indian culture today.

The rise of Shah Rukh Khan can be understood as a metaphor for a country changing at breakneck pace. During the 1990s, India underwent avalanches of change. In 1991, under the threat of imminent fiscal collapse and facing an inability to repay World Bank loans, the government introduced wide-ranging economic reforms. The centralized socialist economy was dismantled. Several major industries were deregulated and multinational corporations were allowed entry. In the same year, satellite television—CNN, STAR TV, MTV—arrived.

For fifty years since independence, India had struggled with a stagnant economy. Economist Raj Krishna labeled it the "Hindu rate of growth," which averaged just 3.5 percent annually. India's first prime minister, Jawaharlal Nehru, envisaged a "socialist pattern of society," which would combine the best of socialism and capitalism so that Indians could enjoy both economic egalitarianism and democratic freedom. Instead, the extreme protectionism and state-controlled public sector created the "License Raj," a Kafkaesque maze of regulations and permits that forced businessmen and ordinary citizens customarily to use bribes and "contacts" in high places. The License Raj distorted the economy and filled the markets with low-quality, made-in-India goods that were two or three decades behind the West. Factories were forced to produce goods in line with centrally mandated Five Year Plans on the Soviet model; producing *more* scooters in a year than the annual quota allowed for was as much of an official sin as producing fewer. In this environment, even ordinary American products such as Kellogg's cereals and Levi's jeans were considered status symbols. They implied that one had the money and good fortune to travel to foreign lands. America, with its vast supermarkets groaning with consumer delights, was a faraway paradise.

The reforms changed the urban Indian landscape. Suddenly cereals, jeans, and dozens of other branded products were available at the corner store. Television, which earlier featured hours of staid, government-run programming on two state-run terrestrial channels, now boasted dizzying alternatives. There were dozens of cable channels, inexpensive enough to be bought by anyone who could afford a television set. Tedious political speeches and discussions on agriculture were replaced by glitzy, titillating shows such as *The Bold and the Beautiful* and *Baywatch*. The West, with its seductive promise of modernity, glamour, and a sumptuous lifestyle, entered middle-class homes.

As India's economic growth rate rose beyond 7 percent in the 1990s, the middle classes with their increased spending power came to the forefront. The Delhi-based National Council of Applied Economic Research, which prefers the term "consuming class," estimated that in the mid-1990s this consuming class was 32.5 million households or 168 million people. (By 2005, experts estimated that the middle class numbered over 250 million people—that is only 50 million less than the total population of the United States.)

Globalization, and the ensuing consumerism and competition, created an enormous cultural churning. The conventional rules no longer held. Negotiating between tradition and modernity, between new desires and deep-rooted expectations, the middle class was wracked by confusion and insecurity. Stress, depression, divorce, long considered ailments of the affluent West, became more widespread. The Indian family, women's roles, marriage, and relationships were irrevocably redefined.

These shifts were paralleled by various reactionary trends, particularly the rise of a muscular Hindu right wing. In December 1992, Hindu fundamentalists destroyed the Babri Masjid, a disputed religious site in North India. Riots followed. Mumbai, long heralded as India's most cosmopolitan city, was torn apart by two spells of rioting. According to the government-ordered *Srikrishna Commission Report*, 900 people died and 2,036 were injured. Over 50,000 were rendered homeless. The patina of globalization couldn't camouflage or quell the religious conflict, poverty, corruption, and violence that simmered underneath. A sleepy society, mired in 5,000 years of culture and tradition, wrestled with the "shock of modernity" and asked itself: What does it mean to be Indian?

Shah Rukh Khan provided one very persuasive answer. In films like *Dilwale Dulhania Le Jayenge* (The Brave-Hearted Will Take the Bride, also widely known as *DDLJ*: 1995), *Dil To Pagal Hai* (The Heart Is Crazy: 1997), *Kuch Kuch Hota Hai* (Something Is Happening: 1998), *Kabhi Khushi Kabhie Gham* (2001), and *Kal Ho Naa Ho* (If Tomorrow Comes: 2003), he told Indians that an Indian could be a hybrid who easily enjoys the material comforts of the West and the spiritual comforts of the East. You didn't have to choose between the two; the twain could meet without friction or confusion. So in *DDLJ*, Shah Rukh's character, Raj, is a London-born Indian who drinks beer, wears a Harley-Davidson jacket, and is clearly a European man-about-town; but Raj doesn't take advantage of his intoxicated heroine because he "respects an Indian woman's honor." Shah Rukh's subsequent characters also reiterated this idea, that the international-designer-label exterior cannot undermine an essential Indian identity. Shah Rukh personified the new millennium Indian who combines a global perspective with local values and is at home in the world.

Shah Rukh became both the face and the catalyst of the new consumerist society; he was one of the earliest Bollywood stars to plunge into advertising. Shah Rukh rarely met a product he could not endorse. He sold everything from Pepsi-Cola to Tag Heuer watches. The commercials accentuated his screen persona and helped transform the actor into a brand.

A popular song from a film released in 1955, *Shri 420* (Mr. 420), puts it aptly:

Mera joota hai Japani
Yeh patloon Englistani
Sar pe lal topi Rusi
Phir bhi dil hai Hindustani

My shoes are Japanese
These pants are British
The cap on my head is Russian
But my heart is Indian.

In 1955, this cosmopolitanism was perhaps a cherished hope for most Indians; today, it is an inescapable reality. Shah Rukh Khan, like Marilyn Monroe, is an icon for an age. This is his story.

Peshawar: The Street of the Storytellers

The Qissa Khawani Bazaar in Peshawar is a gaudy, vibrant locality resonating with rhythms at once ancient and new. Both sides of the main road are crammed with shops that seem to have arranged themselves in no particular order. Doctors offer their services next to bookstores; cloth shops neighbor sweetmeat sellers; *dhabas* (roadside cafés) and *kehwa khanas* (teahouses) compete. Antiques, shawls, Peshawari *chappals* (slippers), dry fruits, and lentils weigh down the shelves. The air is heavy with noise, people, and the pungent smells of meats grilling on coals, freshly baked bread, and mounds of fresh fruit. Above the shops are residences and behind them *mohallas* (colonies) of tapering, multilevel houses connected by a labyrinth of gullies so narrow that in some spots two people passing each other must do it sideways.

For centuries, Peshawar has been perched at a religious, historical, and geographical crossroads. The city stands near the eastern end of the Khyber Pass, and has long been a natural stop for travelers en route to the subcontinent. Kings, armies, invaders, and traders have all passed through Peshawar. In the mid-nineteenth century, Sir Edward Herbert, the British commissioner in Peshawar, described the Qissa Khawani Bazaar as the "Piccadilly of Central Asia." Travelers paused in the market to drink the local green tea called *kehwa* and exchange *kissas*, or stories. In the past, professional raconteurs enthralled large crowds. The name Qissa Khawani Bazaar means "the street of the storytellers." It is fitting that some of Indian cinema's biggest names, whose stories have seduced generations, trace their roots to this space.

In a *mohalla* called Dahkki Nal Bandi stands the house where Prithviraj Kapoor once lived. Prithviraj, a statuesquely handsome man, left Peshawar when he was only twenty-two, traveled two days and nights to Mumbai, and became a leading man in the 1930s and 1940s. He spawned a dynasty of actors and filmmakers. Four generations of Kapoors have fashioned Hindi film fantasies.

Less than five minutes away, in Dooma Gulli, is the house where Dilip Kumar was born. His father, a fruit merchant, shifted to Mumbai in the early 1930s, but every two or three years the children traveled back for holidays. They stuffed themselves on delicacies like *balushahi* and *salone kulche* and spent hours playing games in the eerily dark *tehkhana* (basement). In 2000, when Dilip Kumar, now a worshipped Hindi film actor, returned to this home, he wept and pointed to crevices under the stairs where he hid money as a child. Within walking distance of both these homes, at the end of a narrow lane in the *mohalla* Shahwali Qatal, is house number 1147, where Shah Rukh Khan's father, Meer Taj Mohammad, was born in 1928.

Meer was the youngest of six children. He had four brothers and one sister. His father, Mir Jan Muhammad, was a formidable man who was over six feet in height—so tall that when he died there was no bed in the house large enough to carry him to the burial ground. Meer was the baby of the family. His siblings pampered and protected him. "*Yeh sona puttar hai*" (He is a good son), his elder brother Ghulam Mohammad Gamma often remarked.

The family was in the bamboo trade, but business often took a backseat. Like thousands of ordinary Indians, they were caught up in a more epic struggle: the fight for Indian independence. Meer and his brothers were followers of Khan Abdul Ghaffar Khan, also called Badshah Khan. Badshah Khan was a political ally of Mahatma Gandhi.

Though Peshawar eventually became part of Pakistan, the city has always been closer to Afghanistan in topography, people, and culture. It is home to the Pathans, a physically imposing people known for their brute strength and endurance; a legend in the area goes that Pathans with a blue birth mark on their back are the direct descendents of the Mongolian emperor Genghis Khan.

Traditionally, Pathan culture glorifies martial prowess, but Badshah Khan inspired and sustained an Islamic non-violent movement, earning the title of "Frontier Gandhi." Badshah Khan's *Khudai Khidmatgars* (Servants of God), or Red Shirts, as the British called them, supported the Indian National Congress. The British troops tried to provoke the Pathans into violence—they were jailed, flogged, and tortured—but

Badshah Khan's non-violent soldiers stood firm. In 1937, when provincial elections were held, a coalition government of the Red Shirts and the Congress Party was elected. The province was the only Muslim majority state in which the Congress had significant power.

Meer's elder brother Gamma was a respected political leader. He was a tireless worker organizing anti-British protests and rallies. Meer himself was an in-demand orator—his fiery speeches in Urdu attracted as much attention as his dashing movie star looks. In August 1942, the Congress Party launched the Quit India movement, which demanded the immediate end of British rule. The party called for non-violence, but when the government arrested most of the Congress leaders including Nehru and Gandhi, the agitation turned aggressive. Bombs exploded, government buildings were set on fire, and there were mass arrests. Almost a thousand people were killed and 60,000 arrested. Among these were Meer and Gamma. Meer, then enrolled at King Edward College, was in and out of jail for the next two years. Though none of the other siblings had even finished high school, they encouraged Meer to study. Concerned that the political and social unrest would adversely affect Meer's education, his brothers sent him to Delhi. In 1946, Meer enrolled as a law student at Delhi University.

A year later, on August 15, 1947, India became an independent nation. But the euphoria of freedom was stained by the bloodshed of Partition. In five weeks, Sir Cyril Radcliffe had carved Pakistan out of Punjab and Bengal and laid the foundation for decades of animosity and tragedy. In the months before and after Independence, an estimated 11 million people crossed the borders in both directions: Hindus and Sikhs fled to India from Pakistan while Muslims abandoned their ancestral lands and trudged to their new home. A Delhi paper, the

Hindustan Times, reported: "Near Amritsar 150,000 people are spread 60 miles along the road. It is perhaps the greatest caravan in human history." It was also one of the bloodiest. Massacres, looting, rapes occurred on both sides of the border. Hundreds of thousands were killed. The birth of two nations was marred and marked by mass murder.

Overnight, Meer became a man without a country. When Lord Mountbatten, the last British viceroy of India, had announced Partition, Badshah Khan was among the few leaders who had supported Gandhi's objections to the Two-Nation Theory. Both men had assessed correctly that cleaving the country on the basis of religion would only intensify communal violence. The Pathans, though Muslim, wanted to remain part of India, but the landlocked province was handed by the British to Pakistan. Badshah Khan, said the Congress, "had surrendered the Pakhtoons to the enemies in helpless condition." Shortly after independence, he was charged with being pro-Hindu and imprisoned by the Islamic government in Pakistan. His followers, including Meer's family, were forcibly scattered through the country. Gamma would spend the next seven years in prison. Meer's name was also on the blacklist of Red Shirt freedom fighters and he was barred from entering Pakistan. He could never go home again.

During the Partition riots, Meer's Hindu friends at Delhi University had slept in a ring around his bed, determined to protect him from any anti-Muslim violence. One of them was a law student named Kanhaiya Lal Poswal, who belonged to an affluent family and later became a Congress Party minister. In 1949, Meer graduated from the university with a second division (a B-grade equivalent, considered average). He stayed with Kanhaiya Lal for months. What happened next is hazy and curious. Meer then opted not to practice law, but instead embarked on the same journey his son would make forty years later: He went from Delhi to Mumbai to become an actor.

In the 1950s, Mumbai was a kinder, gentler metropolis of 3 million people. Monstrous blocks of skyscrapers hadn't yet distorted the skyline. Illegal encroachments did not blot the sidewalks. The concrete was leavened by swaths of green. There were fewer cars—clunky Indian Fiats and Ambassadors mingled with Studebakers, Dodges, and Buicks left over from the Raj. Trams and rows of art deco buildings gave the city a fashionable charm. The air was heady with the exhilaration of new freedom and possibilities of the future.

After the trauma of Partition, the task of national reconstruction had begun. In his historic midnight address to the nation, India's first prime minister, Jawaharlal Nehru, had proclaimed, "Long years ago we made a tryst with destiny, and now the time comes when we shall redeem our pledge, not wholly or in full measure, but very substantially. At the stroke of the midnight hour, when the world sleeps, India will awake to life and freedom."

Nehru dreamed of creating a modern, democratic, industrialized, secular country. In 1950 he set up the National Planning Commission, which created a blueprint for progress. Increased agricultural output and large-scale industrialization would better the abysmal living standards in the country. Politics was not then the synonym for corruption that it became in ensuing decades, and great hopes were pinned on the success of the Nehruvian state. Author Gurcharan Das writes in *India Unbound*, "It was not unfashionable in thc 1950s for either the old or the young to admit to idealism. . . . It seemed possible to believe then that India would be great because she was good."

The Hindi film industry was also flourishing. The 1950s

were the Golden Age of Hindi film. The films made during this creative and commercial renaissance set the standard for later mainstream cinema and influenced generations of directors and actors. During World War II, raw stock was tightly rationed at 11,000 feet for the final release print. The number of Hindi films made fell from 154 in 1935 to 78 in 1941. But immediately after the war, with rationing gone, production doubled as hundreds of independent producers, flush with war profits, entered the movie business. The output increased from 73 in 1945 to 150 in 1946.

The producers, armed with suitcases lined with cash, made offers that actors couldn't refuse. Through the 1930s and 1940s Hindi films had been dominated by a Hollywood-style studio system, in which directors and actors were salaried employees. Actor Dev Anand, whose puffed hair and lilting dialogue delivery defined style for a generation, was contracted to the Prabhat Film Company for 400 rupees ($9), of which 35 (80 cents) were cut as income tax. But now the influx of independent producers altered the economics, and it became difficult for studios to hold on exclusively to stars and technicians. A 1951 Film Enquiry Committee report states that within three months of de-control, "over 100 new producers entered the field" and "within three years of the end of the war, the leadership of the industry had changed hands." In 1953, the Prabhat Film Company closed. A year later, another leading studio, Bombay Talkies, ceased production.

There was a migration of talent from Lahore, the other center of film production, which was now in Pakistan. Mumbai became a mecca for producers, directors, actors, musicians, writers, and poets. These men and women refined and redefined the mainstream Hindi film. They used the popular narrative form but imbued it with personal sensibility, creating a layered and sophisticated cinema. The output was staggering in its range, depth, and artistry.

Italian neorealism inspired Bimal Roy, one of Hindi film's greatest directors. His cinema blended social issues and a naturalistic style with songs. Guru Dutt, who was also a popular leading man, created hauntingly poetic, angst-ridden dramas of love and longing in the increasingly materialistic world of post-Independence India. In 1957, Mehboob Khan made *Mother India*, a searing story of a peasant woman who single-handedly raises her two sons but is forced to kill the younger one when he becomes an outlaw. In 1958, *Mother India* became the first Hindi film to be nominated for an Oscar. It didn't win. Mehboob Khan lost by one vote to Federico Fellini's *Nights of Cabiria*, but *Mother India* gave Hindi cinema some of its most enduring themes: the mother as an iconic moral center, the rebel son, the importance of honor and sacrifice.

Three actors dominated the screen in the 1950s. Dilip Kumar, a handsome, melancholic man with an understated acting style, was best suited to tragedy. Raj Kapoor, also a celebrated director, embodied joy. He propagated uncomplicated, utopian themes in the persona of a Charlie Chaplin–inspired Tramp figure. Dev Anand, the definitive debonair, brought stylized acting and a Western panache to Hindi film. These men personified the dreams and aspirations of a long-subjugated country taking baby steps into freedom and modernity.

One of the biggest productions at the time was a film called *Mughal-e-Azam* (The Great Mughal). The film was based on the legend of Anarkali, a palace courtesan who falls in love with Prince Salim, the son of the mighty Mughal emperor Akbar. The director, K. Asif, was an illiterate man with a grandiose 70-millimeter dream that he was determined to transfer to celluloid. But circumstances that varied from finances to fatalities conspired against Asif. The making of *Mughal-e-Azam* was as dramatic as the film itself.

Mughal-e-Azam was in production for fifteen years. Chandra-mohan, the actor selected to play the lead, died after ten reels were shot, and the film had to be scrapped and re-started. Some of the scenes were so complicated that they took three days to light and as many weeks to shoot. Asif was unwilling to compromise on anything, whether it was the costumes or the singers, so tailors were brought in from Delhi to stitch the elaborately embroidered costumes. Renowned classical singer Ustad Bade Ghulam Ali Khan was hired for a staggering 25,000 rupees ($550). The shooting days added up to a year and a half and the film's budget totaled an unprecedented 15 million rupees ($335,000). The cast included hundreds of junior artists (extras) who were kept on standby just in case Asif *saab* decided to fill up the frame.

Meer made his way to the sets of *Mughal-e-Azam*. His fine Pathan features are said to have increased the number of women at political rallies in Peshawar. Perhaps he hoped that his good looks would propel him to stardom. Meer later told his children that he was offered second lead and that Madhubala, the ethereally beautiful star of the film, even seemed to find him attractive. But Surinder Kapoor, one of the assistants on the film, told a less fanciful story.

When Meer introduced himself as an actor, he was cursorily told to stand in the line for extras. Affronted, he left immediately. Though Meer seemed serious about acting—Surinder Kapoor said Meer even took up smoking to make his voice heavier—he didn't have the stomach for the daily grind and humiliation. Meer gave his acting career only one more shot. He tried to meet Ashok Kumar, a leading actor of the times, but couldn't get past the watchmen. He gave up on his dreams of working in films but continued to live in Mumbai for a year. He would spend his time taking walks on beautiful windswept Marine Drive and drinking cups of bitter tea. Meer started to fall sick often, and eventually his friend Kanhaiya Lal convinced him to return to Delhi.

Meer was still unemployed when he met Fatima Lateef. He was twenty-nine. She was thirteen years younger and, in every way, his opposite. Meer was a tall man with an athlete's body. There was not an ounce of extra flesh on him. His skin was fair, almost translucent, so that the blue veins underneath showed. He dressed simply in Khadi kurta pajamas or flowing Pathan suits.

Little provoked Meer. He was a serene, smiling man with an irreverent sense of humor and the patience of a mule. When he disapproved of something, he only said "*Yeh halal nahin hai*" (This is not *halal*, this is not permitted). A lover of books and poetry, Meer could recite lengthy Urdu verses. He was unhurried in his speech, stance, and outlook. Meer's constant companion was a small bag that contained his *paan*-making paraphernalia. When someone requested a *paan*, he would take inordinately long, meticulously cutting *supari* and mixing *chuna* so that every nuance in the betel-leaf flavor was perfect. His friends often joked that by the time Meer made the *paan* they would be asleep. For Meer, life was a ritual to be lived with grace and goodness.

Fatima was short and slightly plump but equally attractive. Her fair skin was offset by long black hair. She had a mercurial temper. Fatima grew up in Hyderabad with the customs and airs of royalty; she used to dry her hair on the *udd*. That is, she would spread her tresses on an upturned basket, which had incense and charcoal underneath. Years later, Shah Rukh would recall the intoxicating perfume of his mother's hair. Fatima had three sisters, but none matched her milky complexion and she was, friends said, more pampered. Her father was a senior engineer with a high-ranking job in the government, but Fatima was not as educated as Meer. She had a fierce, impulsive spirit. A few years after marriage she requested a family friend to take her to a wrestling match. When he refused, she went alone.

They met by chance, and for Meer, it was love at first sight. One day, while visiting her father in New Delhi, Fatima was involved in a serious car accident near India Gate, a popular tourist spot. Meer happened to be taking in the sights as well. He pulled Fatima out of the mangled car and rushed her to hospital. In the best Bollywood tradition, Fatima needed a blood transfusion and Meer's blood group matched hers. But even a Hindi film writer couldn't have scripted what happened next. Upon hearing that her daughter had had an accident, Fatima's mother, who was pregnant with her fifth child, had a miscarriage. She too needed blood and her blood group was the same as her daughter's. Meer gallantly traveled to Bangalore, where the family lived, to donate blood.

Despite Meer's chivalry, Fatima's parents weren't overly enthusiastic about the dashing young man keen to marry their daughter. He had a degree but no family and no job. In fact, one of the reasons put forth to stop the marriage was that since Meer had donated blood, he was technically a blood relative and could not marry into the family. But Meer persisted. He wooed Fatima with cars borrowed from Kanhaiya Lal and delectable sweetmeats. In February 1959, Meer and Fatima were married. After the marriage ceremony, the wedding procession returned to Kanhaiya Lal's house in Rewari. Kanhaiya Lal was now president of the Municipal Committee, and the entire village showed up to celebrate the couple. Wedding guests remembered that the strapping Meer blushed like a bride.

3

A "Lady-Killer" Is Born

Shah Rukh Khan was born on November 2, 1965, at the Talwar Nursing Home in New Delhi. He was Meer and Fatima's second child. Their daughter, Shahnaz Lala Rukh, was born in 1960. Shah Rukh's birth was complicated. The umbilical cord looped around his neck. Though the condition has been known to cause asphyxiation, retardation, and even death, Shah Rukh emerged unscathed. A nurse interpreted the deadly cord around his neck as a blessing of Hanuman, the divine monkey-god. The child, she predicted, would be very lucky.

This wasn't immediately apparent. When Shah Rukh was born, his father was in a financial slump. Meer's partners in his transport business had cheated him and the venture had to be shut down, like several others before it. Meer dabbled in furniture and once ran a canteen at the famous National School of Drama. But his successes were small. The family hovered at the edge of genteel poverty. Shah Rukh believed that his father, who had a law degree and was fluent in six languages, was too honest to be rich.

Shah Rukh was born on *Mangalwar*, a Tuesday. Fatima often told him that he was a *Manglik* child. But Hindi was not her native language; Fatima was an Urdu speaker from Hyderabad. So Shah Rukh was never sure what exactly his mother meant: that he was born on a Tuesday, or that he was born under the *Manglik* astrological sign, which is considered unlucky by Hindus.

They lived in Rajinder Nagar, a dowdy housing locality in west Delhi. Meer's various business ventures stretched their meager finances, and the family struggled to maintain the sheen of refinement. Meer did not have the guile for business. They were, at times, forced to borrow money. This enduring financial grind did not dampen Meer's morale. His spirit was *shaiyrana*. That is, Meer was a romantic who, in the tradition of the best Urdu poets, embraced life with an old-world chivalry. In the face of all calamities, Meer kept his sense of humor. Affectionately he called his wife *Kanha*, an Urdu word for dimples. He imbued their routine, humdrum life with such wit that even the mundane became magical.

Fatima had less patience with poverty. Meer's stubborn refusal to use his political contacts—he was a certified freedom fighter on a first-name basis with Prime Minister Indira Gandhi—and his tolerance even for cheating partners frustrated her. She used to call him an "honest failure." Once, after an especially fiery fight, she shifted to Kanhaiya Lal's house for a few days. Every few years the family shuffled from one small, run-down rented apartment to another.

It didn't help that both Meer and Fatima were inordinately easy with their meager monies. Extravagant hospitality is central to the Pathan way of life—in Peshawar, it is said that when a guest is invited to a wedding, he must bring at least four friends with him to honor the host. The people of Peshawar are often described as *Khurren log*, that is, people who eat with their hearts. Meer continued these traditions. Both Meer and Fatima were fond of eating and they maintained an open house. Friends recalled impromptu feasts of succulent meats cooked Hyderabadi style and Peshawari delicacies such as *raan* and *gosht*. Their house was unkempt, but the dining table was usually laden.

Meer was a simple man who needed little beside his bitter tea and *paan*, but Fatima was more stylish. She was especially keen that her children enjoy material comforts. Shah Rukh and his elder sister, Shahnaz, grew up in a buffer zone created by Fatima. They were barely aware that there was a discordant note in their near-idyllic childhood.

Shah Rukh inherited Meer's serenity. As a toddler he spent hours playing on a small pink toy piano. At three he was so tranquil that Fatima sometimes dashed out to do chores, leaving him alone at home. Family folklore has it that on one such occasion a cobra slithered into the living room. Like much of Delhi then, Rajinder Nagar was a mixture of concrete and jungle, and snakes in living rooms were not unheard of. Shah Rukh was sitting on the *deewan*, a low, platform-like sofa. He had spilled ink around himself and the snake couldn't come any closer because the thick wetness wouldn't let it move.

Shah Rukh was a sickly, accident-prone child, suffering from bouts of malaria, ruptured back muscles, and frequent dog bites. But the illnesses didn't seem to sap his spirit. He spent hours in his own company. In a small storeroom he created a secret lab in which he melted his mother's lac bangles. A favorite game was creating a make-believe universe on the *deewan* in which he, in red underwear and towel tied on back, was Superman and the pillows were the bad guys. Shah Rukh would pummel the long cylindrical pillows till the cotton inside flattened out. The villains lost each time. Shah Rukh was already a hero.

He also had lots of friends. They played cricket on a dusty patch of land near the house, sometimes until midnight. Fatima and Meer did not believe in rigorous parenting. It was an easygoing house with few rules, even for Shahnaz. As long as the children received good grades, they weren't forced to study. Sometimes they were allowed to skip school for no other reason except that they "didn't feel like going."

Their religious education was equally informal. Fatima was a more traditional Muslim than her husband. She endeavored to say her *namaaz* (prayers) the prescribed five times a day. But Meer's faith was flexible. Meer was devoutly secular and encouraged the same in his family. The trauma of Hindu-Muslim riots during Partition had not eroded the lessons he imbibed from Badshah Khan: that all men and religions are equal. Meer's closest friend, Kanhaiya Lal, was a Hindu. Though it was considered blasphemy for Muslims, there was even a picture of the Hindu god Jagannath in the house. Unlike Fatima, Meer rarely fasted during the month of Ramadan. Sometimes, as a joke, Meer would turn off Fatima's alarm so she couldn't wake up before sunrise to eat the *sehri*. On Sunday the children went to the mosque with their uncle. Sometimes, when a *Kazi* came home to teach them the Koran, Shahnaz and Shah Rukh would run around the house trying to hide from him.

Meer and Shah Rukh called each other *yaar*, a variation of the Pathan *yarra*, or friend. Meer was as much friend as father. He imparted to Shah Rukh his off-kilter sense of humor. On the other hand, Fatima was a screamer who sometimes punished the children. Meer was gentler. He encouraged his children to read and regaled them with stories of the freedom struggle. In this home, bedtime stories weren't fairy tales—Aesop's fables were the only fiction the children heard. Instead Meer told them inspiring, real-life sagas of brave men like Badshah Khan and Saifuddin Kichlu, who devoted their lives to the cause of an independent India. Meer told his children about days spent in British jails. When Badshah Khan came to Delhi, Meer took Shah Rukh to meet him. He also took him to hear a fiery orator named Atal Bihari Vajpayee who would one day become prime minister.

Summers were spent in Bangalore at their maternal grandparents' luxurious home. Meer never accompanied his family on these trips—he was too proud to accept his in-laws' hospitality. At four, Shah Rukh was already performing: when he danced to the radio, his aunts smiled and said, "Lady-killer *banega*" (He will be a lady-killer). At home, the radio had pride of place. The family could not afford television. Every evening they gathered in the living room to listen to the only station available at the time, the state-controlled All India Radio. The program usually consisted of news and Hindi film songs. Shah Rukh pirouetted around the room, especially if the song was from a film starring the actress Mumtaz. He entertained the family by imitating Mumtaz's hip-swiveling walk and coquettish mannerisms.

Mumtaz was a glamour doll from the 1960s. She wasn't a classic beauty, but she had a perky elfin charm, which suited the kitschy lightweight films the industry was churning out at the time. The social concerns and more serious tenor of the 1950s cinema had given way to unadulterated escapist romp. Hindi films had discovered color: in 1960 only one color film was released but by 1970 color was the norm. Foreign locations were the rage, as were sparkly, swinging fashions. In zip-on saris and five-inch-high bouffant hairdos Mumtaz danced, mostly in breezy romances and family dramas.

This increasing frivolity and Westernization didn't impress the critics. Baburao Patel, editor of the most influential film journal of the time, *Film India*, trashed these lightweight confections as a "rape of Indian culture" and "stinking rubbish about cultural mongrels." But Shah Rukh was wholly seduced. He said that Mumtaz "was the most important cause of my tilt toward anything that vaguely had to do with the performing arts." This early passion was perhaps a hint of things to come: Three decades later, Shah Rukh became a superstar acting in the 1990s version of these candy-floss films, which were as much about foreign locations and designer clothes as romance and family values.

Bollywood was at first a bribe. In the first grade, when he was seven, Shah Rukh routinely failed his Hindi language tests. Once Fatima promised him that if he managed to get a perfect score on the next test, she would take him to see a Hindi movie in a theater. Shah Rukh, whose preferred studying style was cramming the night before exams, studied till dawn and got full marks. Fatima took him and Shahnaz to the Vivek Cinema Hall in Patel Nagar to see *Joshila* (Zesty).

The film, a not particularly zestful thriller starring Dev Anand, was already a flop—tickets were easily available before the show started. But Shah Rukh was thrilled by its feeble twists and turns. The excitement of standing in line to buy a ticket, the squeaking sound the folding chairs made when pushed open, the hard Rexene cushioning, the smell of stale popcorn, and images flickering in the vast thousand-seat theater made an indelible impression. Shah Rukh was so short that he had to sit on his mother's purse to see the screen. But he fell in love with the movies. A few years later Shah Rukh's passion found a face: Amitabh Bachchan.

Amitabh Bachchan is Hindi cinema's most resilient superstar. But even in his youth, Amitabh had nothing of the fair, chocolate-boy handsomeness that the industry preferred in its leading men. He was lanky, brooding, and attractive in a sullen way. A haunting bleakness hovered about his eyes, even when he did comedy. He seemed like a man with a bruised soul. In the 1970s, Amitabh redefined heroism and Hindi cinema.

Superstardom, that mysterious condition when an actor transcends mere fame and becomes a myth, is a product of talent, luck, and timing. In the early 1970s, the industry was ripe for change. The old guard of actors had passed on the baton to a new romantic star, Rajesh Khanna. He held the nation in thrall (many of his blockbusters starred Mumtaz). At his peak, female fans wrote him letters in blood. But after a blaze of unprecedented glory—he had eleven hits in three years—he was headed for burnout. In 1972 the unthinkable happened: Rajesh Khanna delivered six flops in a row. The signature mannerisms, crinkling eyes, and crooked smile didn't work magic anymore. Filmmakers too seemed at a loss. The surefire formulas of locations in Technicolor, fashion, and melodrama weren't filling up the theaters. The audience was growing restless, perhaps because the cloying sweetness on-screen had so little to do with their reality.

The 1970s were India's decade of discontent. The post-Independence optimism of the 1950s and 1960s had given way to a deepening disillusionment with authority. The legacy of altruism and integrity left behind by the leaders of the freedom struggle had been replaced by corruption and cynicism. Politics was no longer the domain of honorable men. The post-Nehruvian establishment was an amoral morass of strategists, sycophants, power brokers, and opportunists who worked for individual gain rather than the national good. The use of violence for criminal and political ends was on the rise.

In 1971, Indira Gandhi led her wing of the Congress Party to victory in the national election on the strength of her slogan, *Garibi Hatao* (Remove Poverty). But the government had no plan in place to implement this winning declaration. Inflation and unemployment rose dramatically. The population, increasing at 12 to 13 million annually, was nullifying the economic gains. Prosperity seemed a faraway pipe dream. There were mounting protests and calls for "Total Revolution" led by the frail Gandhian Jayaprakash Narayan. One Congress state government fell and others were threatened. Tensions heightened. When the Allahabad High Court found Indira Gandhi guilty of electoral misconduct in the last election, there were loud cries for her resignation. Instead of resigning, she declared a national state of emergency.

On June 26, 1975, India went from a democracy to a dictatorship. The constitution was suspended. Political opponents were rounded up at midnight and imprisoned. The media was muzzled. Over the next twenty-one months, until the emergency was lifted on March 23, 1977, the state machinery—police, judiciary, bureaucracy—was irretrievably weakened. At one point more than 100,000 people languished in jail without trial. The common citizen believed that law and order had broken down. The mood in the country was hopelessness and frustration. On the streets, a new morality was taking shape.

Amitabh Bachchan gave a face to that ethos: He played a grim urban vigilante. Three seminal films, all written by the pioneering script-writing team of Javed Akhtar and Salim Khan, shaped his persona: *Zanjeer* (Shackles), in which he plays an honest cop traumatized by his parents' massacre; *Sholay*

(Embers), in which he is a taciturn mercenary who sets out to capture a murderous bandit; and *Deewaar* (The Wall), in which he is a tragic, haunted mafioso named Vijay. When Vijay refuses to pick up money tossed at him, saying, "*Main aaj bhi phenke hue paise nahin uthaatha*" (Even today I don't pick up money thrown at me), he articulated the seething anger of a generation of Indians.

Amitabh Bachchan was box office gold. The scalpers who loiter outside cinema halls still speak longingly of the glorious days when they sold four-rupee (less than one-cent) *Sholay* tickets for 500 rupees ($11). Bollywood folklore has it that a scalper named Prakash, who operated outside Delhi's Plaza Cinema, eventually made enough money to buy himself a small house, which he decorated with *Sholay* posters. Amitabh inspired absolute devotion, the extent of which became apparent in June 1982, when, while shooting an action sequence for a film called *Coolie*, Amitabh fell onto the edge of a steel table and ruptured his intestines. It was a life-threatening injury. India came to a halt.

Then Prime Minister Indira Gandhi flew to Mumbai to visit the ailing superstar. Fans, directors, co-actors, and technicians kept a constant vigil at the Breach Candy Hospital. Hundreds came forward to offer their blood and vital organs. Throughout the city, Muslims and Hindus organized prayer meetings to invoke their gods. A producer, S. Ramanathan, took vials of Amitabh's blood to temples in South India to be blessed. Actor Puneet Issar, whose fist triggered the accident, received death threats and was called Nathuram Godse. In the national imagination, the scared, struggling actor was on par with the man who killed Mahatma Gandhi.

The unceasing chorus of prayers pulled off a miracle. When Amitabh's battered body refused to respond, the doctors gave up hope. For a few seconds, Amitabh was clinically dead. He had no pulse or heartbeat. But then a new steroid, administered as a last-ditch effort, kicked in. His wife, Jaya, who stood at the foot of the bed praying, said, "Look, his toes are moving." Like in the movies, Amitabh vanquished evil and returned triumphant to the studios. In the next two decades, Amitabh's Angry Young Man persona hardened into a stereotype.

Like millions in India, Shah Rukh walked the Amitabh walk (a sinewy, panther-like gait) and talked the Amitabh talk (a low baritone). He put talcum powder in his hair to imitate a character Amitabh played in a *Seven Brides for Seven Brothers* remake called *Satte pe Satta* (Seven on Seven). Shah Rukh thought even Amitabh's bad films were good. He saw them all. His theater companion was a girl a few years older than he was. Her name was Amrita Singh.

Amrita's mother, Rukshana Sultana, was a friend of Congress leader Sanjay Gandhi. Though mostly known as a well-connected socialite, Rukshana also worked to promote Sanjay's controversial Family Planning program in the Muslim-dominated parts of the city. Fatima had also taken a job: she had been appointed as a special magistrate in the Juvenile Court. The two women often worked together in the Old Delhi area. Amrita was in the same school as Shahnaz. After school, the three hung out together, usually at Amrita's posher house. She tried to teach Shah Rukh how to swim and in the process almost drowned him. They spent hours concocting fanciful dreams of getting rich quick and talking about Amitabh Bachchan. Amrita said that "Shah Rukh wanted to be Bachchan and I wanted to be romanced by Bachchan." Both achieved their ambitions: Shah Rukh eventually took over the mantle of superstar hero from Amitabh Bachchan; Amrita became an actress and played his love interest in several films.

But at the time they were content to watch his movies sitting in the cheap first-row seats, which cost one rupee seventy-five paise each (less than one cent), because they couldn't afford more expensive tickets. Films were followed by intensive discussions and mimicry sessions, mostly at Amrita's house. When they had money, they bought the sound tracks of Amitabh's films. They memorized his dialogue and imitated his famous style.

At school, Shah Rukh's talent for mimicry was winning him fans. Teachers would invite him onstage at functions to do the latest impersonations of Hindi film actors. His imitations of filmmaker Raj Kapoor and Gabbar Singh, the bandit from *Sholay*, were especially popular. At home, Shah Rukh and his friends put on plays on the veranda. They rigged up a curtain for their makeshift stage. Often, Shah Rukh was writer, director, and lead.

When Shah Rukh was seven or eight, he started to write poetry, simple rhymes about everyday things: an aunt who wore jarring bright pink lipstick, Meer trying to soap stubborn *paan* stains off his hanky. A typical poem went like this: *Log kehte hain meri aunty ke hont gulabi hain, main kehta hoon meri aunty ki aankhen sharabi hain* (People say my aunt's lips are pink, I say my aunt's eyes are intoxicating). Meer noted these rhymes in a book. He encouraged Shah Rukh's poetic inclinations with glorious stories of the great Urdu poets: Mirza Ghalib, Mir Taqi Mir, and even the subversive Chirkeen, who wrote first-rate poetry on only one topic: human feces. Shah Rukh believed that his phenomenal success as a romantic hero came, at least in part, from these early lessons in unrequited love and longing. "At heart," he said, "I'm a poet, perhaps a more materialistic yuppie poet, but a poet all the same."

Shah Rukh was also part of the Chhabra Ram Leela. The

Ram Leela is an enactment of the epic *Ramayana* onstage. It is part of the festival of *Dusshera*, which falls usually at the end of September and celebrates the victory of Lord Ram over the ten-headed demon god Ravan. In Delhi's *maidans* (playing fields), giant effigies of Ravan and his two brothers, Meghnath and Kumbhakaran, are erected. On the last day of the festival, these are set on fire.

Over the ten days of *Dusshera*, the *Ramayana* is performed in parts over several evenings, leading to the grand finale when Ravan is killed. In this cosmic battle between good and evil, Lord Ram is helped by a *Vanar Sena*, an army of monkeys. Shah Rukh was cast as a monkey warrior. The stage was set up in an open field near the house and, even though the performance ran late into the night, Meer and Fatima never objected. Performing in this makeshift theater was great excitement for Shah Rukh.

There wasn't much pressure to emote or learn lines. The *Vanar Sena* was only required to eat bananas and march into Ravan's kingdom, Lanka, shouting "*Bol siyapati Ramchandra ki jai, Pawan Putra Hanuman ki Jai*" (Praise to the commander Ram, praise to Hanuman, son of the wind). Life backstage was raucous: the actor playing Ravan often got drunk, perhaps to add weight to his ominously theatrical "hoo-ha-ha" laugh. Sometimes a male actor played the part of Lord Ram's wife, Sita. The performance was chaotic and unapologetically loud. Even the makeup was melodramatic. Through the chilly nights, the kids gorged on *gajak* and *revdi*. Shah Rukh loved it. Sometimes he was the filler between acts, reciting his poems to the restless audience. Sometimes people gave the charming boy one or two rupees for his effort. It was the first time he was paid to perform.

No-Man's-Land

In 1980, Meer took a fourteen-year-old Shah Rukh to Pakistan. It was their second visit. After repeated requests, the Pakistani authorities had finally given Meer a visa in the mid-1970s. He had applied earlier when his sister and later a brother nicknamed *Brahamachari* (bachelor), because he had never married, had died. But the blacklisted freedom fighter was rejected both times. The authorities relented only when Meer pleaded that he be allowed to meet with his family before they all passed away.

The journey was long and arduous. Father and son first traveled by train to Amritsar and then to a small border town named Attari. This was the only official road crossing between India and Pakistan. Meer and Shah Rukh walked across the designated no-man's-land between the two countries to Wagah in Pakistan and traveled on to Peshawar, to Meer's family home. On the way, Meer told Shah Rukh stories of his childhood and how much Shah Rukh resembled *Brahamachari,* who'd also had a talent for mimicry and playing practical jokes.

The first visit, made when Shah Rukh was twelve, was a happy memory. The ancestral *haveli* was large and teeming with people. Several generations lived together as a joint family. Shah Rukh had met far-flung relatives and romped with cousins his age. His first cousin Mansoor Khan Mir recalled Shah Rukh entertaining the family by dressing up as a girl with *kajal* in his eyes and flowers in his hair. There were several beautiful, fair-skinned female cousins. They couldn't step outside without their heads covered, but at home they wore elaborate makeup. They took Shah Rukh with them to the teeming markets. He watched Pakistani movies and even traveled to see the Khyber Pass. But on the second visit, the veneer of affection wore thin. A common friend warned Shah Rukh that his cousins were being nice to him only because they wanted Meer to leave his share of the property in Pakistan to them.

Shah Rukh did not believe this, but as they walked back across the border, he saw new anguish in his father's eyes. Meer had left behind a family and life in Peshawar to pursue his ambitions in Delhi. But there, too, his ventures had failed. He was literally and metaphorically in no-man's-land. A few months after the journey to Pakistan, Meer fell ill. Shah Rukh believed that his father died later that year as much from unhappiness as from cancer.

When a blister on his tongue persisted for months, Meer went to see a doctor. The diagnosis was oral cancer. Meer's tongue bled. He could not eat, and soon he was unable to talk. In six months, the handsome, strapping man was reduced to a skeleton, bent over with the fatigue of pain. He had to be carried to the bathroom. At times, blood gushed out of his mouth like a geyser and splattered walls two feet away.

At first Meer wrote instructions for his family but as the

disease ravaged his body, his writing became unsteady. He was too weak even to pick up a pencil. Shah Rukh and Meer then communicated through signs and gestures, playing a poignant game of dumb charades. It was a strange sight, a boy who can talk gesticulating for a man who can hear, but perhaps both preferred the silence. Toward the end, even gesturing became difficult for Meer.

Despite the quick corrosion of Meer's body, Shah Rukh never believed that his father would die. It annoyed him to watch doctors clinically poking and tapping Meer's shrinking body. The stench in the ward was overwhelming. Meer shared the room with three other patients, and an empty space usually meant that one more had succumbed. Like most sons, Shah Rukh believed his father was a superhero who would defeat the disease. A few days before his death, Meer actually seemed to be improving. He was discharged from the hospital. At home, he shaved and ate some ice cream. The blue marks on his cheek from chemotherapy were fading. He looked better than he had in months.

Even when Meer was rushed back to Safdarjung Hospital, Shah Rukh was unperturbed. By now, hospitals were a familiar routine. Shah Rukh did not visit his father through the day. At around 2 A.M. on September 19, a nurse called to tell the family that Meer was dead. Fatima did not break the news to Shah Rukh immediately. She just said Meer wanted to meet them. This time Meer was lying alone on a gurney in another hospital room. His mouth was slightly parted and his eyes were half shut. His body was icy cold. Shah Rukh furiously rubbed his feet, trying to infuse some warmth. The sight of blood trickling out of his father's ear would stay with him his whole life. Fatima and Shah Rukh returned home early in the morning. The driver had left by then and Shah

Rukh got behind the wheel of their Fiat. When Fatima asked him when he had learned to drive, he replied, "Just now."

A light rain started as they lowered Meer's body into the ground. Bhavanimal Mathur, an old family friend, said it was as though nature itself was mourning the loss of a fine man. Fatima was devastated but she did not have the luxury of mourning for Meer. She had little money and two children to raise. When she married, Fatima had been a child herself. Naïve and temperamental, she was almost too spoiled to tend to home and hearth. But experience honed her into a strong, willful woman who refused to allow the untimely death of her husband to damage her family. Fatima was already working as a magistrate. She took over the family business interests, running a small restaurant called *Khatir* and an agency for oil.

Meer's death derailed Shahnaz's life. Even as children Shahnaz and Shah Rukh had distinct temperaments. Shah Rukh was driven and forceful, almost seething with a quiet determination to get ahead. Shahnaz was impulsive and reckless. She was more complacent, happier to dream than to do.

Shahnaz was much closer to Meer than Shah Rukh. Meer especially chose her middle name, Lala Rukh, which means "beauteous like a poppy." He liked the name so much that he had suggested it to Kanhaiya Lal when his daughters were born. But Kanhaiya Lal thought the name was too foreign and exotic for his rural surroundings. Over a decade later, when his own daughter was born, Meer took great pleasure in naming her Lala Rukh. True to her name, Shahnaz had grown into an alluring woman. Her light eyes and fair skin attracted a legion of suitors.

At the time of Meer's illness, Shahnaz was a student at Lady Shri Ram College. Meer had insisted that she live in the college hostel. He believed that it would be an additional education. The hostel had helped to shield Shahnaz from the grind of Meer's deterioration. When Meer died, Shah Rukh went to the college to fetch his sister. Fatima had instructed him not to tell Shahnaz and he spent most of the rickshaw ride home looking away from her. She reached the house unaware that her father was dead. They were living then in a matchbox-sized apartment in Safdarjung. As Shah Rukh and Shahnaz walked up to their second-floor flat, Shahnaz noticed the flurry of movement. She asked Shah Rukh what was going on and he mumbled something about Meer being unwell. Shahnaz walked into the house. When she saw Meer's body, swathed in white, lying inert in the center of their tiny living room, surrounded by wailing women, Shahnaz collapsed like a tree felled by an ax. Her fall shattered glasses of water that were placed on the floor. For days, Shahnaz did not shed a tear. Instead she retreated into a depression from which she would never fully emerge.

Shah Rukh was two weeks short of his fifteenth birthday. He never wrote poetry again. Without Meer around to record them, the jejune rhymes no longer seemed special. Shah Rukh grieved, exhausted and fiercely angry, but he bounced back without pause. His eighth-grade teacher, Seetha Venkateshwaran, recalled, "He wasn't the type to miss school and his mother wasn't the type to make him stay back. He just moved ahead."

St. Columba's School, where Shah Rukh was enrolled in kindergarten in January 1972 when he was six years old, is an imposing institution spread over several acres of south Delhi. Founded by the Indian Province of the Congregation of Christian Brothers, it was started on April 29, 1941, with thirty-two boys. The school's reputation grew with its size. By 1955 the students numbered 2,200 and a new building had been added. The Irish brothers were famous for discipline. Up to the late 1980s, corporal punishment was used at St. Columba's. Smaller children were spanked. Older ones were caned on their backsides—a few whacks meant sitting on a sweater or bag all day to cushion the cuts. And the eldest boys were rapped on their knuckles and fingertips. On cold winter days the canes connecting with frozen fingertips caused immediate blisters. The brothers hid canes in their robes. If a rule was broken, punishment was immediate and agonizing.

The school insisted on clipped nails and short hair. Anybody with hair over the designated length was sent from school to the barber on the sidewalk at the nearby Gole market. Shah Rukh, blessed with a dense, unruly mop, made this trip often. It would be 7:30 A.M. and the barber had usually just woken up. He'd have morning breath and eyes full of sleep, but he always began the haircut with the same question, "What style haircut do you want, Dharmendra or Amitabh Bachchan?" Years later, Shah Rukh knew he had attained stardom when hairstylists told him that clients were asking for the Shah Rukh Khan cut.

The specter of cane-carrying priests and the lengthy roster of rules at St. Columba's didn't deter Shah Rukh. He was a master prankster. His best tricks were witty, audacious, and usually put his budding acting talent to use. In the ninth grade, he borrowed an Amitabh Bachchan line from a film called *Kaalia* to convince a teacher that his parents and the school administration had mistreated him. The teacher was his only tenuous support. Considering this and his fragile mental state, he told her, she should allow him to skip some upcoming tests. "*Mere liye toh oopar bhagwan hai, neeche aap. Beech mein Yamraj talwar le kar vaar kar raha hai,*" he said. (For me, God is above and you below. In between, Yamraj, the Lord of Death, is attacking me with his sword.) The implication being that the teacher was the only one who could save him from destruction. She bought it and allowed him to miss the tests.

By the eleventh grade, Shah Rukh was more daring. Once, when class got unbearably monotonous, he feigned an epileptic fit. He fell on the floor and started frothing at the mouth. His friends, in on the con, convinced the teacher, who happened to be wearing suede shoes, that the only way to rouse Shah Rukh was by making him smell a suede shoe. The teacher promptly volunteered his. Finally they carried him and the shoe out on the pretext of taking him to a doctor. They loitered outside school while the teacher hopped around with one shoe all day.

On occasions, when the joke went too far, Fatima was summoned to school to discuss her errant son. But Shah Rukh never crossed the line enough to invite suspension or expulsion. Good grades gave him leeway. So did his sporting activities: Shah Rukh played hockey, football, and cricket and led the school teams in several sports. "He was a boundary breaker," said his middle-school headmaster, Brother Eric D'Souza, "but he was also smart enough to live on the edge and not get caught."

Brother D'Souza was the resident rock star at St. Columba's. He stretched the definition of both teacher and priest and was a seminal influence in Shah Rukh's life. Eric was only in his twenties, but being younger than the other teachers wasn't his only distinguishing feature. Eric had long hair and he played the guitar. In charge of several co-curricular activities, he hung out with the boys after school and gave their adolescent angst a sympathetic ear. Students could gather in his room for a dose of music and advice. Eric initiated them into the latest Western chartbusters, including Pink Floyd's excitingly subversive "Another Brick in the Wall." He remembered each boy by his first name. He was brimming with new, dynamic ideas. Eric introduced computers to the school, writing a textbook for the students himself.

But the priest was no slouch in the severity department. He insisted on academic brilliance and caned students when they fell short of their potential. If a student was capable of getting 95 out of 100 marks, 90 were not good enough. Eric, who was nicknamed *Kauwa*, or Crow, by the other boys because he had a hooked nose and dark skin, tried to instill in them the necessity of thinking out of the box and continuously raising the bar. He was equal parts nightmare and role model.

In 1983, Eric cast Shah Rukh in his first major role: that of the wizard in a musical called *The Wiz*, based on *The Wizard of Oz*. There was stiff competition but Shah Rukh got the role because, Eric said, "he was versatile and had enough self-belief to be goofy if necessary." Shah Rukh had so much confidence that he even attempted to sing the songs in the musical, but he couldn't pull it off. Eric, who had a soaring, sonorous voice, and another boy, Palash Sen, who would grow up to be a famous vocalist, were Shah Rukh's first playback singers (that is they actually sang the songs, which he lip-synched onstage).

The highlight of Shah Rukh's school days was the creation of a "gang." On September 9, 1984, eighteen-year-old Shah Rukh and four of his closest friends formed the C-Gang. The C stood for "cool." Coolness was the group's mission, function, and reason for being. The boys worked toward it. Vivek Khushalani was the rich kid. His father brought T-shirts from America for the gang. Each shirt had the C-Gang logo and the member's name at the back. Raman Sharma's cousin, a graphic designer, created the logo. She painted a tiny but visible C-GANG on their white uniforms so that even in school their special status was underlined. The other members were Bikash Mathur and Shah Rukh's closest friend, Ashok Vassan. Outside school, the designated C-Gang uniform was gray Nike shoes, blue jeans, and white T-shirts. The boys had laminated identity cards made in a shop in Connaught Place for 25 rupees (50 cents) each. The cards had a picture of the bearer and the date the gang was started, 9-9-84.

The dictatorial brothers allowed the C-Gang to thrive at St. Columba's, perhaps because it was mostly innocuous posturing. Drugs, alcohol, and sex were still not the adolescent rite of passage they would become a decade later in Delhi. The C-Gang's rebellion was confined to being cool. Even when the boys broke rules, it was always just short of being illegal. One night they ran away from their respective homes, each one saying he was spending the night at another person's house. For a few hours they watched planes land from a spot near the Delhi airport called Jumbo Point. The police found them playing hockey on the road and detained them until dawn. This was the extent of their teen spirit.

All five boys came from different backgrounds. Raman's father was a pilot. Vivek's was a businessman who manufactured equipment for oil and gas wells. But these disparities were rarely discussed. They hung out at Nirula's Café in Chanakyapuri and played video games for 25 paise (a fraction of a cent) each in the basement of the Chanakya movie theater. For these outings they pooled their meager pocket monies. When they could, they went bowling at the Qutab Hotel bowling alley. They could rarely afford five-star hotels, and nobody talked about whose father was richer. The boys went to parties dressed in identical C-Gang clothes and often forced the other dancers off the floor by doing the moonwalk and break dancing. They spoke in language left over from Hollywood films: "Yo," "Yaooza," and "Hang ten!" were favorite expressions.

Hollywood was the sacred source of all that was trendy. Made-in-U.S.A. labels were fiercely desired status symbols. Not all the C-Gang members were affluent enough to go abroad; Shah Rukh didn't travel to the West until he was twenty-eight years old. But like city youth across the country, they imbibed the talk, the walk, and the attitude from American films. Ironically, many of these movies were B-grade, and almost all were dated. Stringent import laws meant that Hollywood products would only hit Indian screens a good twelve to eighteen months after a U.S. release. Which meant that long after American teenagers had stopped shearing sweatshirts to look like Jennifer Beals in *Flashdance*, Indian teenagers would be aping the fashion.

But even passé Hollywood glamour was preferable to Bollywood. Hindi films were decidedly down-market. The youth and intelligentsia in urban India looked down upon Bollywood as opium for the unwashed masses. This disdain wasn't unfounded.

The 1980s were the dark ages of Hindi film. New technologies had altered the entertainment environment. Bollywood was thrown off balance, and even the most successful filmmakers found themselves flailing around, trying to regain their rhythm. In 1982, color television came to India. The videocassette recorder, or VCR, followed soon after. For the first time, the audience had a choice. Movies were no longer the only option. In the year 1984–85, the color television industry grew at an astounding 140 percent. For a certain class of people going to the movie theaters became both unnecessary and unattractive.

There was little to draw them out. Hindi films were in an artistic wasteland. Amitabh Bachchan still ruled the roost. In May 1980, *India Today*, the country's leading weekly newsmagazine, anointed him "The One Man Industry." But this colossal clout at the box office had stifled creative vision. Amitabh's directors, afraid to tamper with his superhero image, continued to flog the Angry Young Man formula until it turned flaccid. After a decade of Amitabh's vigilante fists, music had been relegated to the sidelines. Songs were merely fillers. So were the actresses. The heroines in Amitabh's films were largely glamorous damsels in distress who provided visual relief from the violence. The titles reveal how a world-class actor calcified into a cliché: *Desh Premee* (Patriot), *Andhaa Kanoon* (Blind Justice), *Inquilab* (Revolution), *Aakhree Raasta* (The Final Road), *Shahenshah* (Emperor). It's difficult to determine whether the uninviting content deterred viewers or whether the indifference of viewers forced filmmakers to woo them with even more coarse content. But theater audiences now largely consisted of lumpen young men, or what the Bollywood trade calls the "front benchers." They seemed to prefer basic action and loud emotion.

A slew of directors—who had originally worked in the Tamil film industry in south India—catered to the front benchers. From 1983 onward there was a spate of shrill, gaudy melodramas. Hindi cinema has never placed a premium on subtlety, but even by Bollywood standards these films were grossly over the top. *Himmatwala* (The Brave), the most successful of the "south-style" films, featured a fantasy romantic song. These sequences, in which the leads are transported by romantic emotion to places of stunning beauty, are a Bollywood staple. But here the leads found themselves on a beach, performing hyper, acrobatic dance steps amidst hundreds of brightly painted earthen pots. The pots made such an impression that a year later, another film, *Tohfa* (The Gift), had the same actors on a similar beach doing furious dance steps in gigantic concentric circles of brass pots. Dharmesh Darshan, a leading director from the 1990s, summarized the movement succinctly, "Suddenly, Bombay cinema instead of national going international became national going regional."

It is a testament to Amitabh Bachchan's talent that even when his films faltered in the 1980s, his fan following didn't. This included Shah Rukh. Shah Rukh continued to be a devotee, memorizing dialogue and sequences—a favorite was a line from *Shahenshah*: "*Rishtey mein toh hum tumhare baap lagte hain, naam hain Shahenshah*," the tough street vigilante played by Amitabh growls, his right arm inexplicably covered in chain mail (Think of me as invincible and be afraid; they call me Emperor). But alongside the faux street grit of Bachchan, Shah Rukh cultivated the swagger of John Travolta in *Grease*. His references were Bill Cosby and *Family Ties*. The walls of his bedroom were adorned with posters of Cheryl Ladd and Samantha Fox.

In January 1985, Shah Rukh graduated from St. Columba's. He was given the Sword of Honor, the school's highest award, presented to the student who excels in academics as well as sports and co-curricular activities. Shah Rukh, then nineteen, was the star of the year.

The rigid Christian environment of St. Columba's and the friendships he cultivated over thirteen years set Shah Rukh in a Westernized mold. He was articulate, erudite, and, in many ways, already the yuppie he would play in films a decade later. But that was not the whole story. Shah Rukh's urbane sheen and sophisticated English were leavened by a rough earthiness. One of the earliest film directors to hire him was an art house auteur named Mani Kaul. He was adapting Fyodor Dostoevsky's *The Idiot*. Though Mani Kaul felt that Shah Rukh had too much of a "baby face" to play the sinister Rogozhin, he still cast him because he found Shah Rukh "a strange mix of someone beautiful and slimy." Shah Rukh was equal parts sophisticated *haut bourgeois* and lumpen ruffian.

This was appropriate to the city he grew up in. Delhi is a peculiar mix of urban and rural. Posh housing colonies stand next to villages. In some areas only a stretch of road divides sprawling homes worth millions of rupees from mud hutments. The crumbling ruins of earlier centuries jut out at impossible angles, reminding residents of the rich history of the city. The earliest architectural relics in Delhi date back to 300 B.C. Delhi has been the capital city of seven empires, and in it several cities collide: the New Delhi built by savvy Punjabi businessmen who arrived during Partition; the old Delhi of Mughal emperors; the colonial Delhi designed by British architect Sir Edwin Lutyens; and the rustic Delhi, coarse and brutal like the neighboring states of Haryana and Uttar Pradesh.

At St. Columba's, Shah Rukh was the unfailingly courteous, diligent student. His seventh-grade teacher, Savita Raisingh, recalled showing Shah Rukh's meticulously neat, indexed homework to other students as an example. Every day, on the bus ride home, he would help her carry her books. But Shah Rukh was equally fluent in the more uncouth culture that flourished outside. Hindi *gaalis*, or curse words, peppered his language. Fights were not uncommon. Shah Rukh saw knives pulled and blood flow. He followed Meer's golden rule: if the opponent is bigger, hit him on the head with a rock and run.

When he was twelve years old, Shah Rukh went to the Uphaar cinema in Green Park to see the Amitabh Bachchan film *Parvarish* (Upbringing). Two friends were with him. Tickets were sold out and the three boys started negotiating with the black market man outside the theater. They were surprised when he offered to sell them tickets at the regular theater sale price. The boys agreed and Shah Rukh went with the scalper into the underground parking lot to conduct the transaction. But the regular-priced tickets had a hidden cost. In the darkness of the parking lot, the scalper unzipped his pants and asked for a favor.

Shah Rukh was initially afraid. He ran away. But later on he and his friends had a good laugh enacting the scene. The incident did not damage Shah Rukh. "It wasn't a moment that scarred me or even made an impression," Shah Rukh said. "It was all part of growing up." He imagined that the man is perhaps still a scalper, selling tickets now for Shah Rukh Khan films.

These contrasting tones were instrumental in Shah Rukh's success as an actor. Though he became famous playing the rich romantic hero, he retained a basic Everyman sensibility that connected across audiences. Amitabh Bachchan played the ordinary man who takes on the system, but he was very much a star on a pedestal. He inspired a reverential low-angle view. But Shah Rukh Khan remained the superstar boy next door. The audience viewed him as an ideal husband, son, brother, friend. He wasn't an inaccessible celestial being, but simply the most charismatic member of the family.

You Should Be in the Movies

"You should be in the movies." The first person to tell Shah Rukh this was a man called Barry John. It was the summer of 1985. The setting was appropriately gaudy. They were at a party in south Delhi's Saket area. Disco lights glared. The makeshift dance floor was packed with heaving, sweaty college students. Shah Rukh, a ferociously energetic dancer, whirled around like a dervish, break dancing and twirling on his head.

Through June and July, Shah Rukh had been working in a production of *Annie Get Your Gun*, performed by the students of Lady Shri Ram College. The college had roped in the city's leading theater company, Theater Action Group, or TAG, to put on the musical with the students. Barry John was the founder and director of TAG. Since it was a big production, male dancers were auditioned and selected from outside the company.

Barry wasn't sure what prompted Shah Rukh to audition: the play or the famously attractive ladies of Lady Shri Ram College. Most of the casting had been done by the time Shah Rukh arrived and he had to settle for the part of a singer-dancer in the chorus. But after the show was done, Shah Rukh joined TAG. Barry was his first and only acting teacher.

Barry was born and raised in the United Kingdom. He was part of the first wave of hippies who hit India in the late 1960s. The flower power movement was at its peak. Like much of his generation, Barry grew his hair long, wore kurtas, and listened to Ravi Shankar. He was, he said, "anti-war, anti-government, anti-money, anti-establishment." But Barry was too conscientious to be an authentic hippie. While the others spread out to Goa and Kulu Manali to smoke pot and meditate, Barry did theater. He came to India in 1968 to participate in a project in Bangalore and stayed on. In 1973, Barry created TAG.

Performing English theater in India is a pursuit of passion. Even in the late 1980s, when there were fewer entertainment options, the audience was spare, the money negligible, and the impact limited to a sliver of the urbane upper classes. The TAG core group consisted of twenty-odd people who were driven solely by their love for theater. The company staged at least two plays every year. The members multi-tasked, so actors were also in charge of sponsorships, public relations, marketing, props, sets, and costumes. Since most had day jobs, rehearsals were held daily from 6 to 9 P.M. at the Father Agnel School. Whoever wasn't required in the scene being rehearsed went on tea runs. Occasionally a sponsor would come forth and they would get paid 100 or 200 rupees ($2.25 to $4.50) per show.

Barry was not a snob. So TAG productions ranged from ambitious adaptations of Shakespeare plays to popular Neil Simon comedies and children's plays. The group had an unspoken but distinct class system. One lot of players was senior both in age and experience—many of them later became successful on film and television. The rest were freshers, which included Shah Rukh and his friends Benny Thomas and Divya Seth. Shah Rukh didn't quite fit in with the older set. They spoke in clipped British accents about Brecht and The Method and he, with his Amitabh Bachchan hangover, was theatrical in the Bollywood sense of the word. Shah Rukh's cultural references were more pedestrian. He was keenly intelligent, but he wasn't an intellectual.

The seniors flaunted what TAG's executive director, Sanjoy Roy, dubbed "a mansion and cars lifestyle." They partied at Bally High, the posh Chinese rooftop restaurant at the Maurya Hotel. Some had high-ranking day jobs. In Delhi's class-obsessed culture—where you live defines who you are—Shah Rukh's down-market address confirmed his outsider status. The congested Gautam Nagar colony, where Shah Rukh stayed in a stiflingly narrow, three-storied house, was not a name to be dropped. But what the freshers lacked in sophistication and knowledge they made up for in energy and enthusiasm.

Unlike the older players, who had lives outside the theater, Shah Rukh, Benny, and Divya had little else to occupy their energy or imagination. This was the magic hour of their lives: that cusp between school and career when there are no responsibilities and everything seems possible. Shah Rukh enrolled at Hans Raj College for a degree in economics, but his real education started in the evenings with TAG. After rehearsals, they ate *parathas* at a roadside stall near the Moolchand flyover, watched grainy movies on video, and passionately discussed acting.

Bollywood was not part of these discussions. Shah Rukh was an unapologetic movie buff. He watched Hindi movies almost daily. Fatima's sister, who now lived in London, had sent them a VCR and every night Shah Rukh and Fatima settled in front of it. Shah Rukh pressed his mother's feet as the drama unfolded. Shah Rukh knew obscure details about long-forgotten films and actors. He could persuasively discuss the merits of Pran, a leading villain from the 1950s. He fantasized about being heroic like Amitabh Bachchan, but he did not want to be a hero. Shah Rukh, whose success became the stuff of Bollywood folklore, never aspired to be a contender.

He had more practical ambitions about short films, television, and advertising. Benny and Shah Rukh had a long-standing joke about someday starting an advertising agency called the *Nahin Na*, or No, Agency. Each commercial they created would work with the word No, as in: "Do you wish to have fifteen children? *Nahin Na*? Then use Nirodh condoms." The two advertising moguls would own a three-level building so that they could have apartments on the top floor, the agency on the bottom, and a discotheque with pool tables in between.

Fatima was perhaps the only one who cherished Bollywood dreams. She was exceptionally supportive of Shah Rukh's acting. She did not demand that he help run the business or contribute to the family income. Shah Rukh would occasionally help out by running chores for the restaurant or doing some bookkeeping, but nothing more. His friends dropped in to the restaurant for free meals. Because their more conservative parents disapproved, they often brought their girlfriends to Shah Rukh's house. Fatima didn't ask questions and instead mothered them with affection and food. She rarely interfered in Shah Rukh's life. He would come home at 2 A.M. and ask for a cup of tea and she would, without question or irritation, get up to make it. She believed that her son, brown, scrawny, with a live-wire intensity and a big mop of hair, was the next Dilip Kumar. Fatima was Shah Rukh's first and biggest fan.

Barry was an astute and patient teacher. His style was not authoritarian. He gently honed students into becoming performers. Barry's method was the workshop. Students would grapple with characters and situations. Barry rarely told a student how to act. Instead, he would question each expression and gesture, helping the actor to chip away the excess and arrive at the core of the character. They trained extensively in the use of space and movement, and did mime exercises with masks. A few days before show time, Barry would give a few suggestions to polish up the final act. Critically, the interpretation of the character came from the student. Barry was the guide. Shah Rukh said he learned a vital lesson in these workshops: that "there is no right or wrong way to do a scene. The Method is what works for you. The barometer ultimately is how many people like it."

What worked for Shah Rukh, in theater and later in television and films, was energy. Shah Rukh was a flamboyant actor. His performances were gymnastic, forceful, and extravagant. He had spontaneity and physicality, not gravitas. Even as a student struggling with the ropes of theater he was larger than life. Which is perhaps why his most successful performances were in plays for children. He was selected to play major roles in boisterous comedies such as *Old King Cole* and *The Incredible Vanishing*.

Children's theater required a broader acting style. The modes of expression were physical: pratfalls, kicks, slaps. In these plays, the sportsman was as evident as the actor (fittingly he got a TAG football team started, which played matches on the weekends). Shah Rukh was an unrestrained performer. At one point in *The Incredible Vanishing*, he was required to thump another character on the back. He did this with gusto. After the first few performances, the actor told Shah Rukh to stop hitting him so hard. In the next performance, Shah Rukh hit harder and added a few extra thumps for effect because it got a bigger laugh out of the children. Even in those days he had a fairly good idea of what worked with the audience. The impact was what mattered. An actor had to do whatever it takes to get it.

Shah Rukh spent five years with TAG. In this time he did not, in Barry's words, do a "serious or strong role." His persona was exuberant, comical, and, invariably, lightweight. There were flashes of the future star in plays such as *Baghdad Ka Ghulam*, an adaptation of an Italian comedy about mistaken identity, in which Shah Rukh successfully played a swashbuckling romantic hero. But Shah Rukh, as Barry said, "never did a Hamlet." His signature performances relied less on internalization and more on what Barry called "advertising," or outward display. Barry's suggestion that Shah Rukh do Hindi films was a backhanded compliment.

For more serious material, Barry usually turned to an actor called Rituraj. Rituraj had joined TAG in 1981, when he was only sixteen years old, and matured into the company's favored leading man. There was, he recalled, perhaps one production in his ten years at TAG in which he did not get the lead. In Delhi theater then, Rituraj, a more intense and subtle actor, was a superstar. "When the curtain used to rise," he said, "I could hear whispers in the audience. They were saying my name. I loved it." Like Shah Rukh, Rituraj also moved to Mumbai in the early 1990s and became a successful television actor, but unlike Shah Rukh, he could not make the leap to films. "Perhaps I'm a coward," he said, "or maybe I didn't believe that much in myself. That was the large difference between Shah Rukh and me. He was always the guy who believed in himself."

In 1990, Barry directed a play called *Whose Life Is It Anyway?*, about a paralyzed sculptor who fights for the right to die. The lead spends the duration of the play lying in bed. Shah Rukh wanted to play the sculptor, but Barry was not convinced he could carry the role. It had too much stillness, both literally and metaphorically. They argued about the casting choices but ultimately Rituraj played the sculptor and Shah Rukh did the cameo of a ward boy, who is cheerful, comic, a positive life force in the grim, death-ridden environment.

A few years later, Shah Rukh would tell journalists that as an actor he had only five expressions but he was a success because his rivals had only two. From the time he started performing professionally, Shah Rukh's acting was as much about charisma as craft. "Shah Rukh may not have been the best actor of his period," Sanjoy Roy said, "but even then he was a star." The debate about Shah Rukh's skills started during his TAG days—when a performance went acutely over the top, his friends joked that Shah Rukh "had broken the roof." It continued long after he became a globally recognized actor. If Amitabh Bachchan was defined by a mercurial intensity, Shah Rukh's keynote was innate buoyancy. An energetic determination tinted every role he played. He was first, foremost, and instinctively an entertainer. "The essence is can I make you laugh, can I make you have a good time?" he said. So Shah Rukh evolved into what he called "a great star actor. I always play a role as Shah Rukh Khan playing a role. It's never the role being essayed by Shah Rukh."

Ironically, this high-beam star quality brought him his first few rejections. Apart from the TAG play, Shah Rukh was also passed over for the lead in the first film he ever acted in, a small, eccentric movie made in 1988 by director Pradip Krishen and his writer-actor companion Arundhati Roy, called *In Which Annie Gives It Those Ones*. The film, set in a Delhi architecture school in 1974, was, in Arundhati's words, "lunatic fringe cinema." The actors were unknown. The language was Delhi "Hinglish," a riotous blend of English and Hindi with a smattering of Punjabi. So a typical scene would be:

BIGSHIT: *Pata nehi yaar Annie ka kuchh*. I asked him in the bogs and he started giving it those ones.

RADHA: What?

BIGSHIT: *Voi apne* usual ones about rural urban nexus and fruit orchards. (*Putting on a Punjabi accent*) *Bhai,* I'm just a simple *seedha sadha* man. *Yeh sab merey palley nahi padta*.

The main characters were peculiar, bell-bottom-wearing students. The lead character, Annie (not a woman as the name suggests but a burly man named Anand), had spent four years in fifth year and raised chickens in his dorm room. *In Which Annie Gives It Those Ones* had a wonderful low-budget-grunge vibe. It was a witty and insightful comment on the stagnant education system and college life in India.

Pradip and Arundhati were marginal players in India's art

house scene. The "off-beat" Hindi film came into vogue in the early 1970s. Though the movement never acquired the stature or impact of the *Nouvelle Vague*, these filmmakers, like their French counterparts, attempted to create a new language of film. Several state-funded institutions gave the movement a fillip. In 1960, the government had set up the Film Finance Corporation—in 1975 it became the National Film Development Corporation—which supported and financed "parallel" cinema. Simultaneously, the Film and Television Institute of India in Pune created a new generation of technicians and directors who were schooled in world cinema and eager to explore new ways of storytelling.

Their inspiration was Italian neo-realism and Satyajit Ray's 1955 classic *Pather Panchali* (Song of the Road). In 1969, Bengali director Mrinal Sen made the first Hindi art house film: *Bhuvan Shome* (Mr. Shome). *Bhuvan Shome*, the story of a dour railways officer who finds personal freedom, was austere, expressionistic, and exhilaratingly new. Its critical and commercial success encouraged a slew of filmmakers to abandon mainstream diktats. So the actors, usually new and possessing no star appeal, were shorn of glamour; the settings were realistic; the stories, typically, were issue based; and there were no songs.

The New Wave threw up several outstanding names and films. Director Shyam Benegal's first film, *Ankur* (Seed), made in 1974, was a riveting statement about the oppression of peasants. Benegal's seed spawned a school of auteurs. In 1983, Govind Nihalani, who was Benegal's cinematographer on *Ankur*, made *Ardh Satya* (Half Truth), about an honest policeman who is brutalized by the system. The film worked critically and commercially (Bollywood promptly co-opted the theme, and Amitabh Bachchan spent many screen hours as an honest cop caught in the quicksand of corruption).

Over the next two decades, however, Hindi art house cinema fell into a typically mainstream trap. The early flashes of brilliance fossilized into uninspiring, rigid patterns. Art films established their own star system—the most in-demand were the quartet of Naseeruddin Shah, Om Puri, Shabana Azmi, and Smita Patil. The themes—oppression of the poor and women in rural India, the caste system, the corrupt establishment—were recycled. Arundhati labeled it "behalfism," that is, middle-class urban people making films on behalf of rural folk. The films were often painfully self-conscious and dreary. A story goes that director Raj Kapoor once attempted to watch Mrinal Sen's 1984 film *Khandhar* (The Ruins). The movie was about a lonely woman who lives with her blind, invalid mother in a sprawling but ruined ancestral house. Half an hour into the ponderous film, Kapoor yawned, stretched, and declared loudly enough for the entire theater to hear, "*Bas ab aur nahin*" (Enough, no more).

By the late 1980s and early 1990s, art house cinema was gasping for breath. The paucity of distributors and viewers confined it to festivals and television. *In Which Annie Gives It Those Ones* was telecast once on the late-night slot on Doordarshan, when few people saw it.

The film had several parts for young actors. Pradip and Arundhati were coming off a massive failure. An ambitious twenty-six-part television serial they were making called *Bargad* (The Banyan Tree) was called off after two years of research and writing and fifty days of shooting. Arundhati writes that she and Pradip "were still mourning the loss of our stillborn story," when *In Which Annie Gives It Those Ones* started to fall into place. For Pradip, one of the hardest aspects of *Bargad* had been working with "mini-stars," that is actors who were recognized but not quite big league. He dubbed their acting style "*daraaz-kholna*," or opening drawers, meaning that for every scene they would open a mental drawer and find a performance they had seen somewhere and been impressed by. Instead of attempting to create something unique, they would reduce the role to something that had already been done.

For the film, Pradip was determined to find new actors by holding intensive workshops. Hinglish was essential to the texture of the film, and finding actors who could speak it authentically was critical. Pradip approached TAG. In April 1988, fifteen actors, including Shah Rukh, Rituraj, Benny, and Divya, started to participate in workshops held in a small house in Chanakyapuri. Pradip used video as a tool to familiarize the actors with the intimacy of cinema and relax in front of the camera. It was the first time Shah Rukh saw himself on-screen. To get into character, the men sprouted beards and let their hair grow. Three times a week for six weeks, they strived to become the people Pradip and Arundhati had created. Each one hoped to land a major role.

The two leads in the film, Annie and Radha, were already cast: an actor called Arjun Raina would play the idiosyncratic idealist Annie, and Arundhati was going to be Radha. But there were a slew of other attention-grabbing characters. The best male role was that of Radha's boyfriend, also called Arjun.

Rituraj got Arjun. The competition for the third lead of the film was stiff, but Rituraj instinctively knew he would get it. "I've been writing a diary since I was eleven," he said. "When I read the script for the first time, I went home and wrote 'I'm going to be doing Arjun in this film.'" Divya got to play Lakes, an annoying, prim student who flirts with her teacher hoping to pass but who fails anyway. Benny got to play Rashid, another student. Shah Rukh was cast as a character with not even enough screen time to warrant a name. He was simply "Senior," the gay college gossip who appears in exactly four scenes. He speaks in only two. In the others, he is just one more face in a group of students.

Shah Rukh's stratospheric career is at least partially the result of a series of fortuitous upgrades. In nearly all the early television serials and films, he was either the second or third choice for the role or he was originally cast as a minor character that evolved into the lead. *Annie* was perhaps the first and only downgrade Shah Rukh would ever experience. He came in as a senior TAG actor and became an extra.

The fairy-tale success in his later years did not blunt the hurt and acute shame of this rejection. It wasn't just that he wasn't good enough, but that his peers were better. *In Which Annie Gives It Those Ones* was about the vulnerability and tenderness of youth. Shah Rukh, Pradip said, was so confident and smooth that it went against the grain for him to play such awkward, clumsy characters. "In a sense, he was already in the heroic mold and there were no heroes in our film."

Shah Rukh's first scene ever in a film has him standing at a door explaining to a fresher why a classmate from Uganda grinds his teeth while sleeping. His hair is plastered down with oil and parted in the middle. One hand is in a cast. Wearing a short Chinese robe, he looks decidedly fey. Shah Rukh says, "He does it when he's dreaming of Idi Amin. . . . Idi Amin killed his Pop . . . *kabhi toh* it's *itna* loud you can hear it in the corridor." Before he did the shoot,

Shah Rukh told Pradip and Arundhati two things: that he would one day win an Oscar, and that he would win it for playing a gay role.

Even after he was anointed King Khan, Shah Rukh did not forget this first failure. In 1997, Arundhati Roy won the Booker Prize for her stunning first novel, *The God of Small Things*. It was a national celebration. Shah Rukh Khan, now a star, was asked to grace a function in her honor. He declined.

Scandal in Panscheel Park

For Indians, Marine Drive is the unmistakable symbol of the city of Mumbai. The spectacularly curved six-lane road runs about two miles from the city's business district, Nariman Point, to its most exclusive residential area, Malabar Hill. It's flanked by the Arabian Sea on one side and a row of art deco buildings on the other. Marine Drive defines Mumbai in the way that the Statue of Liberty does New York or the Eiffel Tower Paris. The windswept promenade, the dramatic curve of the streetlights, and the ceaseless parade of walkers, hawkers, children, and lovers embody the frenzied and fragile spirit of the city.

Movies have only added to its allure. Generations of directors have shot on Marine Drive. The promenade has seen it all: romantic duets in the rain; high-speed car chases; sad sequences with lonely, homeless heroes sleeping on stone benches. Sometime in 1990, a scene rich in drama, bravado, and heartache, typical of a Bollywood movie, played out on Marine Drive. Except this was real life.

Shah Rukh stood on the parapet on the Marine Drive overpass. He had spent the night, sleeping intermittently, at Bombay Central railway station. He was disheveled, sweaty, and bleary-eyed. He was also hungry. Shah Rukh had recently sold his Pentax camera for about 4,000 rupees ($90), but between him and his friends, Benny Thomas and Ashish Mittal, the money had quickly run out. The past few days had been a haze of desperation and frustration. Dawn had just broken. Shah Rukh looked at the brightening sky and declared in a determined voice, "One day I'm going to rule this city."

Shah Rukh had come to Mumbai to look for his girlfriend, Gauri Chibba. He was unfamiliar with the city. He did not know where she was staying, but he knew that she loved to swim and so was likely to be around a beach. He also knew that the chances of finding her were slim. But then the odds had always been stacked against them.

Romance in urban India comes with a set of taboos. Of these, the proscription against Hindu-Muslim relationships is the strongest and the thorniest. India is an acutely divided country. The relations between the minority Muslims and the majority Hindus are, at best, in a state of simmer. The two communities are scarred and separated by a long and bloody history. On the streets, divisions are real and palpable. A person's last name denotes his religion, and even educated, affluent, and secular families balk at the idea of intermarriage. Gauri was Hindu.

Shah Rukh first saw her at a party. These gatherings were the Indian version of American teen parties. They started at six in the evening and usually wrapped up by nine—the hosts pulled down curtains to get a nocturnal ambience. There was no alcohol. The boys stood on one side and the girls on the other. When a popular song started, the boys were expected to make the first move and ask the girls to dance. The most sensational part of the evening was slow-dancing cheek to cheek.

By now, C-Gang members were into making moves, so after a tennis match with a girl, Vivek would casually drop the line, "Babe, the ball is in your court now. It's up to you to reject it or give me a love game." Some of them had girlfriends. But Shah Rukh, who would become the romantic fantasy of millions of women, was a clumsy suitor. He was petrified of talking to girls and too shy to slow-dance at the party. He noticed Gauri's maroon corduroy jeans. She was only fourteen. He was four years older, but she was more fashionable than he was. She had wavy brown hair descending below her shoulders and a perky, upturned nose. Gauri wasn't a classic Indian beauty with large eyes and fair skin, but she was alluring and relaxed enough around boys to make conversation. Shah Rukh got her phone number the third time they met, on October 25, 1984.

Their first date lasted all of five minutes. Gauri lived in Panscheel Park, a genteel, upper-middle-class enclave of bungalows and row houses in south Delhi. The hub of action was the expansive British-style Panscheel Club. The club was crawling with Panscheel Park matrons who spent afternoons at the cards table while their children swam and played badminton. It wasn't the ideal place to conduct a secret romance. But a young, broke couple courting in Delhi didn't have many options.

The date was chaperoned. Shah Rukh was accompanied by Raman, another C-Gang member. The boys drove to the club on Shah Rukh's uncle's beat-up scooter. Shah Rukh and Gauri sat by the pool and nervously sipped colas. Raman killed time elsewhere in the club. Then it was over. But the scooter's rickety engine gave way. It refused to start. Raman and Shah Rukh pushed it down the road, desperately hoping that Gauri wouldn't notice their un-cool, tattered vehicle.

Through these furtive meetings and missives sent through friends, a relationship developed. Their romance had a Bollywood-like innocence to it. Gauri's father, Ramesh, was a retired army officer. She lived in a joint family. Her maternal uncle Tejinder Tiwari and his family lived in the house. The two families also worked together, running a successful garment export business. In a home full of relatives, cousins, and servants, subterfuge was essential.

Shah Rukh and Gauri developed an elaborate system of deception. He could not telephone her directly because a boy calling frequently would attract attention. So Shah Rukh would get other girls to ask for her. They would say "Shaheen" was calling, which Gauri would recognize as code for Shah Rukh. Gauri wasn't allowed to date, but she would meet Shah Rukh at parties where she would come with her girlfriends. He made history notes for her and taught her how to drive. They would wander around the sprawling Jawaharlal Nehru University campus, hug for a few moments, and then go back to their homes.

Both were young and immature. Their relationship was bumpy. Despite his cool C-Gang posturing, Shah Rukh was a claustrophobically possessive boyfriend. He objected to her wearing white shirts (they might be transparent) or leaving her hair untied (she might be too striking). Swimsuits were anathema. If she so much as spoke to another boy, he flew into a rage. Shah Rukh had what he described as "a small-town middle-class mentality." At one point Gauri decided that she had had enough. For six or seven months she avoided Shah Rukh, refusing to meet him or come to the phone when "Shaheen" called. Then, without telling him, she went to Mumbai for a holiday.

Shah Rukh, bewildered at her silence, called Gauri's friends. As per her instructions, they revealed nothing and instead, he recalled, lectured him in patronizing tones about how time changes relationships (he would hold this against them even after the tumultuous love story ended in a happy marriage). But Shah Rukh was not so easily eluded. He called her house, changed his voice to sound like a girl's, and asked for Gauri. He was informed that she was in Mumbai. Like a true Hindi movie hero who will not be cowed by logic, he followed her.

Shah Rukh came to Mumbai with two friends, 10,000 rupees ($225), and the shaky theory that since Gauri liked swimming, he was likely to find her at a beach. The first few days of the mission were spent in luxurious comfort at a friend's empty apartment in the posh Cuffe Parade area. But then the friend's parents returned from vacation and the three boys found themselves out on the street. The money soon ran out and Shah Rukh was forced to sell his camera. The boys slept on benches and at railway stations, washed up in hotel bathrooms, ate food from street stalls, and wandered around Mumbai looking for the girl who loved to swim. But Gauri was nowhere in sight.

On day eight, distressed and heartbroken, the boys decided the search was futile. Ashish was especially weary since the other two were using their meager money to buy cigarettes instead of food. They used the last few rupees they had to buy train tickets back to Delhi. But Shah Rukh refused to give up without exploring one final stretch of beach in north Mumbai. A few hours before they were scheduled to take the train, Shah Rukh found Gauri at the distant Gorai Beach.

But even this lovelorn expedition didn't convince Gauri that Shah Rukh was the man for her. After returning to Delhi, she told him that she needed space and thought they should take a break from each other. It was, he said, "the usual shit that girls talk." But it broke his heart. He also stepped back from the relationship and immersed himself in theater. Nearly four months later, Gauri sent Shah Rukh a letter saying that she missed him. She came to see him and said that she had met other boys, but she didn't want to do that anymore. She liked him. "We resolved then," he said, "in our heads and hearts that we would marry."

When Shah Rukh declared his intent of becoming the ruler of Bombay at dawn on Marine Drive, Benny punctured the golden movie moment by laughing loudly and saying, "Shut up, don't talk shit." This stubborn defiance in the face of misery was typical Shah Rukh. But it wasn't merely a fanciful boast. Shah Rukh was already on his way to ruling the city.

The medium of ascent was television. The 1980s were for Indian television what the 1950s were for Indian film: a creative and commercial explosion. Viewers still did not have choices; cable television entered the Indian market only in 1990. But the country's single channel, the government-run Doordarshan, reinvented itself. By the end of 1982, Indian viewers could at last watch color television. In July 1983, the Information and Broadcast Ministry relaxed sponsorship guidelines and invited private producers to create programming.

Until then, television had largely been political propaganda—

the ministers of the day cutting ribbons, giving speeches, visiting afflicted areas—and crushingly boring educational shows, all in relentlessly bleak black-and-white. Doordarshan created all of the programming with the aim of social change, not entertainment, which prompted at least one critic to comment that "tedium is the message." Suddenly there was color and there was fun, even if it came with an occasional moral attached. Comedies such as *Yeh Jo Hai Zindagi* (This Is Life) and soap operas like the 156-episode *Hum Log* (We, the People) captured the Indian imagination. A story in the newsmagazine *India Today* reported that in 1985, 2 million television sets were sold. That is, four Indian homes acquired a television set every minute of the day.

Doordarshan, which had made a net income of 7.7 million rupees ($170,000) in 1975, recorded advertising revenues of 1.61 billion rupees ($36 million) in 1988–89. The channel continued to be dogged by charges of corruption and nepotism—getting shows approved at the Doordarshan office in Delhi, the infamous Mandi House, necessarily involved kickbacks to the bureaucrats. But many of the shows created at the time are benchmarks of Indian television: Govind Nihalani's searing Partition drama *Tamas* (Darkness, 1986), director Ramesh Sippy's epic soap opera, *Buniyaad* (Foundation,1986–87), and *Nukkad* (Street Corner, 1986), a tragicomic sitcom about several colorful characters who live on a street corner. In 1987–88, an estimated 60 million people watched the religious epic *Ramayana* every Sunday morning. Newspapers reported that television sets had become temples, with viewers burning incense as they watched Lord Ram battle Ravana.

Shah Rukh's television break came with a serial called *Fauji* (Soldier). It was written and directed by a large and jolly man named Colonel Raj Kapoor. Raj, who had a loud laugh and a propensity for poor jokes, was destined for Bollywood. In 1931, while his mother was giving birth to him, his father was attending the premiere of the first Hindi talkie, *Alam Ara* (The Light of the World). In his college days, Raj was friendly with the more famous Kapoor brothers—Raj, Shammi, and Shashi—and had acting ambitions. But his father would not allow Raj to enter such a disreputable profession, and he was forced to join the army instead. Raj's father died in 1970. In 1975, after twenty-six years of service in the army, Raj opted for early retirement and went into the movies. Raj took on roles in several films as a character actor. But ironically, he had his biggest success when he returned to the life he had abandoned.

Fauji was Raj's tribute to the army. The thirteen-part serial followed the lives of a batch of army cadets as they trained to become commandos. Raj wanted to show how boys become officers and gentlemen, but he did not want a Bollywood-style gloss on the transformation. His aim was a realistic slice of military life.

Shah Rukh was introduced to Raj by Raj's son-in-law Kamal Deewan. Kamal, who dealt in real estate, was showing Fatima some houses. When he heard that her son was an actor, Kamal suggested that Shah Rukh meet Raj. Shah Rukh was already then working in a serial called *Dil Dariya* (A Heart as Vast as the Ocean), being made by reputed film director Lekh Tandon. Lekh and the Colonel were close friends—Shah Rukh would shoot the first four episodes of *Fauji* during the lunch breaks of *Dil Dariya*.

The audition for *Fauji* was a nearly mile-and-a-half run at 6:30 A.M. Raj wanted to make sure that the boys he selected were fit, punctual, and disciplined. Some of the aspirants gave up halfway through, but Shah Rukh kept pace with Raj. The run was followed by an impromptu boxing bout. Raj found Shah Rukh "correct," but initially gave him only a small role. Raj wanted his son Bobby to play one of the lead characters, Abhimanyu Rai. But Bobby was already the cameraman on the serial. Being actor as well would be a logistical nightmare. So Raj upgraded Shah Rukh to Abhimanyu's role. The actors trained for a week at the Rajputana Rifles Regimental Center in Delhi. When shooting started, Raj kept a barber on set to make sure his actors didn't look like the fake, long-haired army men of Hindi movies.

Fauji went on air on January 19, 1989. The first episode started with the assertion that "all incidence [*sic*] & characters of this serial are based on thruth [*sic*] but for security reasons we have changed the names, locations and at few places, the uniforms." *Fauji* was technically sloppy, but the narrative had emotional heft. The male bonding and hesitant romances worked well as a soap opera with a dash of patriotism and valor. The serial became instantly popular. The camera loved Shah Rukh. He wasn't photogenic or fiercely handsome, but his charm spoke to viewers. A series of fortuitous coincidences also worked in his favor. One of the other leading actors said in a press interview that *Fauji* was just another ordinary serial until he, star that he was, agreed to act in it. He later claimed that he had been misquoted, but Raj was upset. Another actor refused to show up for a shoot because he had a fight with an assistant who brought him cold tea. By the fifth episode, Raj was scripting with Shah Rukh at center stage. He became the character with the most compelling love angle and the best action in combat sequences.

As a young boy, Shah Rukh had nurtured dreams of becoming an army officer. In seventh grade, he had even visited his class teacher's husband, a retired brigadier, and seriously discussed the possibilities of army school with him. Shah Rukh believed that being an army man was a "very proud thing." It was fitting that a serial about the army brought him his first taste of fame. When Shah Rukh walked on streets, people stared and occasionally shouted his name: not Shah Rukh Khan, but Abhimanyu or *Fauji*. Among his growing tribe of fans was the Chibba family in Panscheel Park.

For Gauri's father, Ramesh, *Fauji* was pure nostalgia. It took him back thirty years to his own days at the academy. One episode showed Shah Rukh giving drill orders to his subordinates. He did it with the requisite clarity and brevity. Ramesh was impressed by Shah Rukh's acting skills and his ability to master a difficult routine that many army men struggle with. Ramesh had no idea that the actor was dating his daughter. One time, when the family went out for dinner, they saw Shah Rukh sitting in a restaurant. Curiously, he was wearing a shirt that their company had just made for a French buyer. These garments were not available in the market. "Look," Savita said, "there's the *Fauji* boy wearing our shirt." Tejinder wondered if someone had stolen it from the factory. Gauri, who was also present, feigned ignorance of both the man and the shirt she had presented to him.

Eventually the scandalous rumor of a Hindu-Muslim romance reached Gauri's house. Bewildered and hurt, her parents grappled with the gossip. They were not overtly religious people. They didn't believe in elaborate rituals and *pujas*. In fact, Ramesh and Savita had had a love marriage, a rarity for their generation when most young people settled for marriages arranged by parents. They were liberal and loving parents, but Gauri falling in love with a Muslim boy was beyond their comprehension. Gauri had always been a docile, undemanding child. When she was a baby she'd cried so rarely that Savita wondered if her daughter was abnormal. It seemed inconceivable that the same child could transgress in this manner. Ramesh said, "I believed I had failed in my training."

One day Ramesh heard that Gauri was in the Panscheel Club with a boy. He hurried there immediately, but Gauri's cousin, Priyanka, saw him coming and warned Gauri. She ran away while Shah Rukh hid his face with a badminton racket. The couple decided it was time to confront the family with the truth, one by one. Shah Rukh began by softening up the least aggressive member of the family, Gauri's aunt Neeru. Neeru was like a surrogate mother to Gauri. She had helped raise her. Shah Rukh and Gauri met Neeru at a restaurant and, almost as though he were applying for a coveted job, Shah Rukh presented Neeru with his various awards and certificates. He also offered, in jest, to change his religion. "I will become a Hindu," he told her, "and change my name to Jitendra Kumar Tully. But how will I get uncircumcised?" Despite the off-color humor, Neeru liked Shah Rukh enough to convince her husband, Tejinder, to see him. Tejinder also approved. He suggested that Shah Rukh come to a party at the house and meet the parents.

At the party, many guests recognized Shah Rukh as the *Fauji* boy. Ramesh was intrigued to see him. He asked Shah Rukh his name. Flustered, Shah Rukh blurted out, "Sir, you may have seen my serial. They call me Abhimanyu in the serial." Ramesh said, "Forget about the serial. What is your name?" and Shah Rukh replied, "Sir, my name is Shah Rukh Khan." Ramesh realized that something was "amiss." He told Shah Rukh, "There are some decent people here and I don't want to create a scene. You'd better leave now." Before leaving, Shah Rukh went into the kitchen and thanked Savita for feeding him *pakodas*. She wondered why the polite, fine-looking man from *Fauji* had to leave so early.

For Ramesh, Shah Rukh's acting career was an even bigger problem than his religion. Ramesh had served as an aide to the president of India, Zakir Hussain, and had had the opportunity to interact with film actors. His impression of them was uniformly unfavorable. In the 1980s, middle-class Indian children did not aspire to work in Hindi films. Children from respectable families became doctors and engineers or joined the civil services. Bollywood, with its lax morals and excesses, was seriously suspect. It was a decadent hothouse of over-paid, over-sexed, over-pretty people who made mostly bad films.

Savita said she "nearly had a heart attack" when she discovered who Gauri's boyfriend was. "As a television star, I loved him," she said, "but as a prospective son-in-law, I hated him." Savita sought a famous astrologer's advice on how to thwart the relationship but was told that it could not be done. Meanwhile Gauri's older brother Vikrant was also keen on protecting his sister's honor, especially from a Muslim boy who had no father and limited job prospects. Vikrant had a reputation of being a *goonda* (thug). He threatened Shah Rukh with a gun, but the posturing didn't scare his sister's suitor. Tejinder, who believed that Shah Rukh was worthy, advised Ramesh and Savita to make their peace. He told them not to get bogged down by religion or what people would say. "*Banda dekho kaisa hai*" (See the boy's character), he told them. The relations in the Chibba house were under great strain.

At one point, in desperation, Gauri advised Shah Rukh

to lie. He had 28,000 rupees ($445) in his bank account. She suggested that he tell her parents that he had 20 lakh ($45,000). Shah Rukh called Tejinder. "I can't do that," Shah Rukh said. "Why?" Tejinder asked. "Just say it, I'm with you. They will faint if you tell them 'I've got 28,000 rupees and I'm taking your daughter to Bombay.'" "No, they won't," Shah Rukh replied, with absolute conviction, "because before going, I'll give them the assurance that I'm going to be a successful star. You see, Amitabh Bachchan has retired, Dilip *saab* is very old, and after that I can see only one person and that is Shah Rukh Khan." Shah Rukh always knew that one day he would rule the city.

The Television Years

On a clammy morning in 1990, Shah Rukh landed in Mumbai. A television company with the peculiar name Iskra had summoned him to the city. Shah Rukh readily adjusted to scruffy accommodations and long working hours, but with travel arrangements he always played the star: he would not take a train. As a concession to the producer, however, he was willing to take the cheapest flight available or even pay for the ticket himself. Iskra got him a ticket for an Air India flight that left Delhi at 4:30 A.M. and headed overseas after a brief stopover in Mumbai.

Shah Rukh ceremoniously bid farewell to his family and TAG friends. This was his big break: an opportunity in mythical Mumbai. He was on his way to fame and riches. Nothing could stop him now. But two hours later, when he landed in the city, there was no one from the production company at the airport. Roy Tellis, the assistant who was supposed to fetch Shah Rukh, had overslept.

Shah Rukh waited at the airport, anxiously scanning the

bustling crowds. Flights carrying Haj pilgrims to the Middle East were scheduled for departure, and the airport was swarming with Muslim women in black *burkhas*. But there was no one from Iskra. Shah Rukh panicked. What if the call was an elaborate hoax? he thought. Suddenly Iskra and its sister concern Rogopag sounded like packaging companies. Mumbai was a frightening foreign space; he had been to the city only twice before. But the shame of returning to Delhi from Mumbai airport as an unsung failure was equally daunting.

Shah Rukh shut himself in a phone booth. He started searching his pockets for coins. He was going to call his mother and tell her that his big break was just a bad joke. By now tears were streaming down his face. The women walking by the booth noticed him. Some recognized the *Fauji* boy, frantic in the phone booth and crying. These phantom-like figures floating around in black pressed against the glass of the booth. "Son, don't worry," they said, with their hands up in blessing. "We'll remember you in our prayers at the Haj. You will become a famous actor."

Iskra and Rogopag were the collaborative companies of three directors: Kundan Shah and the brothers Saeed and Aziz Mirza. Kundan and Saeed were both graduates of the Film and Television Institute of India in Pune. Their leftist art house sensibility was evident in everything they did: Iskra, which means "the spark," was the name of a newspaper started by Lenin. Rogopag came from *Ro.Go.Pa.G.*, a 1963 film that consisted of four short films directed by avant-garde directors, including Jean-Luc Godard, Paolo Pasolini, and Roberto Rossellini. Kundan, Aziz, and Saeed, tutored in the traditions of Godard and Fellini, dreamed of changing if not the world, at least cinema and television in India.

Kundan Shah's first film, called *Jaane Bhi Do Yaaro* (Who Pays the Piper), was a dark, achingly funny satire on corruption in urban India. The film, made in 1983, had become a cult classic and established him as a distinctive and original voice. When Shah Rukh's TAG buddies found out that he was going to Iskra, they had made one request: that Shah Rukh kiss Kundan's feet. Saeed Mirza had also built a reputation for making uncompromising, realistic cinema. Iskra's television show, *Nukkad,* was both critically acclaimed and popular. At the time, Kundan, Saeed, and Aziz were reverentially referred to as the Brahma-Vishnu-Mahesh, or holy trinity, of Indian television.

The trinity had noticed Shah Rukh in *Fauji*. He was raw, but he stood apart from the other actors. There was vigor in his performance. When Shah Rukh met Aziz—he had finally called a friend who gave him a ride from the airport to the Iskra office—there was an immediate connection. Shah Rukh reminded Aziz of his son Haroon. Shah Rukh was hired to act in two serials that the company was making. He found both work and a surrogate family.

Shah Rukh started shuttling between Delhi and Mumbai. Aziz and his wife, Nirmala, took him in. Nirmala (who died in June 2003) was especially concerned about the young boy fending for himself in an unfamiliar city. At times Shah Rukh slept on a sofa in the Iskra office. Often Haroon and Shah Rukh camped out in an empty apartment that the family owned. Haroon, five years younger than Shah Rukh, became his confidant. Shah Rukh spent the day in shootings and meetings while Haroon attended college. In the evening the two played a vigorous game of volleyball, ate dinner with Aziz and Nirmala, and then headed back to their apartment. On the way they stopped at the Prabhadevi telephone exchange so Shah Rukh could make two long-distance phone calls: one to Gauri and the other to Fatima, who was increasingly ill.

Shah Rukh acted in three serials for Iskra: *Umeed* (Hope), *Wagle Ki Duniya* (The World of Wagle), and finally *Circus*. The last was intended for their usual in-house lead actor, Pavan Malhotra. But Malhotra was offered a lead in a film called *Bagh Bahadur* (The Tiger Dancer) and could not adjust shooting schedules. Shah Rukh stepped in. *Circus*, telecast in 1990, was the last television work Shah Rukh did at the time. Kundan, Saeed, and Aziz took turns directing the twenty-episode drama about life in an Indian circus. Shah Rukh played Shekharan, the circus owner's son who returns from studies abroad and tries to convince his father to sell the dying enterprise. The circus, he argues, can hardly compete with modern modes of entertainment like cinema, video games, and television. But as he spends time in the circus, he is slowly seduced by the magic of this intriguing world.

The serial was shot on location with a real circus. The cast and crew traveled with the Apollo Circus. Over a three-month period they toured small towns and villages in the states of Goa and Maharashtara. The circus was a distinct universe with its own rules. It was another kind of showbiz, tattered and shrinking but still full of passion and intrigue. Girls and boys stayed separately and were strictly forbidden to get involved romantically. Naturally, it happened all the time. An act in which a girl balanced another girl and a boy in a barrel on her feet worked as a postal service. The girl and boy in the barrel exchanged notes while inside the drum and carried them to their quarters. The highest ambition for these young men and women was to become trapeze artists. Many died or were maimed in this quest. But no one quit because this was the only life they knew. Living with these performers for weeks on end taught Shah Rukh a critical lesson. "*Ho gaya to kartab, gir gaya to hadsa*," the circus artists said: If you can pull it off, it is art. If you fall, it is an accident.

An actor named Ashutosh Gowariker played one of the trapeze artists. Unlike Shah Rukh, Ashutosh's acting career stalled at insipid character roles. So eventually he switched tracks, became a director, and went on to win an Oscar nomination for his third film, *Lagaan* (Land Tax). In 2004, he also directed Shah Rukh in the critically acclaimed *Swades* (Our Country). But in *Circus*, Ashutosh was one of the many actors who slept eight to a dorm in various stages of undress. They would shoot most of the day and play cards for small stakes till dawn. Raju Bulchandani, the production person in charge of wake-up calls, was partial to Shah Rukh and always woke him up last. He would stagger into the bus, barely awake. While the shot was being lit, Shah Rukh would shave and bathe, usually in the open, with a *lota* and bucket.

Shah Rukh did not tone down for television. His acting was as flamboyant as it had been onstage. "He was so boisterous," said Ashutosh. "If there was an emotion given to him, he would multiply it twenty times. What was amazing was his attitude: 'This is the way I act. Is there any other way to do it?'"

Shah Rukh's rapid-fire dialogue delivery and high-speed heroism attracted some unlikely admirers. Uber-arty director Mani Kaul found in Shah Rukh something "tragic—unrequited. I was attracted to his voice," he said, "an unstated whimper." Mani's films usually featured lesser-known actors or non-actors, and Shah Rukh, by now, was a semi-famous face. But Mani bent his rules and offered Shah Rukh a role in an adaptation of Dostoevsky's *The Idiot*. Like Kundan and Saeed, Mani was an Institute graduate and a prominent figure in the art house movement. However, even the art house crowd considered his cinema esoteric. His best films were stylized and breathtakingly beautiful but exhaustingly impenetrable.

Shah Rukh was not instantly seduced by film. He was fiercely driven, but his ambitions were not centered on becoming a Hindi film hero. He wanted to be a famous television personality, someone like Oprah Winfrey, with a signature talk show. His aim, in Haroon's words, "was to be the king of television. He knew it would be a good place to reign." Gauri's vehement anti-Bollywood stance also smothered his enthusiasm. In their relationship, being Muslim had already been a hurdle. Being a Muslim who was a Hindi film hero would strain his faltering love story even further. But Mani Kaul did not make "Hindi films." Mani's world was separate and isolated from Bollywood. Besides, the film was designed as a four-part mini-series for television. Aziz advised Shah Rukh to work with the director for the experience. *The Idiot* was one of the first books that Meer, his father, had given Shah Rukh. Meer had bought it at the Russian Cultural Center in Delhi for four rupees (one cent). Out of sentimental reasons and sheer curiosity, Shah Rukh agreed to do *The Idiot*.

Mani rarely acted out scenes for his actors. Instead, he described the action using a precise pace and tone, hoping that the actor would pick up the cues. Mani's directions were as brilliantly cryptic as his films. At one point, he instructed Shah Rukh to touch his hair "not as if it is hair but a possibility." Another time Mani took Shah Rukh to the seashore and advised him to "be like the seventh wave, not the third or the fifth, but the seventh." This was an exercise in *dhyaan,* or meditation, designed to improve the actor's focus. *The Idiot* was telecast on

Doordarshan in 1991. Mani also edited it as a film but, like *In Which Annie Gives It Those Ones*, it was never released.

Around the same time, another classic novel was being translated into Hindi film. Ketan Mehta, who had graduated from the Institute after Mani, Saeed, and Kundan, was retelling *Madame Bovary* as *Maya Memsaab*. He saw some episodes of *Fauji* and *Circus* and immediately called Aziz to ask, "Who is this brat?" Shah Rukh was cast as one of Maya's lovers. The film was highbrow and deliberately opaque, but it was one step closer to mainstream cinema. In one sequence, Shah Rukh even got to frolic with the heroine amidst scenic snowy hills in a typical Hindi film fantasy. Inevitably, Bollywood came calling.

At the time, Hindi films were in a creative intermission. Amitabh Bachchan's Angry Young Man had run his course, but a new heroic persona had still not materialized on-screen. However, the wave of violence and gore that Amitabh's success had generated seemed to be ebbing. In 1988 and 1989, two saccharine love stories swept the box office. Both *Qayamat Se Qayamat Tak* (From Eternity to Eternity) and *Maine Pyar Kiya* (I Have Loved) had new actors, soothingly melodious music, and minimal bloodshed. Viewers, numbed by two decades of violence, once again reveled in the sweetness of first love. Instead of tiring anti-establishment rhetoric, these films featured hesitant lovers shyly holding hands and singing songs. They launched the careers of two actors who, along with Shah Rukh, would dominate Bollywood over the 1990s: Aamir Khan and Salman Khan.

Suddenly new aspirants had an edge in Bollywood. Producers hoping to replicate the success of these films were casting newcomers as leads, along with reputed character actors for "padding." Shah Rukh had already generated considerable buzz on television. "It was like a movement," said Amrita Singh, Shah Rukh's childhood friend who had moved to Mumbai in 1981 and become a successful heroine. "You actually heard the chariot coming into Mumbai with Shah Rukh Khan on it."

But Shah Rukh wasn't interested in doing love stories with padding. He refused films and, on occasion, irked established producers by asking for a script. Once Feroz Khan's office called. The actor-director was Bollywood's Marlboro Man. He wore Stetsons, chewed on cigarettes, and spoke, inexplicably, in a thick American drawl. When Shah Rukh said he wanted to see the script, the assistant balked. "You want Mr. Feroz Khan to tell you the story?" to which Shah Rukh, always quick on the draw, replied, "So should I ask a guy on the road to tell me the story?" Post-success, Shah Rukh's cocky irreverence was labeled as wit, but coming from a newcomer, it was a serious affront. Feroz Khan did not call again.

In the late 1980s, bound scripts were a rarity. Bollywood was a frenzied, chaotic cottage industry. Actors signed for as many as five to seven films and sometimes shot for three in a day, flitting from one set to another. It wasn't unusual to find crews waiting hours for the stars to show up or scenes being written on the set. An apocryphal anecdote from the time involves a busy writer who once inadvertently mixed up scenes for two different films that were being shot simultaneously. Both crews shot the wrong scene before realizing it was from another film.

In late November 1990, Haroon and Shah Rukh were mulling over coffee at 2 A.M. in a suburban hotel called Bandra International. Their mood was especially grim. Haroon was then also dating a Hindu girl. The two spent endless hours fretting over their respective love lives and moaning about a callous world that has so many issues with two decent

Muslim boys who happen to love Hindu girls. "We were two good souls," said Haroon, "deprived of the women we loved." As they were leaving, a man stopped them and asked, "Are you Shah Rukh Khan?" This was Anwar Khan, who would later become Shah Rukh's agent. Anwar introduced Shah Rukh to an actor-producer named Viveck Vaswani. Viveck, prematurely bald and constantly talking, was a rare entity, a south Bombay boy obsessed with film.

The city of Mumbai is actually two cities. Each has a distinct mood, resonance, and culture. Sobo, or south Bombay, is old money, art deco and Victorian architecture, and trendy world-class restaurants. The government offices, Mantralaya, the Bombay Stock Exchange, and the city's premier business district, Nariman Point, are all at the southern tip of the city. The north, or suburbs, is new money and new construction. It's flashy and unapologetically *filmi*. Most of the film and television industry resides and works in the burbs between Mehboob Studios in Bandra and the sprawling Film City Studio in far-north Goregaon.

An actor's address reveals his rank. Strugglers stay in far-flung suburbs, but as they become successful they head south, moving from Malad and Kandivali to Versova. Bollywood's A-list lives in Juhu and Bandra. Here star homes are landmarks. People routinely use them as markers, as in, "Take a left at the Bachchan bungalow." Earlier, suburbanites had few options and trekked south across the city to find decent movie theaters, five-star hotels, and high-end shopping. But through the 1990s, the burbs metamorphosized. Shiny, gleaming multiplexes, luxury hotels, and fancy apartment buildings altered the dowdy landscape. The traffic now travels in both directions, but for Sobo residents, going north of Worli still feels like leaving the country.

Viveck grew up in Cuffe Parade, the spiffiest, southernmost tip of south Mumbai. In his posh school and college, Bollywood was considered low class. But Viveck skipped his cricket coaching and extra study tuitions and instead went alone to watch Hindi movies. Like Shah Rukh, he started his career acting in television serials. At the time, Viveck was producing a film for G. P. Sippy, who was famous for having made the then-longest-running film in the history of Indian cinema, *Sholay*. Viveck and Shah Rukh shook hands and exchanged telephone numbers.

A few weeks later, on December 17, Viveck happened to be in Bandra again. The film he was producing was being shot on Linking Road. The teeming crowds gaping at the stars Raveena Tandon and Salman Khan aggravated the sweltering heat. Viveck's assistant suggested that he go kill a few hours in an air-conditioned coffee shop. Viveck didn't want to sit alone, and remembered that Shah Rukh had mentioned that he lived close by. Coincidentally, the same day, the *Sunday Review* section of the *Times of India* newspaper had carried a story on *The Idiot*. Shah Rukh got special attention. The article said: "Shah Rukh Khan, the live wire, so far confined to sitcoms, is spoken about by the unit as a *kamal ka* actor. The impossible to please Kaul raves about him: 'Must make a film just with him. What a character, he understands everything, gives so much more than he is asked to.'"

Viveck was intrigued and impressed. He called Shah Rukh, but no one picked up the phone. So Viveck located his house and knocked on the door. Though it was late afternoon, Shah Rukh was still sleeping, and he took several minutes to rouse himself. When Shah Rukh finally opened the door, Viveck dramatically declared, "I'm going to make you a big star."

Life After Death

Death created a star.

On April 15, 1991, Fatima died. Death came furtively, as it had for Meer a decade ago. An innocuous sore appeared on Fatima's foot. She was diabetic and the wound refused to heal. Her deterioration was sudden and quick. In a few weeks, she stopped wearing shoes because it was too painful and started shuffling around in airline slippers. In a few months she was in Batra Hospital fighting multi-organ failure.

Fatima was a dynamic woman who had single-handedly raised two children. Like an indestructible, pint-sized tank, she had battled on alone without losing her fire or her sense of humor. In the early days of hospitalization, Fatima joked with Shah Rukh's friend Divya that the IV holder hooked on her looked like a *chota sa cup* (tiny teacup). Once, when Aziz Mirza visited, she made him wait outside while she combed her hair and placed her *dupatta* (scarf) correctly on her head. But as illness wracked her body, her spirit broke.

Fatima, who had believed in her son's magic long before anybody else, did not live to see him soar. One day Shah Rukh hooked up a television set in her room to show her some episodes of *Circus*, but she was deliriously ill and did not comprehend much.

The diagnosis was septicemia, an irreversible poisoning of the blood. Fatima slipped into a coma. Her body started shutting down. When the doctors suggested that her family members come to meet her immediately, Shah Rukh understood that it was only a matter of a few hours. Until then, few people had been allowed into the intensive care unit. Shah Rukh refused to let his mother go without a fight. Numbed by grief, he prayed alone in the hospital parking lot. He was convinced that if he repeated his favorite prayer 869 times, Fatima would live. *Nasrun minal lahi wah fatahun kareeb*, he mumbled, over and over again. It was a sportsman's prayer that means, God give me the strength to win. His uncle came to the parking lot several times to fetch him, but Shah Rukh spent half an hour praying amidst cars. By the time he got to his mother's bedside, she was barely breathing.

Shah Rukh believed that death comes only when a person is completely content. So he tried to hold on to Fatima by making her feel unhappy. Sitting by her bed, he narrated to her the litany of all the bad things he would do if she left him: He would not take care of Shahnaz, he would fail as an actor, he would do everything to ensure that their lives were a mess. A tear fell from one eye. Fatima was clinically dead and the tear was perhaps an involuntary spasm of the body. But Shah Rukh took it to mean that she had heard him but was by then so close to God that she knew that her son was lying. For a fleeting moment, Fatima looked as attractive as she had before sickness sapped her. Her glazed eyes and cracked lips seemed to regain their lost vitality. Shah Rukh combed her hair and kissed her. Then there was a flurry of movement to shift the body. In an overpopulated country, beds in the intensive care unit are always at a premium.

At the burial ground, Shah Rukh sat by Fatima's side. When the *maulvi* interrupted his meditation, insisting that he join in the last prayers, Shah Rukh swore at the priest and nearly got into a fight with him. "I just wanted to look at her face that I would never see again," he said. "I wanted to touch her skin. I wanted to take away some memory, something tangible that I could retain." When they buried Fatima, he finally wept.

Shah Rukh sank into a fog of despair and anger. For the first few days he refused to eat. Getting him to take a sip of water was a task. He was dry-eyed and shattered. When Divya suggested going to the cemetery he refused, saying there was only earth there, not his mother. Every inch of his home and the city reminded him of his loss. Shahnaz retreated further into an inaccessible silence and aggression. Ten years ago, much of Fatima's jewelry had been sold to pay Meer's hospital bills. Fatima's own sickness had plunged the family further into debt. Shah Rukh began to feel suffocated in Delhi. Two weeks after his mother's death, he packed his bags, took his usual after-midnight Air India flight to Mumbai, and landed at Viveck Vaswani's house at 5 A.M. "Let's make films," he said.

Since his dramatic declaration at Shah Rukh's door, Viveck did his best to fulfill his promise of making Shah Rukh a star. Viveck recalled the first meeting a little differently. He said it was not he but Shah Rukh who pronounced that he would become the biggest star in the history of Indian cinema. But Viveck had become Shah Rukh's friend, philosopher, and guide. "We could match each other cigarette for cigarette, coffee for coffee, chips for chips, insomnia for insomnia," Viveck recalled. After their second meeting, Shah Rukh moved to Viveck's house in Cuffe Parade. They spent nights watching movies, mostly from the front-row seats.

For most actors in Bollywood, stardom remains a chimera. Figures have never been substantiated, but industry insiders casually declare that about 200 to 300 people come to Mumbai every day to become actors. They toil for years on the periphery, looking for a way in. Aptly, the industry calls them "strugglers." Bollywood folklore abounds with stories of fine young men and women who have wasted their lives chasing stardust: they can be seen at the edge of the frame as extras in a party scene holding a gaudy drink in their hands. One rare success story, such as Mumtaz, who started as a B-grade heroine opposite a famous wrestler-actor, became a leading lady, and retired after marrying a millionaire, inspires thousands more to leave home and make the pilgrimage to *Mayanagri* (City of Illusions).

The star system came to Hindi films in the 1940s. In the early years, the system allowed outsiders in. Stars such as Dharmendra and Rajesh Khanna were ferreted out by talent hunts (in 1958 and 1964). But over the decades, Bollywood turned into an insular, impenetrable fortress run by several generations of the same families. The independent production houses, which replaced the studios, are family concerns, so it isn't unusual to have a film with one member of the family as director, another as producer, and a third as star. Successful actors, and technicians too, give their siblings a leg up by working with them. Fathers and sons in Hindi movies are sometimes real-life fathers and sons. Here nepotism isn't a backroom business tactic. It's a birthright.

Stardom is as much about talent and charisma as the family name. Every year, sons and daughters are launched with much fanfare. Reams of newsprint are devoted to their films and to comparing their looks and skills to those of their famous parents. Conventional wisdom dictates that the audience would rather see a newcomer who has inherited the aura of an adored star than a complete unknown. Star children bask in the reflected glory of their parents. Their failures are more easily forgiven. But every few years, like the warrior Abhimanyu who broke a formidably elaborate battle formation in the *Mahabharata*, an outsider breaks through the ranks of these privileged few.

Amitabh Bachchan's father, Harivanshrai Bachchan, was a famous poet and intellectual. Before becoming an actor, Amitabh worked with a freight company in Kolkata. Jackie Shroff grew up in the tenements of south Mumbai. But these successes are as rare as a Hindi film without romance. Many of the stars are second-generation film industry. Some, like Kareena Kapoor, are fourth-generation actors. Kareena's great-grandfather, Prithviraj Kapoor, was also a resident of the famed Qissa Khawani Bazaar, where Shah Rukh's father, Meer, was born. Kareena's father, mother, sister, uncles, and first cousins have all been actors. Film acting is imprinted in their DNA.

Shah Rukh joined films a year after Amitabh announced that he was taking a break. Exhausted by both his spectacular success as an actor and his scandal-ridden failure as a politician, he took a five-year sabbatical. His last film was *Khuda Gawah* (God Is Witness) in 1992. He returned with *Mrityudaata* (Angel of Death) in 1997. Amitabh had redefined the Bollywood superstar. Before him, Rajesh Khanna had evoked a similar euphoria, but Rajesh's reign had been short-lived and his downfall sudden. Like a powerful narcotic, Amitabh had hooked the nation for almost two decades. He had raised the bar for stardom. When Amitabh retired, there were several talented, successful heroes, but none dazzled the audience as he had.

The leading contenders were Sunny Deol, Anil Kapoor, and Jackie Shroff. Anil was the son of producer Surinder Kapoor, who was once an assistant on *Mughal-e-Azam* and who had befriended Meer. Sunny's father, Dharmendra, was an astonishingly handsome man who had come to Mumbai from a village in Punjab and become a star. Jackie was the man from nowhere who made the miraculous leap from the villain's sidekick to leading man. The young lover-boy roles, mostly college romances in which the hero and heroine lip-synched melodious songs before being torn apart by disapproving parents or difficult circumstances, were divided between Salman Khan and Aamir Khan. These fresh-faced boys (one the son of a famous writer and the other the son of a producer) were the new teen heartthrobs.

Shah Rukh was very definitely not the familiar struggling actor with a gym-toned body, painstakingly preserved looks, and an obsequious manner. He was respectful but not slavishly fawning, even with the biggest names in the business. Shah Rukh was arrogant about his talent and bewilderingly confident about success. He was defiantly unkempt. His clothes were crumpled. His hair had a life of its own (in the early days when he couldn't afford gel, Shah Rukh tried to contain it with a homemade mixture of Camlin glue and water). He was scrawny, with undying dark circles under his eyes because he was an insomniac and rarely slept before 2 A.M. "He didn't give a shit," said Rajiv Mehra, who directed Shah Rukh in *Chamatkar* (Miracle). "He was completely unlike somebody who had come to sell himself." Producer G. P. Sippy, who in forty years in the business had seen dozens of stars shine and sputter, was more frank. "His hair is like a bloody bear's," he declared after a two-minute meeting with Shah Rukh. Sippy unequivocally turned down Viveck's proposal to make a small-budget film with Aziz as director and Shah Rukh as lead.

Shah Rukh did not look like a Hindi film hero. Unlike Salman and Aamir, he wasn't fair-skinned or conventionally handsome. But Viveck believed that Shah Rukh could become a star and he marketed his friend fiercely. He took Shah Rukh everywhere, from producers' offices to parties, and introduced him as the "next biggest superstar in the history of Indian cinema." No television star until then (or since) had made a successful transition into cinema, but Shah Rukh's television serials worked as his "résumé." Despite his grungy looks, the offers came fast and furious.

A new director named Raj Kanwar offered him *Deewana* (Crazed Lover). Raj had already tried to cast several other actors but nothing had worked out, because the role was a second lead. Rajiv met Shah Rukh for *Chamatkar*, a romantic comedy and ghost story rolled into one. Hema Malini, a breathtakingly beautiful heroine from the 1970s, wanted Shah Rukh for her directorial debut, *Dil Aashana Hai* (The Heart Knows the Truth). Rakesh Roshan, an A-list filmmaker, was looking to cast a young boy in a two-hero film called *King Uncle*.

Shah Rukh was a reluctant "next biggest superstar." He was deeply ambivalent about working in mainstream Hindi movies, mostly because Gauri strongly disapproved (Amrita Singh remembered that Shah Rukh carried a black-and-white picture of Gauri, which he bashfully showed everyone—

Amrita, a more pragmatic actor, dismissed his affections as "baby love" and advised him to dump Gauri if she disapproved of his career choice). Shah Rukh had met producers and mulled over their offers, but despite Viveck's persistent lectures and advice, he had not committed to any film. But Fatima's death made the decision for him. Bollywood seemed to be the only option. Work would be his therapy and allow him to combat the overwhelming depression. Within a few days of returning to Mumbai, he signed four films. In a little over a year, Shah Rukh had achieved more than many Bollywood aspirants do in a lifetime of struggle.

Even G. P. Sippy changed his mind. Viveck and Aziz wanted to make a film called *Raju Ban Gaya Gentleman* (Raju Becomes a Gentleman). The title came from a song Aziz's mother used to sing when she gave her sons a bath: "*Ek paise ki ghadi churaiyee, do paise ki chain; Raju ban gaya gentleman*" (He stole a one-paise watch and a two-paise chain; Raju became a gentleman). Loosely inspired by Raj Kapoor's 1955 classic *Shri 420*, *Raju Ban Gaya Gentleman* was the story of a small-town boy who comes to Mumbai for a job and is momentarily dazzled by the bright lights of the big city. Power and money make him lose his way, but the love of a simple, middle-class girl draws him back to the right path.

Sippy insisted that Viveck consider other, more saleable stars as lead. But when Shah Rukh became a newcomer with four brand-name production houses backing him, Sippy decided to gamble as well. But with a caveat in place: The film would be made with only 6 million rupees ($135,000). Viveck hustled and sweet-talked actress Juhi Chawla into playing Shah Rukh's heroine. Juhi had been Aamir's heroine in the runaway hit *Qayamat Se Qayamat Tak*, and Viveck told her to think of Shah Rukh as the "next Aamir Khan." Juhi had heard of Shah Rukh but had not seen *Fauji*. They met only when shooting started. She took in Shah Rukh's scrawny frame and untidy hair and, the same night, called Viveck to scream: "Eeek, this is the next Aamir Khan?" In all the films he signed, Shah Rukh wasn't the first but the second or third choice. On June 26, 1991, Shah Rukh did his first Bollywood shoot, for *Dil Aashna Hai* at the Convent Villa in Versova.

The decision to do films and move to Mumbai pushed Shah Rukh's relationship with Gauri to a head. Gauri's parents were still staunchly opposed to Shah Rukh, but Gauri understood that their passion would not survive separation and the scandal of the Hindi film industry. "If I didn't marry him at that point," she said, "I would never have married him." Though she was only twenty-one and just out of college, Gauri decided to take a leap of faith. Shah Rukh convinced her that they would try it for a year. "One year of honeymoon," he said. If she didn't like Bollywood, he would quit. When Ramesh and Savita realized that their daughter was adamant, that she wasn't going to change her mind, they acquiesced.

Shah Rukh and Gauri married on October 25, 1991, the anniversary of their first interaction seven years earlier. They married in court, and then a traditional Hindu wedding followed, in which he rode to the venue on an elephant. Only three people from the film industry were at the wedding, Viveck, Rajiv, and Aziz, but the wedding had a unique Bollywood touch: Shah Rukh wore suits borrowed from the *Raju Ban Gaya Gentleman* costume department. Unlike his father, Shah Rukh was a boisterous groom. He danced at his wedding, longer and harder than anyone else. He was still only when he sat by his mother-in-law's side, holding her hand for half an hour. As the wedding approached, Savita had become extremely agitated and nervous. She didn't enjoy her daughter's wedding because she was afraid that right-wing Hindu or Muslim organizations would try to disrupt the proceedings. She was also anxious about their future. Shah Rukh could sense her distress and wanted to reassure her that he could and would look after her daughter.

The next day the newlyweds left for Mumbai. Rajiv was on the same flight they were on and he found himself worrying for Gauri. "You could see her nervousness," he said. "She didn't know whether she was coming or going." Viveck's wedding gift to the couple was three nights at the Sun 'n' Sand Hotel. He didn't want them to start worrying immediately about where they were going to live. They eventually moved into Aziz's empty flat in Bandra, where they lived for five months, subsisting mostly on eggs. The only furniture they had were two mattresses, a refrigerator, a television set, and a cooking range. Gauri refused to buy furniture until they moved into their own apartment.

Although Shah Rukh had started shooting for *Raju Ban Gaya Gentleman* earlier, the first film to release was *Deewana*, on June 25, 1992. *Deewana* is the story of a young girl whose rich husband is killed soon after marriage by scheming relatives. In a dramatic departure from Hindi film formula, her mother-in-law encourages her to marry again. Shah Rukh plays the brash, arrogant man who enters her life and helps her to love again. But just when the couple seems settled in domestic bliss, the first husband returns.

At the time of release, director Raj Kanwar was in Punjab after making a trip to the religious shrine of Vaishno Devi. It is a pilgrimage filmmakers often make before their film hits the theaters. The goddess, they hope, will help them conquer the box office. The distributor of *Deewana* suggested that Raj come with him to drop the prints at the theater. The show was to begin at 10 A.M. When they got to the theater at nine, they found it deserted. Raj was saddened by the silence greeting his directorial debut. He was angry with the distributor for releasing his film at such an awkward hour, but the distributor assured him that all would end well. A half hour later, they swung back for a second look. The theater was swarming, mostly with college kids. *Deewana* was a hit.

The length of Hindi films, three hours and sometimes longer, makes an intermission necessary. In *Deewana*, Shah Rukh appears on the screen only after the second half starts. The mother-in-law is consoling her widowed daughter-in-law. She says: "*Waqt hi tere zakhmon pe marham rakhega*" (Only time will heal your wounds). The camera cuts to Shah Rukh. His first few shots have him zooming down the Marine Drive overpass on a motorbike—fittingly, it is the same place where only a few years ago Shah Rukh had stood and angrily declared that one day he would own Mumbai. He is wearing a brown leather jacket, jeans, and a white T-shirt. His hair flops, without style, into his eyes. He does daredevil acrobatics on a motorbike and sings, "*Koi na koi chahiye pyar karne wala*" (I need someone to love). Shah Rukh has bravado, but he's not particularly striking. His C-Gang friend Vivek Khushalani observed that he was so little changed that it "almost felt like he left from Delhi, got to the set, and they filmed him."

Mani Kaul had once asked his music teacher, the great classical vocalist Ustad Zia Mohiuddin Dagar, "When will there be another Tansen?" Ustad had replied, "When there will be an audience for him." Perhaps the same was true for Bollywood. A superstar was created because the audience was ready for him. When Shah Rukh came into the frame, the crowd reacted like the screen had emitted an electrical charge. They roared their approval with deafening whistles and screams. The noise filled Raj's ears. He said he felt that his heart would stop beating. It was almost as though, starved of a god after Amitabh, the audience had already decided to make Shah Rukh the next idol.

The extended Chibba family—Gauri's grandmother, parents, aunt, uncle, nephew, and niece—piled into the family van and went to Delhi's Sapna Theater to watch their son-in-law make his Bollywood debut. It had been years since they had gone to a cinema hall to see a Hindi movie; cable and video had made it unnecessary. Tejinder's son Rustam, then nine, was especially excited because he had never been to a cinema theater before. While Tejinder was a Hindi film aficionado, Ramesh knew little about the industry. How, he wondered, would they know whether the movie was or wasn't a hit? The audience's boisterous approval of Shah Rukh provided the answer. After the film, Tejinder called Shah Rukh and told him, "You *are* a superstar."

Super Brat

Rose petals perfume the air at the tomb of Hazrat Khwaja Moinuddin Chishti. The shrine of the twelfth-century Sufi saint draws millions to Ajmer in northwestern India. Both Hindus and Muslims come here on pilgrimage, to tie threads to the latticework of the shrine's marble screen. Each thread reminds the saint of its owner's *mannat,* or wish. It is believed that those who ask with a pure heart do not return empty-handed. The sixteenth-century Mughal emperor Akbar performed the pilgrimage on foot to pray for an heir. His son Jehangir was born soon after.

Sometime in 1990, Shah Rukh, Shahnaz, and Fatima made the trip. Fatima's health was already faltering and Shah Rukh was in charge. As part of the offering, devotees carry a heavily embroidered *chador* on their heads. After Shah Rukh had performed this ritual, he noticed that his wallet was missing. It contained around 5,000 rupees ($110), all the money the family was carrying. He panicked and started looking for it desperately. A fakir standing nearby noticed Shah Rukh's frantic search and asked him what he had lost. Shah Rukh told him it was a wallet with 5,000 rupees in it. "Don't worry," the fakir pronounced, "5,000 has gone; 500,000 [$11,100] will come." And it did. A year later, Shah Rukh went from being a television actor earning 8,000 rupees ($178) per episode to the hottest new actor in the business. At least one magazine reported that he was already asking 2 million rupees ($45,000) for a film.

Deewana was crude and melodramatic. Shah Rukh, in keeping with the rhythms of the film, was equally loud. For Bollywood, Shah Rukh cranked up his acting a few notches higher than he did onstage and on television, hamming with élan. In a scene in which he tells his friends that he is obsessed with the heroine, he bangs his head against the wall dramatically, laughs hysterically, rages, and stammers. But the over-the-top performance established him as an actor with the potential to be a star. Incredibly, even the critics were impressed. Nikhat Kazmi, film critic of the influential *Times of India,* wrote: "Before you dismiss Raj Kanwar's *Deewana* as one more midsummer nightmare, in walks Shah Rukh Khan, the smart young *Fauji* who grapples headlong with the sinking storyline which suddenly begins to ascend dizzying heights. . . . It is a clichéd role but Shah Rukh interprets it with a fresh zeal and wafts across like a breeze in the traditional role of a young man obsessed with love. Angry, confused, tender, mature and childishly rebellious, *Deewana* marks the advent of a new talent."

Shah Rukh won his first Filmfare Award for the film. Instead of one defining award ceremony such as the Oscar, Bollywood pats itself on the back several times a year with dozens of awards, which vary in prestige and glory. The Filmfare Awards, instituted by a leading film magazine called

Filmfare, are the oldest in Bollywood. Unlike the Oscars, none of these awards impact the business of a film or the professional status of an actor, but Filmfare Awards are among the most coveted.

Winning Filmfare Awards was to become a habit with Shah Rukh. He won nearly every year, ranging from the Best Actor to Best Actor in Villainous Role. In the years when he did not win for a performance, he walked away with statuettes for newly created categories such as Power Award and Filmfare's Swiss Consulate Trophy Special Award. But none of the later wins had the frisson of the first for Best Debut. At the function, Shah Rukh was seated next to a leading filmmaker, Subhash Ghai. When Dilip Kumar went onstage, Subhash whispered to Shah Rukh that he must become Dilip Kumar. Subhash meant it as a long-term aspiration and expected a standard self-effacing response like "Oh, if only I could be half the actor that Dilip Kumar is," but Shah Rukh said, "Just wait—very soon I will be Dilip Kumar." Shah Rukh took the black statuette to Delhi to show his friends. After all, he reasoned, they had never seen one before.

The rush of fame and money didn't cushion the culture shock for Gauri. Mumbai was alien, aloof, and always in a hurry. The industry was fraught with intrigues and rivalries, clinging to peculiarly old-world mores. Everybody was arranged in a hierarchy depending on their level of success and when they had joined the industry—you were "senior" to some people and "junior" to others. All seniors had to be addressed with the respectful suffix *ji* attached to their name. Gauri described the first two years as "torture. I didn't know what was happening. It was really crazy and horrible." Every two months, Gauri would escape to Delhi. She tried to fill the empty hours with a career. For a few months she worked at a garment export house. But when Shah Rukh had to go for a three-month outdoor stint to Goa, Gauri dumped her job and joined him.

The Khans refused to toe the conventional Bollywood line on marriage. Traditionally, wives stayed in their husband's shadow. They lived lives of luxury and silence. They were pampered, discreet, and invisible. Even A-list heroines, once married, would quit acting and purposefully slip into oblivion; this was considered proper matrimony-motherhood etiquette. This rule especially applied to star wives. Trade pundits believed that marriage would affect the box office status of an actor. Female fans failed to be as enamored by a romantic hero who, as one producer put it, "was already hooked and cooked." So Aamir Khan, who made his debut four years before Shah Rukh, hid his marital status. His then wife, Reena, made a fleeting appearance in his debut film, *Qayamat Se Qayamat Tak*, but Aamir did not make his marriage public. Only after the film succeeded and Aamir was anointed a star did he emerge from the Bollywood version of the closet.

In contrast, Shah Rukh flaunted Gauri. It was rumored that producer F. C. Mehra had asked Shah Rukh to postpone his wedding until his film *Chamatkar* was released. The director, Rajiv Mehra, denied this, but the story goes that Shah Rukh said he would quit the film instead. Shah Rukh was shrill in his declarations of love for Gauri. In a 1992 interview with *Stardust* magazine Shah Rukh said, "My wife comes first. And I can tell you this much that if ever I am asked to make a choice between my career and Gauri, I'll leave films. . . . I mean I would go insane but for her. She's the only thing I have. . . . I love her body. I am hooked to her." A year later, the same magazine commented on the "devastatingly sexy-looking twenty-three-year-old Gauri." She was, *Stardust* wrote, "clad in a micro-mini. Radiant, confident, smug, almost purring on her star-husband's arm." The couple posed together for magazine covers and Gauri even gave interviews. In June 1994, she told a magazine called *Aura of the Stars*, "What I'm getting out of this relationship is total satisfaction and complete happiness. I don't have any regrets having married Shah Rukh. I can't imagine life with anybody but him."

In the early 1990s, Bollywood was a world in transition. The old order was gasping for breath and the new one hadn't been born yet. The industry was a fussy and formal place, rigid with hierarchies. An inherently conservative North Indian Punjabi culture prevailed. Like the movies it was churning out, Bollywood was rough and unsophisticated. Many artists and technicians were uneducated. The clichéd image of a producer was an oily man in a white safari suit, chewing *paan* and carrying a suitcase stuffed with cash. A handful of men, mostly above forty, wove fantasies for a billion Indians across the globe. The actors, especially the heroines, were baby-faced. But for the technical crew youth was a liability. White hair equaled wisdom, so assistants paid their dues for years before they got the chance to direct their own films. Directors under thirty-five were virtually unheard of. The films were equally fossilized; writer Javed Akhtar dourly remarked that most directors came to him asking for "an original script, which has been done before."

Shah Rukh navigated this tricky terrain with cocky confidence. Unlike most aspirants, he wasn't in awe of the big names. He was, he believed, a serious theater actor, way ahead of these frivolous *filmi* types. He first met Subhash Ghai at a party. Subhash had transformed Jackie Shroff from a semi-junior artiste into a leading man. The press had tagged Subhash "Showman," and newcomers regarded him with a reverence bordering on obsequiousness. Subhash *ji* was a Godfather whose golden touch could put a wanna-be on the fast track to stardom. Subhash shook Shah Rukh's hand and remarked, "I hear you act well." Shah Rukh replied, "Yes sir, I do." Subhash observed that even Shah Rukh's body language was unlike that of most aspirants. "When they first come, newcomers are bent over with their hands folded in supplication," Subhash said. "When they become stars, their hands move behind their backs in arrogance, but Shah Rukh's hands were always straight by his side. His eyes had confidence."

Shah Rukh's volatile temper was more problematic. Among the first lot of films he did was *Kabhi Haan Kabhi Naa* (Sometimes Yes, Sometimes No), directed by Kundan Shah. In what is widely considered to be one of his best performances, Shah Rukh plays a hapless loser who does not win the girl at the end of the film. At the launch of *Deewana*, Shah Rukh had signed *Kabhi Haan Kabhi Naa* for 25,000 rupees ($550). The film was almost completed before *Deewana*, but financial troubles held up the last five days of shoot. It didn't release until 1994.

Most of *Kabhi Haan Kabhi Naa* was shot in Goa. While making the film, Shah Rukh had fierce fights with Kundan. At times they nearly came to blows. Both attributed it to a generation gap. "Kundan is a perfectionist," Shah Rukh said, "My comedy was too labored. He wanted each actor to be a rock he could pick up, place, and shoot." But these petty personal quarrels didn't detract from their commitment to the film. Shah Rukh had a bone-wearying capacity for work. His attitude was: anything for the film. When doing the last shot of *Kabhi Haan Kabhi Naa*, the unit ran out of film stock. The producer, harried by months of delay and plagued by financial problems, refused to buy any more. Shah Rukh knew that Kundan wanted to do another take so he ran to every other unit shooting at the Kamalistan Studio and asked for spare film. But it was past midnight and most of the other units had wrapped up. When he couldn't get any, Shah Rukh sat down and cried.

Shah Rukh's unapologetically brash and impulsive behavior made him prime film-magazine fodder. Over the years, Bollywood has spawned a sub-industry of fan magazines. These are wholly star driven. The loves and lives of actors are the focus and selling point; films are an afterthought. The most influential magazines are in English and combine glamorous pictures with interviews and stories. The first magazine entirely devoted to cinema was the Gujarati *Mauj Majah* (Fun), published in 1924. *Filmfare* began publication in 1952, but the prototype for "fanzines" was set by *Stardust*, which was first published in October 1971. *Stardust*, modeled on the American *Photoplay*, was cannily constructed to titillate. Stories were always scoops. Headlines were controversial and enticing even when the actual stories were not. Gossip columns ran with no bylines. All of this was written in Mumbai Hinglish, that is a blend of Mumbai-style Hindi and English.

Especially since the advent of the scandal-loving *Stardust*, Bollywood has had a rocky relationship with the press. Film magazines carried glossy, flattering photographs, mediated between the industry and its audience, and were a useful marketing and publicity tool. But with the emphasis on gossip and "exposés," they could be equally damaging and vicious. In case of the latter, Indian libel laws were little consolation. Few people had the perseverance for court cases that could drag on for a decade, so stars devised their own ways of dealing with unsavory press. Through much of the 1980s, Amitabh Bachchan did not talk to film magazines. Others decided that blows were better than boycott. Dharmendra once chased a leading gossip columnist named Devyani Chaubal out of a party. In June 1992, actor Anupam Kher slapped a *Stardust* journalist named Troy Rebeiro because Troy wrote an article alleging that Anupam had molested a co-star's sister. At the time, many actors supported Anupam and some even talked of banning the magazine. But, like most controversies, this too fizzled out. Stars and journalists co-existed like a warring couple who couldn't live with or without each other.

Stardust recognized Shah Rukh's "quotable quote" potential even before he became a star. Its then editor, Nishi Prem, was among the first journalists to do a major interview with him. In September 1991, before the release of a single film, when he was only a television star, Shah Rukh filled up five pages of *Stardust* magazine. The headline read WILL SHAH RUKH KHAN'S INTENSITY BURN HIM OUT!? [*sic*]. Nishi compared Shah Rukh to Jonathan Livingston Seagull, "who always wondered why the other seagulls didn't desire to fly higher than they did." Shah Rukh didn't play demure debutant, either. Among other things, he pontificated at length on what ails stars: "It seems like these stars have just come here to earn some money, fame, glory and throw their weight around. Acting be damned. They do not understand the concept of acting. I mean there is no concept. It's become a fad now, like if I like hangers-on, if I get my shoe-laces tied by a spot boy, if I like posing for photographs then I'm a star. . . . Hey, but what about some acting too. I mean,

TOP, LEFT: Shah Rukh's grandfather, Mir Jan Muhammad (courtesy: Mansoor Khan Mir). TOP, RIGHT: Shah Rukh's mother, Fatima Lateef (courtesy: Renu Poswal). RIGHT: Shah Rukh's father, Meer Taj Mohammad (courtesy: Renu Poswal). ABOVE: Meer, Fatima, and Shahnaz Lala Rukh Khan (courtesy: Renu Poswal).

TOP: Shah Rukh in his first major role, as the wizard in a school production of *The Wiz*, a musical based on *The Wizard of Oz* (courtesy: Anshumaan Swami). LEFT: Shah Rukh in his teens (courtesy: Tejinder Tiwari). ABOVE: Shah Rukh and Gauri at a party in 1985 (courtesy: Vivek Khushalani). OPPOSITE, TOP: Shah Rukh in his first film role, as the fey college gossip "Senior" in *In Which Annie Gives It Those Ones* (courtesy: Pradip Krishen). OPPOSITE, BOTTOM: Yash and Aditya Chopra (courtesy: Yash Raj Films/Filmfare).

LEFT: Shah Rukh and Kajol in *DDLJ*, the longest running Indian film ever (courtesy: Yash Raj Films). BELOW: Shah Rukh with director and close friend Karan Johar (picture by Subi Samuel, courtesy: Gauri Khan). BOTTOM: Shah Rukh and Rani Mukherjee in *Kuch Kuch Hota Hai* (courtesy: Dharma Productions).

TOP: Shah Rukh looms large in billboards over Mumbai (picture by Fawzan Husain/ Lens Impressions). ABOVE: Amitabh Bachchan, Rani Mukherjee, and Shah Rukh in *Kabhi Khushi Kabhie Gham* (courtesy: Dharma Productions).

ABOVE: Shah Rukh in between shots in Egypt on the shoot of *Kabhi Khushi Kabhie Gham* (picture by Ayesha Monani, courtesy: Dharma Productions). RIGHT: Shah Rukh with Gauri and daughter Suhana on the set of *Kabhi Khushi Kabhie Gham* (picture by Ayesha Monani, courtesy: Dharma Productions). BELOW: Shah Rukh as the alcoholic lover in *Devdas* (courtesy: Bharat Shah).

TOP: The Khan family: Aryan, Shah Rukh, Gauri, and Suhana (courtesy: Gauri Khan). ABOVE: Shah Rukh in the New York City–based drama *Kal Ho Naa Ho* (courtesy: Dharma Productions).

ABOVE: Shah Rukh with bodyguards on an overseas visit (courtesy: Gauri Khan).
RIGHT: Karan directing Shah Rukh during *Kabhi Alvida Naa Kehna* (courtesy: Dharma Productions).
BELOW: Shah Rukh on the King Khan throne at the LIC Zee Cine Awards in March 2006 (courtesy: Zee Telefilms, Ltd).

where's your professionalism?" After success, the quotes became more self-important: "I am the best and I have to compete with myself. I don't believe in the rat race because I am not a rat. . . . At night before I go to sleep I tell myself I won't let the sun go down on me." By September 1992, *Stardust* headlines were asking: CAN THE INDUSTRY DIGEST SHAH RUKH KHAN'S ARROGANCE? The editor, Nishi, and Shah Rukh made a one-rupee wager. He said that stardom would not change him. She insisted that it would. They never settled the bet.

Like most stars, Shah Rukh found himself in and out of favor with the leading magazines. His relationship with film journalists was prickly. When one journalist asked him about his personal life, Shah Rukh responded with, "I'll break your face." When another questioned his sexual orientation, Shah Rukh said he "caught hold of him and told him, 'Okay, take off your pants—let's make love.'" But Shah Rukh was the master of the sound bite. Articulate and well read, he could speak without pausing for breath on almost any topic. He was entertaining, quick with clever repartees, and unafraid of offending the powers that be. But if one line in an entire article bothered him, he could be equally dismissive and haughty. His relationship with journalists reached a low point with the *Maya Memsaab* story.

In *Maya Memsaab*, based on *Madame Bovary*, Shah Rukh plays the young lover of an older, married woman who is disillusioned by the banality of ordinary life and lives in her own fantasy world. Their relationship is passionate but fraught with conflict, jealousies, and aggression. One scene has the couple making love. It is, by Hindi film standards, explicit. The actress Deepa Sahi, who also happened to be the director Ketan Mehta's wife, is topless. Shah Rukh and Deepa are first shown under white satin sheets but then he pushes her up against a wall. She bites his neck. Finally he tears a pillow apart and scatters feathers all over her.

In 1992, a magazine called *Cine Blitz* published a full-page story under the headline SHAH RUKH AND DEEPA'S STEAMY SCENES REVEALED! The story alleged that Ketan had asked his wife and Shah Rukh to spend the night together at a suburban hotel the night before he shot the scene so that they could "get totally comfortable with each other." The writer continued, "They should not be merely acting the parts but be well and truly involved." The story claimed that the actors had complied and the scene was shot the next day with only the director and cameraman present. This was done so the art house film would have more appeal for festival audiences abroad and, naturally, Shah Rukh had hidden the entire episode from Gauri. As was normal practice with exceptionally slanderous stories, there was no byline. No journalist at the magazine wanted to take responsibility.

The day after the story appeared, Shah Rukh was at a film function where he ran into Keith D'Costa, a *Cine Blitz* journalist. Shah Rukh believed that Keith had written the story and started to abuse him. The same night, Shah Rukh called Keith at his house and threatened to go there and beat him up. The following day he made good on this threat. He ended up at Keith's doorstep and hurled abuses at him in front of his parents. According to Keith, Shah Rukh's exact words were: "You f****** asshole, how could you write that f****** shit about me and a respected actress like Deepa Sahi. Why don't you f****** write about how I am going to f*** you in the presence of your mother and father." Among other things, Shah Rukh threatened to castrate Keith. Keith recalled that Shah Rukh was like a man possessed. Keith said, "The intensity with which Shah Rukh spewed venom and hatred made my skin crawl. I did think that he would hurt me."

On his editor's advice, Keith lodged a police complaint against Shah Rukh. But Shah Rukh continued to call his house and abuse him. Keith filed another complaint and requested police protection. The following day Shah Rukh was arrested. After his shoot wrapped up at Film City, Shah Rukh was taken to the Bandra police station. The police did not actually put him in the lockup. He was, after all, a star. A few of the cops took his autograph. They allowed Shah Rukh to make one phone call. He called Keith and said, "I'm in jail but I'll come f*** you." Around 11.30 P.M., Shah Rukh's close friend Chikki Pandey got him out on bail.

Two years later, another *Cine Blitz* journalist, Virginia Vacha, convinced Shah Rukh that Keith had not written the article. Shah Rukh apologized profusely for his behavior. He hugged Keith and offered to come to his house and apologize to his parents. He also went out of his way to accommodate *Cine Blitz* magazine, doing photo sessions and interviews. But Shah Rukh did not do anything as explicit on-screen again. His romantic persona was passionate and sometimes sensual, but never sexual. The few lovemaking scenes he did in his career were suggestive but not explicit. He never, ever kissed on-screen.

Hindi films have long shied away from kissing. A nation of a billion people presumably has a working knowledge of sex, but Bollywood has long pretended otherwise. All films released in India must be certified by the government-appointed Central Board of Film Certification, which follows a Cinematograph Act formulated in 1952. Though the act doesn't actually ban kissing, filmmakers and reluctant actors have steered clear of forthrightly depicting sexual situations. For decades, kissing was implied by juvenile shots of birds pecking at each other or flowers brushing against each other. Sexuality was sublimated into steamy songs and dance numbers in which men and women, often drenched, heaved and pushed against each other, but their lips never met. This hypocritical conservative streak was finally abandoned at the turn of the millennium when a new breed of filmmakers, actors, and viewers decided that they were indeed mature enough to handle kissing. But even when kissing became all the rage—an actress named Mallika Sherawat shot to stardom with a film called *Khwahish* (Wish), in which she famously kissed seventeen times—Shah Rukh did not relent. He maintained that he was just too shy to do it. Shah Rukh became Bollywood's biggest romantic icon without ever locking lips with a co-star.

Ironically, the actor who was squeamish about sex had no qualms about violence. Shah Rukh loved action movies. His one desire, as he told *India Today* magazine in August 1992, was "to give the Hindi movie creep a whole new dimension." Shah Rukh had started his film career playing a dark character; Rogozhin in Dostoevsky's *The Idiot* is a notable villain in Russian literature. He is a rich merchant's son who squanders his father's fortune. Rogozhin is obsessively in love with an infamous beauty called Nastasya Filippovna, but his poisonous passion is fraught with jealousy. Ultimately, when Rogozhin realizes that he cannot have Nastasya, he stabs her to death. Critics have suggested that Rogozhin, with dark hair and features, is the embodiment of evil, in stark contrast to the light-haired and blue-eyed hero of the novel, Myshkin, who represents the Christ figure. *Rog* in Russian means "horns," lending credence to the interpretation of Rogozhin as the devil. In Mani Kaul's cinematic adaptation, he is Raghujan.

Shah Rukh's pubescent features provide a sharp contrast to the character's actions. In the climax, after stabbing Nastasya, Raghujan chillingly remarks how though the knife was plunged deep, only a spoonful of blood came out. As Raghujan, Shah Rukh was compellingly sinister. But playing bad men in art house adaptations of literary classics was not quite the same as playing bad in a Bollywood film. Being villains was not the trajectory Bollywood heroes traditionally followed.

Until then morality in Hindi films was largely a two-tone affair. Characters were either good or bad; gray shades were rarely part of the script. The conventional hero was modeled on Lord Ram from the epic *Ramayana*, who was a paragon of virtue. In contrast, the villain was unmitigated evil. This one-dimensional worldview can be traced back to the earliest Hindi films, which were mostly costume dramas, historicals, or stories based on religious texts. Even when Hindi cinema moved into modern settings the actors continued to play archetypes rather than characters. The inspiration remained the great Indian epics, the *Mahabharata* and the *Ramayana*, which are peopled by larger-than-life men and women and are concerned with the *dharmic* role of individuals within a society. Human struggles are part of a larger cosmic cycle. And so even contemporary B-grade Hindi films about criminals and their molls alluded to larger battles of good versus evil. The leading-man roles were played by a select group of actors, who were usually conventionally handsome men with light skin. Similarly, the villain roles were also played by a small group of actors, at least some of whom were frankly ugly. There was little room for confusion. As soon as an actor walked into frame, the audience could identify him as heroic or villainous.

There was a small but distinct tradition of the anti-hero. In 1943, actor Ashok Kumar played a thief who reforms himself after falling in love with a physically challenged dancer in *Kismet* (Fate). The film was the first Hindi blockbuster. It ran for three years and eight months at the Roxy Theater in Kolkata. In the 1950s, as film noir emerged in the United States and Europe, Indian filmmakers also started to subvert the heroic image. The most successful actors of the time—Raj Kapoor, Dilip Kumar, and Dev Anand—all played negative characters who are redeemed by the end.

In 1993, Sanjay Dutt played the role of a terrorist in *Khalnayak* (Villain), a much-hyped film directed by Subhash Ghai. The character is a hardened criminal who kills his own father, but the script offers mitigating circumstances to soften the blow of his bad deeds: the terrorist is misguided by a Machiavellian villain. The terrorist is a willing murderer, but even so he does not transgress certain codes of conduct: the heroine roams the jungles with him and sings a suggestive song, which asks, "*Choli ke peeche kya hai?*" (What is under the blouse?), but he does not violate her virginity. Eventually, like most leading men, the terrorist also discovers the *nayak*, or hero, within himself and sets right the wrongs he has committed.

The Bollywood hero, even when he plays the villain, treads carefully. In the *Ramayana*, the hero Lakshman draws a furrow in the earth and asks his sister-in-law Sita not to step outside this *Lakshman Rekha*, or Line of Lakshman, which represents the limits of proper feminine behavior. Like Sita, film heroes also operated within a highly circumscribed moral universe. An unhinged, psychotic hero who murders innocent people, including his girlfriend, was unthinkable. Which is why when filmmakers Abbas Mustan suggested remaking *A Kiss Before Dying*, no actor was willing to do it.

Abbas, Mustan, and Hussain Burmanwala were Bollywood's men in white. The three brothers nearly always wore identical crisp white safari suits. They also made films in tandem. Abbas and Mustan directed (with one finishing the other's sentences), and Hussain edited. They were known as Abbas Mustan, one name with no hyphen. Their nephew Saifu suggested that they see *A Kiss Before Dying*, based on Ira Levin's novel about a coolly calculating college student who murders his girlfriend and then sets out to woo her sister. Abbas Mustan never saw the whole film. Halfway through, the power failed. But the little they saw convinced them that they must remake it.

Refashioning Hollywood was not a novel concept. Bollywood has a long tradition of co-opting and plagiarizing Hollywood ideas. Even Raj Kapoor was inspired by Charlie Chaplin's Tramp figure. He had the talent to infuse Chaplin with an Indian sensibility in films such as *Shri 420*, but lesser talents are happy simply to steal. There is an entire school of writers and directors who take Hollywood films and "Bollywood-ize" them, that is, they dilute the sexual content and add melodrama and songs. Levin's protagonist, played by Matt Dillon in James Dearden's 1991 film version, is downright nasty. To temper the malevolence, Abbas Mustan tacked on a motivation: The hero's family is destroyed after his father is cheated by his business partner. So the hero stalks the partner's family, romances one daughter, kills her, and then romances the other.

These motivations, however, weren't powerful enough to motivate any leading actor to do the film called *Baazigar* (Gambler). Aamir Khan refused. So did Anil Kapoor. Salman Khan's father, the scriptwriter Salim, nixed the idea, saying it was too early for his son to be experimenting with negative roles such as this. Abbas Mustan, scrambling and desperate, thought of Shah Rukh. They had seen his television serials and met him earlier. Though he didn't seem "typical hero material," there was something distinctive about him. The producer, Ratan Jain, wondered if the directors were downsizing their film. Both Aamir and Salman had made their debuts with blockbuster hits. Anil was a senior hero. In comparison, Shah Rukh was a minor player with only one success and too much attitude.

But Shah Rukh was the only actor willing to play a character who throws his nubile girlfriend off a roof without a trace of remorse and then murders her two friends because they might reveal his secret. In September 1992, Abbas Mustan gave Shah Rukh a detailed 1½-hour narration of the story. When they finished, he shook hands with them and immediately started to discuss how he would enact certain scenes. Shah Rukh loved the idea of being bad: "My whole logic is if you tell *Sholay* from Gabbar Singh's point of view, the murders will seem correct," he said. Abbas Mustan worried that audience sympathy may not be with Shah Rukh if he is seen killing an established actress. So new girls were chosen. One was Kajol, from a dynasty of famous actresses. Her mother, Tanuja, and grandmother, Shobhana Samarth, were popular actresses. Through the 1990s, Kajol and Shah Rukh would become Bollywood's most enduring screen pair, with a series of successes. But when *Baazigar* was being made, she was a minor and her mother signed the contracts.

While shooting, Shah Rukh plunged full-blown into extreme villainy. He wasn't hesitant about appearing unattractive or scary onscreen. In certain scenes, he is seen in a tight close-up with eyes bulging, face streaked with blood, and tears and lips quivering so hard that he seems afflicted with a serious tropical disease. Shah Rukh added his own touches to make the character even more malicious. After viciously murdering a girl who has an incriminating photograph, he stares into the camera lens, chews on the evidence, and swallows it. Before tossing his girlfriend off the roof, he gives her an eerie look and says, "I'm sorry." Shah Rukh plays the murderer with clarity and conviction. Many years later, he would tell documentary filmmaker Nasreen Munni Kabir that "playing bad guys was the first creative thought I had. I have lost that youthfulness and urge to swim against the current."

Shah Rukh had so much fun swimming against the current that he agreed to play the bad guy in two other films. One was made at the same time as *Baazigar*. It was called *Darr* (Fear) and was directed by one of Indian cinema's foremost filmmakers, Yash Chopra.

Murder, He Wrote

Little about Yash Chopra suggested romance. He was a bald, aging filmmaker who spoke with a throaty Punjabi accent so thick that his sentences often needed translation. He didn't smoke, touch alcohol, or even imbibe caffeine in any form. His favorite drink was a wholesome milk concoction called *lassi*. Despite spending decades in the business, Yash had acquired little of Bollywood's flashiness. With his singularly staid shirts and habit of addressing everyone younger as *beta* (child), Yash had an avuncular air about him—in fact, many of his actors called him Yash Uncle. Yash had had an arranged marriage when he was thirty-seven. He had two sons, who treated him with old-fashioned reverence. As did most of the industry: Yash Chopra was Bollywood's high priest of romance.

Yash wasn't so much a filmmaker as a school of filmmaking. Over forty years of making successful films, Yash had developed a style that was instantly recognized and widely imitated. The quintessential Yash Chopra film reveled in overblown beauty. The heroine, usually played by the leading actress of the day, was portrayed as an ethereal, virginal goddess swathed in chiffon saris. The romance, conducted in spectacular foreign locales (usually Switzerland), was achingly pure. Yash celebrated chaste sensuality; he was a connoisseur of the rain song, in which the heroine, inevitably wearing white clothes, got wet. But sexuality rarely tainted this sunlit world, and lust, betrayal, jealousy, envy, insecurity, the inevitable untidy debris of relationships, didn't get much screen time either. Above all, Yash propagated family values. His films were filled with rich, beautiful, noble people who struggled gallantly with social and familial obligations.

Through the 1990s, Yash became a movie mogul. His company, Yash Raj Films, grew from a successful but stodgy production house that released one or two films every few years into an integrated entertainment conglomerate. The company dabbled in film production, television software, music videos, and home entertainment. It also included a global distribution network and a music company. The sprawling 180,000-square-foot, state-of-the-art Yash Raj Films Studio opened in 2005. A year earlier, the *Hollywood Reporter* ranked Yash Raj twenty-seventh in its annual list of Top 100 production houses in the world.

Yash's life was the quintessential film fairy-tale story. He had come to Mumbai on January 1, 1951, with 200 rupees ($5) in his pocket. He was then only nineteen. Yash was born in pre-Partition Lahore and was largely raised in the house of his elder brother, B. R. Chopra, who was then a film journalist. In 1945 Yash moved to Jalandhar to continue his education. Just before Partition in 1947, B. R. Chopra moved to Mumbai and became a filmmaker. Yash joined him as an assistant at a salary of 150 rupees ($3) per month. For seven years, Yash toiled as a mid-level assistant. In 1959, B.R. gave Yash a break as a director with a film called *Dhool Ka Phool* (Flower of the Dust). The film about the fate of an illegitimate child was a big success and Yash went on to make four more films for his brother.

Waqt (Time), made in 1965, was the first film to articulate the Yash Chopra method. It was among the most expensive films made until then. Much of the budget was spent on stars and style. *Waqt* is widely acknowledged as the first Hindi film to have multiple stars. It has five leading actors. The frames are soaked in glamour. The ladies, dressed in stylish outfits and diamonds, flit in and out of splendid parties and mansions. The men wear tight fashionable suits, race foreign cars, and play billiards. The film is shot in beautiful locations, such as Kashmir and Shimla. The sets are spectacular. Every mansion in the film, and there are many, has grand pianos and fountains gurgling in the background. The opulence is made more dazzling by color—B.R. had entrusted the company's first color production to his brother.

In 1971, on his thirty-ninth birthday, Yash set up his own production house, Yash Raj Films. Moving out of his brother's shadow was a momentous and traumatic decision. The brothers never spoke out publicly against each other, but industry grapevine was rife with speculation on what caused the break: Yash had recently married, and his wife, Pamela, was cited as a probable cause for the rift between the brothers. B.R. had raised Yash like a surrogate father. Years later Yash would tell his biographer, Dr. Rachel Dwyer, "I respect B.R. very much. I feel my existence is because of him. He brought me up. I behaved badly." But the distress of professionally parting ways with his brother was at least partly assuaged by the success of his first independent production

Daag (Stigma). *Daag*, advertised as "A poem of love," was the unconventional story of a man who lives happily ever after with two wives. It is firmly placed in the Yash Chopra landscape of high emotion, glamorously dressed characters, beautiful locations, and melodious music.

Yash sometimes moved away from this blueprint. In 1975, he directed Amitabh Bachchan in the landmark film *Deewaar*. The searing film played an instrumental part in setting up Amitabh's Angry Young Man image. But a year later Yash turned the image on its head by casting him as a brooding poet in *Kabhi Kabhie* (Sometimes), a love story spanning several generations. Through the 1980s, Yash seemed to lose his Midas touch at the box office. He weathered five failures in a row. In 1989, after a decade of unsuccessfully chasing box office success with action dramas, Yash went back to what he did best: romance. With *Chandni*, a love story about a middle-class girl (who nonetheless dressed in chiffons) and a rich boy, Yash reestablished himself. He did not stray far from his patented formula again.

Aditya, Yash's elder son, imbibed his father's style from the time he could see and listen. As a four-year-old, he wandered around the shoot of *Kabhi Kabhie* with a viewfinder hung around his neck. The heavy instrument occasionally strained his neck, but Aditya refused to let go of it. The monotony of film production did not bore him. His parents had to drag him away from the set. Until he was six years old, Aditya assumed that everyone worked in the movies. Famous actors, directors, music composers were guests at his sprawling house. Cinema was the world. Aditya did not make a conscious decision to become a filmmaker. It was ordained.

Aditya was instrumental in the transformation of Yash Raj

Films into an entertainment powerhouse. His commercial instincts were honed by years of watching movies. Even as a teenager Aditya was studying Indian films. He watched the oeuvre of seminal Hindi film directors such as Raj Kapoor, Bimal Roy, and his uncle, B. R. Chopra, and tried to analyze the mechanics of storytelling: what makes a film work, how masters of the medium manipulate the audience. Every Friday he headed to the nearest movie theater to see the latest Hindi release. This was unusual; industry folk typically watched movies in plush preview theaters with their family, friends, and *chamchas* (sycophants). But Aditya wanted to get a feel of a "real" audience. He researched viewer reactions. He became what the industry calls a "First day, first show man."

From 1989 to 1991, Aditya kept a meticulous record of his film viewing in his Sydenham College notebooks. For each film that he saw, he wrote down the first-week collections, the box office result in the following weeks, and his own prediction for the film. He also wrote a monthly review of overall box office performance. Aditya did not discriminate. He watched hackneyed movies like *Bade Ghar Ki Beti* (The Rich Man's Daughter) with equal enthusiasm (the diary entry reads "an insult to filmmaking"). At the end of each year, Aditya compared his predictions with how films actually fared. He was right 80 percent of the time.

Aditya joined his father as an assistant in 1989. It was an opportune time. With *Chandni*, fifty-seven-year-old Yash was trying to rediscover his inner romantic and his lost box office touch. Aditya's mother insisted that he finish college so Aditya missed some shooting schedules, but he was present throughout the post-production of the film. Before its release, the film elicited what the industry calls "a mixed report." Some people thought the love triangle was clichéd, but Aditya loved it. He predicted that his father had made a "superhit." He was right. *Chandni* rode in on the anti-violence wave that *Qayamat Se Qayamat Tak* had ushered in the year before. It put Yash on the A-list again.

The shy boy who sometimes stammered had grown into an opinionated young man with soaring ambition. When Aditya came to Yash with the idea of a film about an obsessive lover, Yash listened. The 1989 thriller *Dead Calm*, about a married couple whose sailing trip is terrorized by a psychotic criminal, loosely inspired *Darr* (Fear). Aditya envisioned the film as a low-budget, dark movie with no songs or major stars. But actor Rishi Kapoor, who was penciled in to play one of the leads, suggested to Yash that he direct it himself, at which point the film transformed into a lush romance in which beautifully dressed stars gamboled in Swiss locations. It was, per Yash Chopra's prescription, a gorgeous big-budget spectacle with songs.

Sunny Deol eventually played *Darr*'s traditional hero, Sunil, the upright navy commando who battles a disturbed young man. Juhi Chawla was cast as the chiffon-clad beauty, Kiran, who triggers the obsessive stalker. But the Chopras were stumped when it came to casting the third leg of this unconventional love triangle. The character Rahul was a first for Bollywood. Rahul is a lonely, unhinged man who talks with his mother who died eighteen years ago. He pursues the heroine and terrorizes her. When she rebuffs his affection, his unrequited passion turns murderous. Like the lead in *Baazigar*, Rahul kills innocents without remorse. At the end of *Darr*, he follows Sunil and Kiran on their honeymoon. He viciously stabs Sunil and tries to force Kiran into an impromptu marriage with him. *Darr*'s climax has Sunil beating Rahul to a bloody pulp and finally shooting him dead.

Casting-wise, *Darr* was a retread of *Baazigar*. No established hero was willing to play this psychotic lover, even with a director as reputed and experienced as Yash Chopra at the helm. The climax, in which Sunny Deol would pound Rahul into the ground, was especially difficult for other stars to digest. They feared that such a brutal on-screen lashing would diminish their heroic image. Aamir Khan seriously considered the role, but Sunny had a reputation for interference and Aamir was concerned that his senior colleague would force changes in the script. Eventually Aamir pulled out. One schedule of *Darr* was shot without the third lead being cast. Yash spoke to actors Ajay Devgan and Sanjay Dutt. Both declined. The situation was desperate when the name Shah Rukh Khan cropped up.

Aditya had loved Shah Rukh's performance in *Deewana*. Shah Rukh was over the top, but Aditya could see that he was an intelligent actor who was hamming to match the film's melodramatic tone. "Shah Rukh was very watchable," Aditya said. "I saw him as a bridge between the old-school actors and what might be new. What came across very strongly was his eagerness to reach out to the audience." To gauge Shah Rukh, Yash watched a song from the unfinished *King Uncle*. He wasn't impressed. Shah Rukh wasn't his idea of a hero. But Yash agreed to a meeting, which went well. Partly because Shah Rukh had a reputation as a good actor but mostly because the Chopras didn't have a choice, Shah Rukh was cast as the stammering, unhinged, brutal lover in *Darr*.

Over the following decade, Shah Rukh became the resident muse at Yash Raj Films. Both Yash and Aditya repeatedly cast him as the leading man in their projects. Just as the Amitabh Bachchan persona was created by writing partners Salim-Javed and directors Prakash Mehra, Ramesh Sippy,

Manmohan Desai, and Yash Chopra, the superstar Shah Rukh Khan was constructed by Yash and Aditya. Karan Johar, Aditya's closest friend and one-time assistant, developed the image further in his films, which were essentially an extension of the Chopra brand.

Unlike with Kundan, Shah Rukh had no "generation-gap problems" at the Yash Chopra camp. He worked equally well with both the sixty-plus Yash and the under-thirty Aditya and Karan. Shah Rukh's star-actor appeal was the perfect fit for the Yash Raj brand of movies. Their feel-good, simplistic stories about pretty people grappling with matters of the heart amplified his charm. Yash, Aditya, and Karan re-imagined Shah Rukh as a yuppie romantic hero. They created a durable global persona for him, which replaced Amitabh's Angry Young Man. Their fortunes soared together. Their sensibilities defined the decade.

The first shot Shah Rukh did for *Darr* had him surreptitiously entering a party at the heroine's house. The guests are celebrating *Holi*, the Hindu festival of colors. Everyone is liberally soaked in color dyes and therefore unrecognizable. This gives Rahul the anonymity he needs to be near Kiran. As he watches Kiran flirtatiously celebrate the festival with Sunil, he beats the *dhol* (drums) with fanatical energy. Aditya had the confidence that Shah Rukh could act but he was still nursing disappointment over Aamir's rejection. Aamir was already a hot star. But after watching Shah Rukh do the Holi scene, Aditya decided that Shah Rukh would "rock the film." He said, "I knew I was not going to miss Aamir."

Darr and *Baazigar* were made simultaneously. Shah Rukh alternated between playing a psychotic lover and a murderous avenger. This was, according to conventional Bollywood wisdom, professional suicide. If the audience did not accept these morally dubious characters, Shah Rukh's shining career would be over before it began. But each day Shah Rukh chiseled away at Hindi film stereotypes with a wholehearted conviction that the audience would be on his side. He had the confidence that he could make this work.

In 1993, *Darr* and *Baazigar* released within a month of each other. Viewers were hard-pressed to decide which film's antagonist was more deranged and vicious. In *Baazigar*, Shah Rukh's character, Ajay, suggests to his first girlfriend that since her father insists on marrying her to another man, they should commit suicide. After both have written identical suicide notes, he laughs and says he was only joking. He suggests they marry the following day. When they get to the registrar's office, it is closed for lunch so he takes her up to the roof. He says he wants her to be at the top of the world and perches her on the parapet. He kneels down, apologizes, and throws her over. He then casually walks past her bloodied body and mails the suicide note. In the next scene, he pays condolences to the bereaved family.

In *Darr*, Shah Rukh's character, Rahul, is introduced playing a game of "she loves me, she loves me not" while walking on the ledge of a tall building. Later in the film he carves Kiran's name on his chest with a knife. After Sunil and Kiran are married, he defaces their new home with graffiti declaring his love. In the climax, after Sunil has pummeled him, Rahul holds his feet and begs for forgiveness. When Sunil hesitates, Rahul plunges a knife into Sunil's stomach, then apologizes for his behavior but proceeds to kidnap his wife. Incredibly, both films were blockbusters.

For *Baazigar*, the production company, Venus Records and Tapes, organized a traveling premiere. The crew went to several theaters on opening night, mingling with the crowds and taking in reactions. There was a stunned silence during the murder scene, but Shah Rukh's outrageous cruelty did not alienate the viewers. Instead they started applauding as he cleverly exacted his bloody revenge. Shah Rukh's connection with the audience veiled the dubious morality of the script. It was, as he had said, like seeing *Sholay* from Gabbar Singh's point of view. Even as Shah Rukh slaughtered innocents, the audience was firmly on his side. As he murdered, they clapped. The whistling was especially loud when Shah Rukh delivered his famous signature dialogue: "*Kabhi kabhi kuch jeetne ke liye, kuch harna padta hai aur haar ke jeetne wale ko Baazigar kehte hain*" (Sometimes to win something you must lose something, and he who wins by losing is called the Gambler).

The same night, the main cast and crew flew to London. It was Shah Rukh's first trip to the West. The overseas distributor, Eros International, had organized six premieres in three days. Shah Rukh and Gauri stayed at the posh St. James Court Hotel, where they were overwhelmed by the luxury of a three-room suite. The following night, at 3 A.M., a phone call from India woke Shah Rukh. It was Karan's father, producer Yash Johar, calling to say that *Baazigar* was a "superhit."

A month later, in December, the same scenario repeated with *Darr*. The *Darr* climax had deterred many heroes from playing Rahul because they did not want to be beaten up onscreen by another star. But Shah Rukh instinctively understood that the more Sunny beat him, the more the audience would empathize with him. He allowed Sunny to reduce him to a bloody pulp and, as Aditya put it, "walked away with the film." So much so that Sunny protested that the Chopras had shortchanged him. The finished film was not what they had narrated to him. He accused Shah Rukh of manipulating the story to win the viewers. Yash denied this, but Sunny never worked with them again.

Baazigar and *Darr* changed the rules for what constituted a Hindi film hero. It was no longer necessary to be a gentleman. Amitabh Bachchan's Angry Young Man wasn't heroic in the traditional mold, but he was, whether as cop, smuggler, coal miner, or alcoholic, an honorable man. There was nobility in his actions. Amitabh was the permanently lonely outsider who single-handedly took on dozens of baddies, the corrupt establishment, an indifferent universe with dignity and grace. Shah Rukh's characters made these seem like old-fashioned virtues. "The Hindi film hero has changed," Shah Rukh said. "He can die in the film and lose the girl. He can kill people. We don't have to like him, just the story he is telling."

In February 1994, Shah Rukh was nominated for three Filmfare Awards. Though he was a murderer in both movies, *Filmfare* magazine inexplicably found his performance in *Baazigar* worthy of a Best Actor nomination and his role in *Darr* of a Best Villain nomination. He was also nominated as Best Actor for *Kabhi Haan Kabhi Naa* in the Filmfare Critics Award section. Shah Rukh had told Abbas Mustan that if *Filmfare* gave him only Best Villain, he would throw away the trophy. He felt he deserved both awards, or at the least, Best Actor. The award ceremony spanned several hours—at the climax, Shah Rukh walked away with the Best Actor trophy and the Best Actor in the Critics' Award. Through the evening he did not see Abbas Mustan, and they weren't at the after party either. Shah Rukh felt that he could not go home with his first *Filmfare* Best Actor award without paying his respects to the men who had made it possible. So he found out where his directors lived and, despite the late hour, decided to visit.

Abbas Mustan lived in a decrepit area of south Mumbai known as Bhendi Bazaar. Even by Mumbai standards, where roughly 17,550 residents live on each square mile, Bhendi Bazaar is claustrophobically crowded. It is a ghetto, mostly populated by working-class Muslim families. Narrow, dingy buildings five to seven stories high squeeze against each other. Many of the homes are painted a lurid green or blue and lit harshly by tube lights. The brothers lived in a *chawl*, a multi-story building that stacked rows of one-room homes with common public bathrooms at the end of each corridor. Shah Rukh remembered that there were at least ten or twelve people sleeping in the room when he entered. In the ensuing commotion and noise, everybody woke up.

Shah Rukh told Abbas Mustan that he could not go home without their blessing and he touched the brothers' feet. They talked, hugged, and marveled at their success. When Shah Rukh headed out of the house it was almost dawn, but the *chawl* had already come to life. It was the month of Ramadan and people had woken up before sunrise to eat their *sehri*. The news that Shah Rukh Khan was in the chawl spread fast. When he stepped out of the house, Shah Rukh was mobbed.

The next *Filmfare* issue was devoted to the magazine's awards, with interviews with all the winners. Shah Rukh declared: "I've already picked up three. I intend to add at least one to the collection every year. And why not? I'm one of the best actors on the scene today."

The Brave-Hearted Takes the Box Office

The Maratha Mandir Theater is an unlikely setting for history. It is located in a predominantly working-class locality in south central Mumbai. One of the city's biggest railway stations, Mumbai Central, and the State Transport bus terminal are nearby. Each day hundreds of trains and buses offload thousands of passengers who come from dusty, destitute villages in search of the fabled Bombay dream. The streets are lined with cheap hotels and roadside eateries. In recent years spiffy new skyscrapers have started to gentrify the landscape, but the area still retains the feel of an inexpensive first stop for immigrants.

The Mandir Theater, inaugurated on October 16, 1958, was once a Bollywood hotspot. In the 1960s and 1970s, glorious premieres were held here. Live bands played as stars in dazzling fashions descended from imported cars and the paparazzi tripped over each other to get a good shot. But over the decades Maratha Mandir deteriorated. The more affluent viewers preferred to get their *masala* movie fix in snazzy multiplexes, and Maratha Mandir came to be patronized largely by what the trade calls the "masses," or lower-middle-class viewers. But since the mid-1990s, each day at 11:30 A.M. history is made in the vast thousand-seat theater: *Dilwale Dulhania Le Jayenge* (The Brave-Hearted Will Take the Bride), the longest-running Indian film ever, plays one more time.

Dilwale Dulhania Le Jayenge (abbreviated as *DDLJ*) was released on October 20, 1995. After the initial years, the audience at Maratha Mandir consisted mostly of "repeat" viewers, people who have seen the film before. As the story unfolds, they cheer, mime dialogue, and sing along. The screening resembles the performance of a well-known mythological tale in a village square. Scalpers outside the theater speak of favorite clients who have seen the film twenty to thirty times. Some saunter in half an hour late or leave after their favorite scene or song is over. The pleasure is no longer in the artful contrivances of the story; the audience only comes to partake in the telling of it.

DDLJ has become a Bollywood landmark. Since film business in India, especially in the hinterland, is often conducted in cash, box office reports tend to be as wildly creative as the scripts. But it is widely agreed that *DDLJ* has done business worth 600 million rupees ($13.5 million). In 2001, *DDLJ* broke the continuous exhibition record of *Sholay*, the previous gold standard, which had run for five years. An estimated 25 million copies of the *DDLJ* sound track have been sold. The film ushered in a new age in Bollywood. It changed Hindi cinema creatively and commercially by opening up new markets overseas. Aditya Chopra was only twenty-three years old when he wrote and directed the film.

Through the making of *Darr*, Aditya and Shah Rukh had become friends. Yash, Sunny, and Juhi were clearly "seniors," older and more successful players in Bollywood's hierarchy. Shah Rukh hung out with Aditya and his younger brother Uday, who was also assisting. They would come up with wacky ideas and conspire about how best to convince Yash to use them. After the completion of *Darr*, Aditya had started thinking about his own directorial debut. He talked to Shah Rukh about a film called *Auzaar* (Weapon). Shah Rukh assumed that a film with such a high-octane name would necessarily be a "macho, cool dude" kind of movie. Instead, in 1994, Aditya came to Shah Rukh with *DDLJ* and offered him the lead role of Raj.

The film was a deceptively simple story set in London. The hero, Raj Malhotra, is a rich, second-generation British Indian. Born and raised in London, he is irreverent, loud, and flirtatious. But underneath the veneer of cockiness he is an inherently upright, good-hearted Indian boy. The heroine, Simran, is a middle-class girl brought up in the Indian ghetto of Southall. She is spirited but extremely conservative.

Raj's father embodies the rags-to-riches immigrant story. He is a tenth-grade drop-out from Bhatinda who, through sheer hard work, becomes a millionaire. Flamboyantly dressed in chic pants and cravats, he is a permanently jovial man who wants his only child to enjoy all that money can buy. So Raj lives in a mansion and drives a Lamborghini. When Raj flunks his university exams, instead of reprimanding him his father pops champagne, saying that Raj has upheld a long family tradition of academic failure. In contrast, Simran's father is a stern, frugal convenience-store owner who insists that his two daughters grow up in a traditional Indian home unpolluted by the corrupting West. Despite twenty-two years in London, he continues to dress in Indian clothes, makes his daughters pray regularly, and frowns upon Western music and culture.

Raj and Simran take a trip on the Eurail with their respective friends. At first they fight, but thanks to missed trains and faulty car engines, they end up spending one night together—of course without any sexual contact—and ultimately they fall in love. The hitch is that Simran is already engaged. Her father has arranged her marriage with his best friend's son in India. She will soon move to a country she has never visited to marry a man she has never met. Simran has made peace with her fate. When Raj questions her imminent marriage, she says, "*Hamare yahaan toh aisa hi hota hai*" (In our community, this is how it works). But her carefully constructed future falls apart when she falls in love with Raj.

When Simran's father finds out that his daughter has broken his rules, he ships the family back to India. He doesn't count on Raj's tenaciousness. Raj follows Simran back to the Punjab in India. With Bollywood's typical disregard for realism, despite not having her address, Raj effortlessly finds her village and house. But unlike generations of Bollywood lovers before them, Raj and Simran don't elope. Simran is willing to run away from her family but Raj refuses, saying, "I might have been born in England but I am Hindustani [Indian]. I've come to make you my bride. I'll take you only when your father gives me your hand in marriage." Raj stays in the village under a false identity and endears himself to every member of Simran's family. Eventually, after many tears and a little blood have been shed, Raj even wins over Simran's father. *DDLJ* asserts that familial approval is essential for love to thrive. A love marriage must also be arranged. Only then does the brave heart take the bride.

As a director, Aditya inherited the Yash Chopra style. Rich emotions, sumptuous songs, and Switzerland were part of his cinema legacy. But he was also greatly influenced by another young film director named Sooraj Barjatya. Sooraj was a third-generation Bollywood director. His grandfather, Tarachand Barjatya, had set up Rajshri Productions in 1962. Tarachand's three sons and several grandchildren followed him into the business. They belonged to the ultra-conservative Jain community and lived in a joint family, never touching meat or alcohol. They were such staunch vegetarians that their films and television serials did not even have references to eggs. In the decadent and lurid movie world, they were an anomaly.

At the Barjatya office, the brief for movies was simple: "Producing wholesome and musical entertainers aimed at the family, which are Indian in content and spirit." Like Yash Raj, Rajshri also offered family values, but with less opulent packaging. Their films were more homely. In 1989, the company was floundering after a spate of flops when the twenty-four-year-old Sooraj made his debut with *Maine Pyar Kiya* (I Have Loved). *Maine Pyar Kiya* was a romance so chaste that when the boy applies medicine to the girl's sprained calf, he closes his eyes because her ankles are exposed. The film was a monstrous success. Aditya liked it so much that he saw it twice in back-to-back shows. His diary entry reads, "A mind-blowing film, a complete entertainer, deserves all the success it gets."

As it turned out, *Maine Pyar Kiya* was only the warm-up for Sooraj's second act, *Hum Aapke Hain Koun . . . !* (Who Am I to You?). In this film, Sooraj extended two weddings and a funeral into over three hours of celebrations of Indian rituals, nuptials, and the united Hindu family. In

Hum Aapke Hain Koun . . . !, the numerous characters—in-laws, friends, aunts, uncles, even the hired help and the pet Pomeranian—are relentlessly cheerful. There is little plot, dramatic sweep, or character development. The film is mostly a series of happy bonding scenes held together by fourteen songs. Critics savaged it as a "wedding video" but viewers embraced it with such ardor that it became the highest grosser in recent Bollywood history and single-handedly revived the theatrical business. *Hum Aapke Hain Koun . . . !* articulated a value system that *DDLJ* would echo a year later: that the extended family is sacrosanct. It is the foundation of all that is properly Indian. It is what makes Indian culture morally superior. Therefore, individual desires must be sacrificed at the altar of greater social good. *Hum Aapke Hain Koun . . . !* was released in August 1994, a month before Aditya started shooting. It reinforced his conviction in his own story.

Shah Rukh, however, didn't share Aditya's vision. "I didn't like those romantic films from the beginning," he said. "I didn't want to go on a picnic or go to college." The other two Khans, Aamir and Salman, were playing these lover-boy roles with great success and Shah Rukh was happy to be regarded as different. His third attempt at playing a negative hero in a dark, grossly violent film called *Anjaam* (Conclusion) had flopped, but he had a clutch of films in hand. The press positioned him as the "hottest star." The December 1994 edition of *Movie* magazine had Shah Rukh's picture on the cover next to that of Amitabh Bachchan with the headline, HEIR APPARENT?

Traditionally, Bollywood heroes make their debut with a *DDLJ*-style romance. The time-honored formula is simple: Boy meets girl, boy loses girl, boy gets girl, and they walk into the sunset hand in hand. The plot is designed to give the actor enough opportunities to show that he is worthy of being a star. He romances, dances, fights, and lip-synchs melodious songs. Bollywood wisdom dictates that the love story is the safest way for a new face to win over viewers. But Shah Rukh had already had fourteen releases before *DDLJ*, three of which featured him as a decidedly unromantic and un-heroic character. Which was why Aditya wanted him.

Aditya had scripted Raj as a slightly *tedha* (crooked) character. He believed that a touch of impudence is far more attractive to women than the straitlaced piety of most Bollywood heroes. Raj is a transgressor. In an early draft of the script Aditya had him buying condoms, but he later decided that might be going too far and he changed it to beer. Raj flirts outrageously. He is, on the surface, a spoiled, rich jerk. Raj's nobility is revealed when Raj and Simran spend a night together. Simran is in a drunken stupor. When she wakes up the next morning, Raj convinces her that they have made love. But when she breaks down sobbing, he tells her the truth. He shakes her and says, "I'm not scum, Simran. I am Hindustani and I know what honor means for the Hindustani woman. Not even in my dreams can I imagine doing that to you." This scene changes the tenor of *DDLJ*. Aditya believed Shah Rukh could do Raj better than anybody else because he would bring an edge to the role—in this critical scene, at least for a moment the audience would think that Shah Rukh, with his history of bad behavior, could have crossed the *Lakshman Rekha* and had premarital sex.

Over three weeks and several meetings, Aditya tried to convince Shah Rukh to do the film. In their fourth meeting, Aditya told Shah Rukh that he was indeed a star, but he could never become a superstar unless he became every girl's fantasy lover, every sister's brother, and every mother's son. Till then he was, as Aditya put it, "the autorickshaw driver's hero." As Shah Rukh dithered, Aditya thought of alternatives. But one day at Mehboob Studios, on the sets of *Karan Arjun*, Shah Rukh agreed to do *DDLJ*. He still didn't believe in the film, but he loved the climax in which the stern father finally lets go of Simran's hand and allows her to leave with Raj on an outbound train. Many industry pundits were skeptical of Shah Rukh's switch to the lover-boy persona. Shah Rukh drove to the premiere of *DDLJ* with Ratan Jain, who had produced *Baazigar*. "Don't mind," he told Shah Rukh, "but this film will never work. People will not accept you as a romantic hero."

In the movie business, as William Goldman famously remarked, "nobody knows anything." Viewers had responded to Shah Rukh's negative persona with unexpected applause. They now embraced the lover boy with greater fervor. In Mumbai, barring one Saturday evening show, every show in every theater in the first week of the film's release was full. Distributors reported record collections across the country. The critics were equally besotted: In the *Times of India*, critic Khalid Mohamed wrote, "Popular, high-cost cinema has come of age." *Screen*, a trade weekly, headlined the review with: A YOUNG MASTER ARRIVES.

DDLJ became Bollywood's Energizer Bunny—it kept going and going and going. The film took on a life of its own and stayed on the big screen. Each time a milestone was reached—5 years, 300 weeks, 10 years—a flurry of media descended on Maratha Mandir to mark the occasion, but largely the film continued as if on autopilot. It needed no marketing. In the ensuing years, Shah Rukh had several more blockbusters and two children; Aditya got married, divorced and set up a studio; the heroine, Kajol, got married, had a daughter, retired for three years, and returned. All the while, *DDLJ* continued to play.

DDLJ set up a new heroic prototype. Raj replaced Vijay; Amitabh's Angry Young Man image was buried and gone. Raj wasn't an anti-establishment rebel. He was a yuppie who worked the system to get the desired results. He was an articulate global Indian who was equally at ease in a nightclub in Paris or in a village in the Punjab. Raj was trendy and traditional. Depending on the situation, he could be progressive or conservative. He played by the rules but also tweaked them when necessary.

Unlike Vijay, Raj wasn't larger than life. He was scripted, as Aditya put it, "as life. The *herogiri* [heroism] was gone. It was the age to be chilled out." Dramatic dialogue was an essential ingredient in Vijay's heroic persona—decades after the films were made, fans can quote Amitabh Bachchan's powerful lines from *Sholay* and *Deewaar*. But Raj spoke in normal, everyday language. Though he still single-handedly beat up several bad guys, he wasn't overtly macho. In *DDLJ*, Raj sits in the kitchen and peels vegetables with the women of the house. When Simran does *Karva Chauth*, a North Indian ritual in which women keep a daylong fast for the good health and prosperity of their husbands, he starves along with her. In his participation in these rituals and his ease in traditionally female spaces, Raj is unlike the swaggering he-man heroes of the past. He is sensitive, vulnerable, and not afraid to cry. But he also has the strength and guile to outwit the more blatantly chauvinistic men in the film: Simran's father and her boorish fiancé. Raj was the new Indian man.

While making *DDLJ*, Aditya instructed Shah Rukh to

take off his mask. Unlike *Baazigar* and *Darr*, there was to be no showy actor's business—stammering, wounds, or ultra-violence—that Shah Rukh could use. Aditya wanted Shah Rukh to "show himself." Raj, witty and irreverent but also sensitive and insightful, was an extension of Aditya and Shah Rukh himself, who Aditya believed was, underneath the brash attitude, an inherently nice man. Despite his frontier Peshawar roots, Shah Rukh was not a proponent of high-testosterone virility. Barring his C-Gang school friends, he preferred the company of women. Even the male friends he made later in life were, in his words, "not the most macho" (one reason, perhaps, why rumors of homosexuality have dogged Shah Rukh from the time he joined films). Shah Rukh was proud of not cloaking his feminine side. He described himself as a "Pathan who can cry."

Shah Rukh was, as Aditya said, "nakedly honest" in his performance. Even though Amitabh had earlier elicited the same passion, fans rarely thought of Vijay and Amitabh Bachchan as one. Vijay was working-class, seething, and sometimes brutal. Amitabh, in person, was highly cultured and sophisticated. But with Shah Rukh, the distance between actor and image blurred. The audience believed that Shah Rukh *was* Raj. He became, as Aditya had said, every girl's fantasy lover, every sister's brother, every mother's son. In short, a superstar.

Just as Vijay embodied the angst of 1970s India, Raj resonated with the aspirations of a post-liberalization 1990s India. Shah Rukh became the personification of the collective ideals and longings of a country undergoing social upheaval. The decade was a curiously uncertain time in the nation's history. The economic rebirth set off by liberalization created a surge of growth in urban India. The reforms created an air of optimism and confidence. After almost fifty years of economic exile, an unshackled country rushed to catch up with the world, which beckoned from television sets. Lifestyles, attitudes, and social mores underwent cataclysmic change. "*Yeh dil maange more*" (This heart wants more), insisted a commercial for Pepsi-Cola that was launched on August 15, 1990, and soon become a ubiquitous symbol of modern India. Middle-class Indians increasingly aspired to the good life, and the economy offered the opportunity to make at least some of their dreams come true. Unlike previous generations, the new middle class had no guilt or inhibitions about money. Being rich was the principal ideology of the 1990s. Greed, as Gordon Gekko so memorably declared in *Wall Street*, was good.

But the torrent of Western goods and ideas that flooded the country also brought a new morality. Sexuality was firmly out of the closet. Mainstream magazines and newspapers reveled in sleek, semi-clad bodies, while on television middle-class Indians engaged in passionate debates on adultery, homosexuality, and premarital sex. Surveys and media reports revealed that a generation of Indian teenagers was no longer waiting for marriage to find out what the fuss was all about. The media marketed sex and also breathlessly recorded the "*amrit manthan,*" or cultural churning, in urban India. Color supplements, crammed with the latest parties, fashions, and indulgent lives of the rich and famous, became *de rigueur*. A celebrity-obsessed populace eagerly read the society pages of national newspapers, thus creating the Page Three Culture (the *Times of India* featured its gossip and celebrity items on the third pages of its editions). Consumerism was king.

The new seductive ethos altered all the rules. In the cities, children imbibed Western values and affected a language of cool that was incomprehensible to their parents. The family unit faced the added pressure of double-income parents, women's dissatisfactions with their conventional roles, and their desires for autonomy. The old order offered stability but the new was more enticing. New freedoms brought with them new confusions and uncertainties. In the push and pull of a globalized society and economy, the definition of what constitutes Indian was reworked.

This rush into globalization was paralleled by a retreat into a comforting cocoon of conservatism and family values. There was a political resurgence of right-wing Hindu politics with the rise of the Bharatiya Janata Party (Indian People's Party). The BJP offered an unapologetically narrow definition of Indian culture. The debate about what is and isn't Hindustani was pursued in the media, sometimes aggressively on the streets, and in political agendas and government policies. So in Mumbai, the BJP's political ally, the Shiv Sena, annually denounced Valentine's Day as "against the ethics and culture of Indian society" and routinely disrupted the commerce of romance by burning Valentine's Day cards and trashing offending shops. In 1998, Hindu nationalists trained their ire on *Fire*, director Deepa Mehta's film about two lonely, neglected sisters-in-law in a middle-class Delhi neighborhood who find love and sexual satisfaction with each other. Cinema halls screening the film were stormed in Mumbai. A leader of the Shiv Sena's Women's Wing, Meena Kambli, told the media that "films like *Fire* have a bad influence on Hindu culture. The majority of women in our society do not even know about things like lesbianism. Why expose them to it?" These culture wars continued through the decade.

The economic optimism and buoyancy of the new, shiny

India was punctured by communal violence and terrorism. The Mumbai riots in December 1992 and January 1993 and a series of horrific bombings that followed two months later altered the ethos of India's most cosmopolitan city and India itself. In these complicated times, *DDLJ* offered an uncomplicated solution: fusion. Like fusion clothes and fusion food, *DDLJ* suggested a fusion lifestyle. Shah Rukh as Raj was the best of the East and the West. He became all things to all people. He was a yuppie hero whose cool clothes and cooler personal style made him a youth icon. But he also unabashedly celebrated and perpetuated homespun *swadeshi* values. He was moral without being tediously pious. Like millions of urban Indians in the 1990s, Raj negotiated between tradition and modernity. But unlike most real-time struggles, Raj's conflicts were beautifully resolved without any permanent heartache or unsanctioned sex. In Aditya's utopia, the contradictions of past and present, rich and poor, urban and rural, non-resident Indian and local, could comfortably coexist and enrich each other.

Like Amitabh Bachchan and Vijay, Shah Rukh and Raj were a perfect fit. Aditya said, "What comes across most strongly is Shah Rukh's desire to please. Most actors want adoration but they want you to love them for how they look or how they act. Shah Rukh doesn't want you to love him as a star. He is trying in a very strange way through his acting to make you love him. It has a lot to do with the loss of his parents. They aren't there anymore and he's reaching out and substituting their loss with the world."

Two years after *DDLJ*, Yash Chopra directed Shah Rukh in *Dil To Pagal Hai* (The Heart Is Crazy). Like *Hum Aapke Hain Koun . . . !*, *Dil To Pagal Hai* had little by way of plot. It was a typically Yash Raj essay on romance. The film's big idea was that love is destined. Every person is born with a soul mate. God has already decided who your life partner is—it is just a question of finding him or her. The tagline was: "Someone . . . somewhere . . . is made for you." So almost till the intermission, the hero and heroine speak of each other, imagine each other, and pass by each other without ever meeting. The emotional intrigue is further complicated because the hero's best friend is also in love with him. The heroine, Madhuri Dixit, meanders in verdant fields wearing white chiffon while the best friend, Karisma Kapoor, dances in tight leotards. The film is love-lite with an unmatched Western gloss and foot-thumping music.

Shah Rukh played Rahul, the hipper avatar of Raj. Rahul is a flamboyant theater director who lives in a Manhattan-style loft space somehow transported to Mumbai, complete with graffiti on the walls and a Pepsi vending machine. At first, Rahul is a sniggering cynic, but slowly, as he falls in love, he comes to believe that someone indeed is made for him. *Dil To Pagal Hai* had little depth, but that didn't prevent it from becoming a smash hit. Shah Rukh became the poster boy of the sunshine cinema of the 1990s. One year after *Dil To Pagal Hai*, the trendy-yet-traditional formula was refined and taken several notches higher in *Kuch Kuch Hota Hai* (Something Is Happening), the debut film of Karan Johar.

A Global Icon

Karan Johar was a key player in the construction of Shah Rukh Khan as a global icon. For Bollywood, the West had largely functioned as a philosophical conundrum (and, occasionally, a flashy backdrop for songs), but after *DDLJ* and *Kuch Kuch Hota Hai*, it evolved into a market and plot. The U.K. and the U.S.A. became a fount for both full-blown narratives and millions of viewers who paid handsomely in dollars and pounds to watch them. By the turn of the millennium, Hindi films were as likely to be based in New York as in New Delhi.

As the market share became larger, canny directors started to design "overseas-friendly films." These were big-star cast movies with extravagant songs, lavish production, romantic plots, and minimal action. Violence and gore were sidelined by family values. The non-resident Indian wanted, as Karan put it, "one big Indian joyride with good-looking faces, in good-looking clothes, saying beautiful things and preaching the right morals for their children." Shah Rukh's films fit the bill perfectly. *Dil Se* (From the Heart: 1998), ironically an unqualified flop in India, became the first Bollywood film to break into the U.K. top-ten charts. In 2003, a Nielsen EDI survey reported that seven of the top ten Hindi films in the U.K. from 1989 onward starred Shah Rukh.

For the 20 million–odd Indians scattered overseas, Hindi films have always been more than entertainment. They were a way to bind the community, maintain an emotional chord with a distant motherland, and buy, inexpensively, a dose of Indian culture for second-generation children who were growing up as hyphenated hybrids. In 1970s London, a Bollywood film was a social event, a chance for the ladies to flash their silk saris and twenty-four-karat gold jewelry. The *samosas* and *chai* served during interval were as critical as the film itself. Through the 1980s, video and cable decimated the theatrical business both locally and overseas. Non-resident Indians now lapped up the latest Hindi films at home or at the corner Indian grocery store, which doubled as a video parlor. But even though they passionately consumed Bollywood product, non-resident Indians very rarely saw themselves in it.

Hindi films traditionally portrayed the West as *kala pani* (black water), a spiritual and cultural exile. Its corrosive effects could be seen on the non-resident Indian, who was, more often than not, scripted as an irreparable debaucher who had made a Faustian bargain, exchanging his morally superior Indian soul for material comforts. This disapproving tone was set by a 1970 blockbuster called *Purab Aur Pachhim* (East and West), in which a decadent Indian family in London—the son is a hippie and the daughter a nightclubbing tart—is set right by a staunchly upright Son of the Soil, who, in case the audience missed the point, is named Bharat (the Hindi name for India).

Eight years later, another film, *Des Pardes* (Home, Abroad), summed up London in a flurry of images of people kissing in the streets and pornographic posters. This blatant wickedness causes the film's heroine, a virginal village belle from India, to rush home in panic and sing a devotional song: "*Kaise yeh nagaria, kaise hain yeh log, haaye sab ko laga prabhu besharmi ka rog*" (What is this city, what people are these? O Lord, everyone seems to be without shame). These films offered local viewers the small solace that their foreign brethren might enjoy living in the comfortable, clean West, but it was they, struggling with heat and grime and flies, who actually had unpolluted souls.

The Chopras—Yash and Aditya—and their protégé Karan turned these stereotypes on their head and resuscitated the business. In 1997, at the insistence of Aditya, Yash opened a distribution office in the U.K. Their first release, *Dil To Pagal Hai*, netted £1 million. No Indian film had done even a quarter of this business before, at least not officially. A year later, they opened an office in the U.S. with Karan's debut film, *Kuch Kuch Hota Hai*. It broke even *DDLJ*'s record, grossing over $7 million worldwide. Karan's film hit the U.K. top-ten charts at number nine. In South Africa, *Kuch Kuch Hota Hai* raked in more money than *Titanic*.

Kuch Kuch Hota Hai is the story of Rahul, a young widower, whose eight-year-old daughter takes it upon herself to reunite her father with his long-lost best friend Anjali. The first half of the film is an extended flashback to their college days, in which Anjali is an unkempt tomboy who beats Rahul at basketball and teases him about his several bimbo girlfriends. But this strictly back-slapping-buddy relationship changes with the arrival of Pooja, a gorgeous mini-skirt-clad vision with permanently windswept hair. Rahul is instantly smitten. Only when Pooja and Rahul begin to fall in love does Anjali realize that she too loves Rahul. Anjali abruptly leaves college. Rahul and Pooja get married. Pooja dies soon after childbirth, but leaves behind letters for her daughter urging her to find her father's true love, Anjali.

Karan set this gossamer-thin confection in a Neverland that was quite disconnected from Indian realities. With its lockers, cheerleaders, and uber-cool skateboarding students, the college is a *Grease*-meets-*Archie-Comics* fantasy that doesn't faintly resemble any existing educational institution in India. The candy-floss American ambience only grows thicker in the second half of the film, which is mostly set in a children's summer camp.

Shah Rukh is once again Rahul, the college's coolest student. He's so cool, in fact, that he actually wears a necklace that spells out C-O-O-L. In this airbrushed world, accessories and clothes are a key element. Karan was a consummate fashionista. He had designed Shah Rukh's look in *Dil To Pagal Hai,* but the Rahul in that film hadn't discovered labels yet. In *Kuch Kuch Hota Hai*, Karan aspired to set a new style standard in Hindi cinema.

Before shooting started, Karan and his designer friend, Manish Malhotra, made special trips to London for appropriate costumes. (When Karan first suggested this shopping spree to his father, who was producing the film, Yash Johar thought his son had "lost it," but he finally agreed to a budget of 5,000 pounds, which was later raised to 8,000.) To make sure that the audience recognized the effort and money involved, Karan and Manish deliberately chose clothes that prominently displayed their foreign-designer origins. Several had labels emblazoned across the chest. Anjali's first shot has her playing basketball in a DKNY tracksuit. Rahul, more sartorially evolved than his earlier screen avatars, is partial to Polo Sport and Gap.

But these weightless fantasy landscapes of the film are rooted in oversized Indian emotions. Karan wept copiously in movies and he wanted his audience to do the same, so scenes are pitched to wring out every last drop of melodrama. Though the film is set in India, the characters, echoing *DDLJ*, are hybrids. They are modern, articulate people who, underneath the trendy Western labels, proudly preserve their Indian identity. Rahul goes to the temple every week (wearing Polo Sport, of course). Pooja, who has been raised in London and educated at Oxford, dresses like a fashion model, but when Rahul and his friends force her to sing in public, she breaks into a Hindu hymn. The boisterous crowd is stunned into silence. She says, "Living in London and studying and growing up there has not made me forget my roots, and don't you forget that."

In *DDLJ*, Simran's father compares second-generation non-resident Indians to the proverbial washerman's dog, who belong neither to the *ghar* (house) nor the *ghat* (riverbank). But these films assured non-resident Indians that in fact the opposite was true. They did belong. Living in the West had not robbed them of their roots. Indian values were portable and malleable. They could straddle both worlds, just as the characters in *DDLJ* and *Kuch Kuch Hota Hai* did. Both films offered non-resident Indians a palatable India. The poverty, corruption, injustice—all reasons for leaving home, perhaps—were carefully edited out. Instead these films fed a nostalgia for an imagined homeland in which beautiful homes were filled with large, loving families; rituals and traditions remained intact; and children, despite their cool posturing, were happily subservient to their parents.

Shah Rukh was a star who blended, in perfect proportions, Indian and Western culture. So while the local Indians aspired to be articulate, designer-clad yuppies like him, the Indians abroad saw him as one of them. First-generation immigrants hoped that their Westernized sons and daughters would find the elusive cultural equilibrium that *DDLJ*'s Raj had. Second-generation children adored Rahul's suave negotiation of traditions in *Kuch Kuch Hota Hai*. He was someone they could relate to—he looked like them and spoke their language (after *Kuch Kuch Hota Hai* was released, the orange sweatshirts, which Rahul wears in the film, were sold out at the Oxford Street Gap store in London).

Unlike Bollywood heroes of the past, Shah Rukh wasn't verni, a derogatory term for somebody who had studied in one of those "vernacular" schools where an Indian language, not English, is the medium of instruction. He made everything look exceptionally cool, from wooing girls in Switzerland to nestling his head in his mother's lap. *Kuch Kuch Hota Hai* helped to make Hindi films *au courant*. For several generations of Indians, Bollywood became a style guide and a way home.

In Karan, Shah Rukh found a filmmaker who instinctively understood that what was being marketed was not an actor but a personality. Karan further advanced the high-gloss, high-emotion style originated by Yash Chopra. But this evolution was also a sanitization. Despite their ostensible glamour many of Yash's films had dark undertones, but Karan and Aditya, both second-generation Bollywood kids, shared a more rose-tinted take on life. They had, as Yash's biographer, Dr. Rachel Dwyer, put it, "a less complicated view of human beings." Together they took the sting out of love and created comfortable, fluffy fairy tales for adults with Shah Rukh as Prince Charming.

Karan's success was especially spectacular because it was wholly unexpected. Unlike Aditya, Karan grew up without any film ambitions. His father, Yash Johar (who died in 2004), was a Bollywood veteran who had started in 1952 as a production controller and eventually, after working his way up the ranks, launched his own production company in 1976. But Karan treated Hindi movies with an aesthete's disdain. He was an unapologetic south Mumbai snob. Even as a child, he had a keen sense of style (he was pudgy and this made him so self-conscious that he sometimes refused to attend birthday parties). Karan knew Aditya and his younger brother Uday. They met at previews and birthday parties, but Karan told his mother that he couldn't befriend them because they spoke in Hindi about Hindi movies, which was just "too tacky."

But this upturned nose was only a front, cultivated perhaps to match the attitudes of his fashionable friends. Actually, Karan was a closet Bollywood buff. He grew up devouring Hindi movies and reading the trades, but he could never articulate his passion for his father's world. After finishing college, he worked in an export business the family owned, learned French, and made half-baked plans about moving to Paris for further studies.

Aditya laid those plans to rest. Sometime in 1994, a common friend re-introduced the two men. Their personalities were polar opposites. Aditya was an introvert, very guarded in his relationships. He was stubborn, intensely focused, and highly competitive—even losing at a board game would put him in a foul mood. Karan was giddily gregarious. He was hardworking but more relaxed. (The contrast would be underlined in their respective responses to success—after his blockbuster debut, Aditya remained an anonymous recluse.

He blocked out the media so effectively that the audience had little idea what he looked like. But Karan, after his debut, determinedly dropped several pounds and became a glamorous Page Three personality, even hosting a successful chat show called *Koffee with Karan*.) Aditya noticed in Karan what no one had before: a distinctly Hindi movie sensibility.

Aditya started bouncing script ideas off Karan. Eventually he convinced Karan to forget Paris and assist him on *DDLJ*. Karan was the all-purpose handyman on the film. Besides consulting on the script, he also had a small role. His chief responsibility was costumes. Aditya had a more prosaic sense of style, but Karan was obsessive about a film's "look." He was as skilled at ferreting fashions as he was with tweaking scenes. He spent hours trudging through the congested, grungy streets of Goregaon, a far-flung suburb of Mumbai, searching for perfectly matching bangles and *bindis*. He agonized over how to make the heroine, Kajol, look slimmer. Sometimes, between takes on the streets of Switzerland, Karan combed her hair himself.

Through the making of *DDLJ*, Shah Rukh connected with Karan in the same way he had connected with Aditya during *Darr*. Aditya was now at the helm of affairs. Harrowed by the myriad details of making a film, he was overworked and so wired that he barely ate. Karan became Shah Rukh's confidant. They thrashed out script details and improvisations. On the outdoor shoot in Switzerland, Shah Rukh, who had never felt the need to cure his insomnia, made Karan sit up with him on long nights, talking movies. Karan's baby face and fey mannerisms belied his sharp scripting instincts and arcane Bollywood knowledge. They shared a similar wacky sense of humor. Shah Rukh saw in Karan the same wide-eyed earnestness he had seen in Aditya. One day, over coffee in Gstaad, Shah Rukh suggested to Karan that he make a film and said that he would be willing to act in it.

Six months later, Karan went to Rajasthan, where Shah Rukh was shooting, and, sitting on the steps of the Amber Palace, he narrated an underwritten romance about a widower who goes in search of his first love. God, played by some suitably heavyweight senior actor, would have a walk-on part. Karan was petrified that Shah Rukh wouldn't like it, but Shah Rukh didn't discourage the nervous, fumbling boy. "I figured," he said, "if Aditya could be so fantastic, even his assistant director would be good. I was very confident about the way Karan described some scenes. We would have the same team, Yash Johar, Kajol, and we would figure something out."

On October 21, 1997, Karan started filming *Kuch Kuch Hota Hai*. The night before, his mother came into his room and hesitantly asked if he knew how to look through a camera lens and frame a shot. She couldn't believe that her "*pallu ke peeche*" (painfully shy) son was going to direct a movie. Her question was valid. The first day of the shoot didn't go well. The crew was young and raw. Karan and his assistants barely knew which lens to use or how the scenes would finally cut together. Shah Rukh was explaining the technicalities, such as camera right and camera left, on the set. He said, "Karan makes no bones of the fact that his technical knowledge of filmmaking wasn't at its peak when he made the biggest hit of the decade." It hardly mattered. Six months after the film's release, Karan was inundated by Best Director awards. He told the press that Shah Rukh would be featured in every film he made henceforth.

This enduring professional and personal proximity led to rumors that Shah Rukh and Karan were lovers, to which

Shah Rukh replied with his typical wit, "So how did I have two children? Heavy petting?" In fact, Karan was closer to Gauri. Karan treated Shah Rukh with a near-fanatical reverence, but Gauri was his mate. Karan helped her navigate the treacherously shifting loyalties in Bollywood and adjust to her newfound status of superstar wife. "It was easy for me because Karan was there," she said. "I didn't miss Shah Rukh at all. With Karan, time just passed."

The roller coaster of stardom did not shake Shah Rukh and Gauri's relationship apart. After the first few years, Gauri stopped giving interviews. She was a fashionable presence at the city's A-list parties. Occasionally she lent her name to boost a favored designer or friend, but mostly she basked in her husband's glory. Their son, Aryan, was born on November 12, 1997. Three years later, on May 22, they had a daughter named Suhana. Unlike many Bollywood stars, Shah Rukh wasn't dogged by romantic scandal. Gossip magazines occasionally linked him to his heroines and industry grapevine mostly linked him to Karan, but there were no sustained stories of extra-marital dalliances. "There are some promises in my heart about our relationship," Shah Rukh said, "and those I think I have maintained."

On October 8, 1995, Shah Rukh gave Gauri a spectacular birthday present: a sea-facing heritage bungalow built in 1896, sitting on a 26,300-square-foot plot of land. In a city where a cramped 500-square-foot apartment is considered eminently livable, a stand-alone bungalow speaks of serious wealth and power. The property had often been used for film shoots and was hideously run down. But over 4½ years architects and interior designers turned it into a Mumbai landmark.

Mumbai law forbids restructuring of heritage properties so

the exteriors and elevation were left untouched, but the interiors were converted into a sleek, awe-inspiring star home. M. F. Husain, India's most famous living artist, created a painting to match the white-and-cobalt-blue living room. The den had a bar, pool table, juke box, and, like so many of Shah Rukh's films, a cola-vending machine. The family moved into the house in 2000. Five years later, a six-floor building with a movie theater and a swimming pool was built in the open space behind the house. Shah Rukh and Gauri called their home *Mannat* (Wish).

Within *Mannat*, Shah Rukh and Gauri endeavored to maintain a semblance of normalcy. But it was difficult to disconnect the man from the pedestal entirely. The media reported on the minutiae of their lives, from how often Shah Rukh dropped his children off at their school to the salon where Gauri preferred to get her hair styled. Shah Rukh's opinion now carried so much weight that he usually had two. Gauri called him Shah Rukh One and Shah Rukh Two, which she explained as "two sides; one is saying one thing, the other is saying the complete opposite, and both in the space of a minute." Which once prompted writer Javed Akhtar to ask Gauri casually, "How are they?"

This split personality was essentially Shah Rukh's way of dealing with his canonization. He said, "There are two Shah Rukh Khans. Gauri's relationship with the superstar Shah Rukh is strange. She doesn't know him. I don't think she even likes him too much. I don't bring him home and she is very clear that she doesn't want to know him either. But her relationship with her husband Shah Rukh is fantastic. I think superstar Shah Rukh is the only competition she has accepted and settled with. That is a big sacrifice. That is how she's dealt with it. It is a good way. I like the joke in it.

"I have also made sure that superstar Shah Rukh doesn't do anything which disturbs the other Shah Rukh's life. I have never disregarded my personal life. I do believe that Shah Rukh is more important than superstar Shah Rukh and because of that belief the superstar keeps prospering. Because I think my heart is in the right place and that is what you require as an actor. I am just an employee of the Shah Rukh Khan myth."

Brand SRK

"How do we create a character?" writer Javed Akhtar asks in the prologue to Nasreen Munni Kabir's book *Bollywood, The Indian Cinema Story.* "We take the morality and aspirations of society and personify them." Yash, Aditya, and Karan fashioned a superstar for the 1990s. Shah Rukh was no longer an actor playing a part. As director Peter Bogdanovich writes in *Who the Hell's in It*, "All the roles merged into one definitive character, one special folk hero, similar to but not necessarily identical with the original mortal. And this creation became, as director Fritz Lang used to phrase it, a 'valid dramaturgical element.'" Shah Rukh's most successful films had him treading familiar Raj-Rahul territory; his attempts to break out of lover-boy roles met with lesser success. It was almost as if the audience loved him too much to let him be anyone else.

Advertising further perpetuated this monolithic romantic-hero persona. Commercials played a key role in the branding of Shah Rukh Khan. Advertising was a familiar world for Shah Rukh. After graduation he had enrolled in a mass communications course at Jamia Millia Islamia University in New Delhi. The idea of telling stories in sixty seconds fascinated him. He learned how to make commercials and occasionally even acted in a few. In 1989, Shah Rukh did a commercial for Liberty Shoes, which featured him running, much like Rocky Balboa, at the crack of dawn. His payment was only three thousand rupees ($65). The total budget was 60,000 rupees ($1,335). After *Fauji*, Shah Rukh also did several public service announcements, which were directed by Colonel Kapoor.

Advertising continued to be part of Shah Rukh's oeuvre even after he became a film star. Shah Rukh positioned himself as a celebrity endorser available for a price. Over the years he advertised a bewildering array of products ranging from a local biscuit to international brands such as Tag Heuer watches and Pepsi-Cola. His reasoning was practical: He was an indiscriminate endorser-for-hire because advertising money enabled him to do the films he wanted at a reasonable price. Shah Rukh was an underpaid superstar by design. While Aamir Khan was said to charge as much as 70 million rupees ($1.5 million) a film, Shah Rukh was willing to do films for half that price. For preferred producers such as Aditya and Karan, there were no monetary discussions.

Cinema was Shah Rukh's passion, but commercials put bread on the table. Though all contract negotiations were confidential, trade gossip put Shah Rukh's price tag for endorsements at between 40 million rupees ($90,000) and 100 million rupees ($2.2 million). He was, along with Amitabh Bachchan and cricket superstar Sachin Tendulkar, among the highest-paid celebrity endorsers in the country. The money helped buffer the financial vagaries of Bollywood. In a May 1998 interview with *Filmfare* magazine, Shah Rukh said, "I need money for my bungalow, I need money to secure my son's future. I need money to become financially firm. If that means plugging everything from colas to condoms, that's fine by me." There was, Shah Rukh believed, no such thing as overexposure.

For Bollywood, this was a startlingly unconventional philosophy. Star endorsements were as old as the star system; as early as 1929, actress Leela Chitnis assured viewers that her fine complexion came from using Lux. The soap continued to be endorsed by the leading ladies of the day (in 2005, Shah Rukh became the brand's first male model in India). But the Lux campaign was a rarity. Most actors were wary of plugging products. Commercials were seen as a lesser form than film, a downgrade that hinted at unemployment and took the sheen off big-screen stardom. The biggest names in Bollywood looked down upon advertising. When adman Prasoon Joshi approached Dilip Kumar with a lucrative offer, the legendary actor disdainfully rejected it, saying, "*Hum ishtiharon ke liye nahin bane hain*" (I was not made for commercials). Amitabh Bachchan resisted ads for over twenty years, only doing his first commercial in 1996.

Until the 1990s, the Indian advertising industry wasn't keen on celebrities, either. Marketing was in its infancy. The two television channels aired such tedious programs that viewers looked forward to the commercial breaks. Advertising was the entertainment. Budgets were limited, and the *mise-en-scène* was sparse. As Prasoon Joshi said, in those days "just making a commercial was enough." But liberalization altered the market and the marketing business. Multinationals came in with deep pockets and set about registering their presence immediately. In a movie-crazy country, the most effective method to ensure brand recognition was stars.

Pepsi was among the first multinationals to jump on the Bollywood bandwagon. Pepsi commercials were often Indian versions of the company's international advertising. Many were identical copies with Indian celebrities replacing foreign ones. In 1993, Pepsi re-created a highly successful commercial in which Michael J. Fox tries to woo his new next-door neighbor with the cola. For the Indian version, the company wanted Shah Rukh because, as the commercial's director, Prahlad Kakkar, said, "he was cheap and cheerful." Shah Rukh's price tag was 500,000 rupees ($11,000). Prahlad insisted on Aamir, who was then the bigger star and naturally more expensive. Aamir asked for 1.5 million rupees ($33,000), 300,000 rupees more than the commercial's total budget. When Prahlad threatened to walk, Pepsi relented and signed Aamir. The commercial was an advertising landmark and launched the career of future Miss World Aishwarya Rai.

But Shah Rukh's irreverent, youthful image was the perfect fit for the challenger cola. Liberalization had created new opportunities and fueled dreams of the good life. Shah Rukh, the Rajinder Nagar boy who wrote his own destiny and became a star, embodied the new *zeitgeist*. His story connected with consumers. Shah Rukh signed with Pepsi in 1996. The first Pepsi commercial starring Shah Rukh had him matching his wits against a dog and losing. Ironically, Aamir and Pepsi parted ways in 1994—in 1999, he signed with rival Coke—but Pepsi repeatedly renewed Shah Rukh's contract. Shah Rukh became the company's most frequently used celebrity endorser in India.

Shah Rukh's stardom sold everything from Sunfeast instant pasta to Hyundai cars. In 2002, Indica Research conducted a four-city survey on advertising. Not surprisingly, Shah Rukh emerged as the most versatile celebrity endorser. Respondents even associated him with product categories that he wasn't then endorsing, such as banks and branded clothing. Shah Rukh was often criticized for becoming what in marketing jargon is called "a promiscuous brand endorser." At times, his fame cannibalized the product. But mostly companies reported greater visibility and happily shelled out increasing sums of money to retain him. In 2003, Tag Heuer watches launched a campaign with Shah Rukh. By 2005, the company had notched a 60 percent annual growth—management said they had "overachieved" their targets.

A leading advertising monitoring firm called The Agency Source (TAS) tabulated that between 1994 and 2006, Shah Rukh appeared in 281 print ads and 172 television commercials. In 2005 alone, he endorsed approximately 34 different products. Shah Rukh was the ubiquitous symbol and conduit of the new consumerist society.

Shah Rukh and Aamir were among the earliest stars to do commercials in a systematic way. In the ensuing years, the escalating paychecks seduced most other actors. Multinationals offered generous one-time check payments that few could refuse—by the late 1990s, several top-rated celebrities were taking home over 10 million rupees ($220,000) per product. For many actors, commercials became the main revenue source instead of films. The figures were staggering. TAS reported that in 1995, only 15 out of 1,259 ads on television featured celebrities. In 2005, the number of television commercials had increased to 6,000. Of these, 785 featured famous faces.

The constantly running commercials made Shah Rukh

an omnipresent celebrity. He usually had two to three film releases every year, but the Shah Rukh Khan persona was ceaselessly available for consumption on television and in print ads. Gigantic billboards lined streets in cities in India and even in neighboring countries such as Pakistan. Shah Rukh had none of the dark, brooding overtones of the younger Amitabh Bachchan. His positive, energetic presence was, as Professor Gyan Prakash, director of the Shelby Cullom Davis Center for Historical Studies at Princeton University, said, "eminently marketable." Shah Rukh was the perfect deity for a rapidly modernizing India in which media, especially television, had become increasingly important. He evolved from an actor into a brand.

The Shah Rukh Khan brand was innately urban. Shah Rukh was a yuppie who loved and pined in Armani suits, but he rarely got his hands dirty. As he said in *Filmfare*, "In the 1970s, the hero was anti-establishment but I promise a better world. The yuppie doesn't bash a truck full of *goondas* [thugs]. He kills in the stock market." City audiences, with sensibilities honed by half a decade of satellite television, enthusiastically endorsed Shah Rukh's designer-hero persona. But viewers in smaller towns and villages, or what the trade calls B- and C-class centers, could barely connect with these Indo-American fantasies. Nearly three-fourths of India's 1 billion people lived in these areas, but their numbers did not give them box office clout. City audiences paid substantially higher ticket prices than their rural counterparts. Therefore, city theaters promised larger returns to producers, especially after the arrival of multiplexes in June 1997. Bollywood, buoyant on the burgeoning city and overseas market, pushed the small-town audience to the periphery.

The screen milieu was now necessarily urban (Shah Rukh

said distributors checked on his costumes before buying his films—Shah Rukh in Western clothes fetched a higher price than Shah Rukh in an Indian *dhoti-kurta*). The spread of television, better mobility and communications had all contributed to making the city a familiar and flashy trope. The city boasted a superior lifestyle. It was clearly where the action was.

The urban gloss on-screen was also a reflection of the changing demographics within Bollywood. A new generation of filmmakers was coming to the forefront. They were educated, city bred, technology savvy, and bottom-line smart. Raised on Hollywood but firmly grounded in Bollywood, many of them came from film families. Sooraj, Aditya, and Karan were all in their twenties when they made the decade's biggest blockbusters. Their success rewrote the industry rule that a director had to be a forty-plus male who had acquired storytelling wisdom by spending decades assisting a reputed name. Suddenly youth equaled success. In a curious reversal of fortune, even older, more established filmmakers aspired to create "youthful" cinema. Anything *filmi* (loud, gaudy, overtly melodramatic) was out.

In this rapidly modernizing environment, Bollywood was forced to reinvent itself. The industry had traditionally functioned as a bustling bazaar run by independent proprietors. It was a business built on relationships. Contracts were rare, lawyers were unheard of, and the agent, in the Hollywood sense of the word, did not exist. In the late 1940s, "black" or unaccounted-for money had entered the industry and effectively ended the studio system (stars and technicians were offered unheard-of prices by independent producers). Fifty years later, cash was still the preferred mode of payment. Most salaries, from the leading star downward, had some cash component. Every few years, the Income Tax Department would conduct surprise raids on star homes and film magazines would run breathless stories of mountains of cash discovered in a false ceiling in the bathroom or in a bag inside the flush tank.

In this cash-soaked environment, "corporate" was a dirty word. There were few systems in place. Getting financing for a film required as much creativity as actually making it. A-list producers raised money on their reputations, but the rest borrowed money at exorbitant interest rates of 36 to 40 percent per annum or relied on assorted sources who were seduced by the glamour—businessmen, builders, jewelers, traders, and non-resident Indians.

The business ran on the whims of the most powerful, which was, more often than not, the star. At any given time, an estimated 200 Hindi films were under production while the number of saleable heroes—who could bring in a first-day audience—was rarely more than five. The demand for stars so outstripped the supply that producers who were lucky enough to sign them on made sure that these celluloid gods were propitiated and indulged in their every whim. Shootings started not on the time scheduled on call sheets but when the hero arrived. Some actors routinely showed up half a day late.

But as a more sophisticated second generation took over the reins in every sector (even distribution and exhibition), Bollywood's structures were irrevocably transformed. From a nepotistic family industry run by patriarchs, Bollywood began to metamorphose into a sleek and shiny entertainment factory dominated by laptop-toting, BlackBerry-flaunting filmmakers and executives. "Corporatization" became the magic mantra. Though a Hollywood-style infrastructure was still years away, a modicum of order was created. Directors now increasingly worked from scripts instead of the handwritten-on-the-sets sheets of paper that earlier passed for screenplays. Stars, though still notoriously high maintenance, were more disciplined and less likely to arrive six hours late for a shoot. Many, including Shah Rukh, launched their own production houses.

On May 10, 1998, then Information and Broadcasting Minister Sushma Swaraj announced that Bollywood would be given "industry status." That is, Bollywood would be treated on a par with other industries such as telecommunications and steel. For nearly two decades industry leaders had lobbied for this label. Industry status opened up the entry of banks and financial institutions into film production. Earlier, banks refused to touch Bollywood proposals. Films were a shady business in which there was little accounting and no tangible assets—a leading distributor aptly described it as an "*andhera ka dhanda*," a business of the dark, implying that just as a film was screened in the dark, its accounting was also best done in darkness. The Bollywood hit-to-flop ratio stood at 20:80. Financing films was no different from playing the jackpot at the racecourse.

Industry status did not alter the rate of success, but the entry of banks helped to streamline operations. The production of films was necessarily time bound, shooting schedules organized, and accounts detailed with payments made by check instead of cash. In 2001, bank financing—for 4 films—totaled 430 million rupees ($9.5 million). By 2003, the numbers were up to 33 films attracting corporate funds of 1.76 billion rupees ($39 million). Several leading companies, such as Subhash Ghai's Mukta Arts and Manmohan Shetty's Adlabs

Films, were converted into public companies and traded on the stock market. This further forced transparency.

In Bollywood's mildewed, tumbledown studios, the atmosphere crackled. The business was pregnant with possibility. Industry leaders termed it a paradigm shift. Everything seemed achievable—in one interview Subhash Ghai said bigger players could "start a studio . . . make a *Titanic*." But underneath the spiffy suits and corporate-speak, dark undercurrents flowed.

Mobsters and Movies

For Bollywood, 1997 was the year of living dangerously. The siege of terror started mid-year with one swift, brutal murder. On August 12, Gulshan Kumar was shot dead. Gulshan was a dumpy entrepreneur who had once sold fruit juice in the bylanes of Delhi. He had started his own record label, T-Series, which took advantage of the country's lax intellectual property laws and flourished on cheap cover versions of original music. Gulshan's competitors accused him of flouting copyright laws, undercutting, and even piracy, but the label, which also bought and distributed Bollywood sound tracks, was among the largest music companies in the country. T-Series had also successfully segued into film production. Gulshan Kumar was often referred to as the Audio King of India.

The King was gunned down in a suburban Mumbai lane as he returned from his morning prayers. Every day, Gulshan worshipped at a tiny Shiva temple tucked away amidst shanties. Gulshan had discovered the temple four years earlier and then paid to have it beautified with marble. He believed that the Hindu god of destruction was his patron saint, but that morning, as three shooters opened fire, no miracle was forthcoming. The assailants sprayed bullets indiscriminately. Bleeding, Gulshan staggered from home to home begging for help, but the frightened slum dwellers shut their doors on him. He finally slumped against the wall of a common bathroom. Gulshan took sixteen bullets and was declared dead on arrival at Cooper Hospital. The murder was credited to a mafia don named Abu Salem. The media reported that Salem had been calling Gulshan since May that year and demanding that he pay 100 million rupees ($2.2 million) or Salem would kill him. When Gulshan refused, Salem decided to prove that he didn't make empty threats.

The murder sent shock waves through Bollywood. A rich, well-connected businessman had been hunted down in a lane like a stray dog. The implication was that the mafia could get anybody, anytime. The police speculated that Gulshan's killers were new recruits, hired perhaps for as little as 5,000 rupees ($110)—in Mumbai, a hit man came cheaper than a meal at a five-star hotel. In the following weeks, newspapers played a macabre guessing game on who would be the next victim while politicians gave self-important sound bites on the nexus between the mafia and movies. An advertising agency called Da Cunha Associates even created a billboard for Amul Butter, which made a feeble pun on "Film Shooting" and "Killer Taste."

But in the studios the panic was palpable. Many of the leading actors and directors were given police protection. Others hired private security. Overnight, offices and homes were turned into mini-fortresses with expensive surveillance equipment. Bollywood's traditional flamboyance was replaced by gloom. Suddenly there was little show in showbiz. Parties and premieres were canceled. Congratulatory full-page ads in the trade magazines, previously a regular ego-massaging exercise, dwindled. Men and women who had brazenly hogged flashbulbs now kept the media at a distance. "*Humko nazar main nahin aana hai*" (We don't want to attract attention) was a common refrain. Since the mafia usually contacted people on cell phones, people started changing their numbers frequently or just switching phones off. The finance sector was especially panicked—Hindi movies were rarely insured and an actor getting bumped off mid-shoot spelled disaster. A leading financier remarked, "I'll monitor the situation for fifteen days. If nobody gets killed, I'll do business." Bollywood, recently reincarnated in a new corporate avatar and poised to soar globally, was brought to its knees by the infamous Mumbai mafia.

This was a new chapter in the long and colorful history of the mafia and movies in the city. The relationship started in the 1970s as mutual fascination. The early dons, Haji Mastan and Karim Lala, were enamored of the stardust and, perhaps even more, the starlets. Bollywood was equally entranced by these gritty men. There was something grimly heroic in the way these larger-than-life figures beat the corrupt system and created parallel power centers. They were perceived not as common criminals but as modern-day Robin Hoods. Mastan and Lala were invited to *mahurats* and other film functions, where they were photographed with stars. They were called *bhai* (brother).

Through the 1980s, the various factions of the mafia were consolidated under one man, Dawood Ibrahim Kaskar. Dawood, the son of a police constable, did not look particularly sinister, but behind the banal appearance lurked a master criminal. In 1984 Dawood jumped bail and fled to Dubai, but the distance didn't diminish his power. His brothers looked after ground operations in Mumbai while Dawood set the bloodstained machine into motion over the phone from Dubai. In four years he was Mumbai's top gun, with a 15 billion–rupee ($333 million) empire active in construction, narcotics, gold smuggling, and extortion. Dawood revamped the mafia, turning it into a ruthless criminal version of an international corporation. His gang, which recruited hundreds of unemployed and impoverished young men, came to be known as the D-Company.

Like the earlier dons, Dawood was fascinated with film. He graciously hosted stars visiting Dubai. There were extravagant gifts and shopping sprees bankrolled by the don. The lanes of Mumbai buzzed with tales of Dawood's palatial houses, parties, and meetings with starlets. Bollywood was not a reluctant or passive player in this relationship. Dawood *bhai* was understood as a powerful benefactor. People took his name with reverence. Those who knew him and even those who didn't used his clout to "throw flak," as one producer put it. Dawood had a much-gossiped-about affair with an actress named Mandakini. His brother Noora, who fancied himself a poet, even wrote the lyrics for a few films. Inevitably the socializing became business. The mafia first operated on the fringes, dabbling in cable and video piracy, and eventually moved into mainstream production. By the early 1990s, it was whispered that at least fifteen to twenty films were being financed via Dubai.

On March 12, 1993, thirteen powerful bombs exploded across Mumbai. Two hundred and fifty-seven people were killed, 713 were injured, and property worth 267 million rupees ($6 million) was damaged. Intelligence reports said that Dawood had orchestrated the mayhem. It was his answer, as a Muslim, to the demolition of the Babri Mosque by right-wing Hindus in Ayodhya and the subsequent riots in Mumbai, during which hundreds of Muslims were killed and rendered homeless. Dawood's subversive glamour evaporated overnight. The don was now a terrorist.

Five weeks later, Sanjay Dutt, one of Bollywood's biggest stars, was remanded to judicial custody. The Mumbai police had traced an AK-56 assault rifle and hand grenades to him. These weapons had been part of a consignment of arms and RDX explosive, which was used in the blasts. Sanjay was named as a co-conspirator in the blast case and charged with unauthorized possession of weapons. In 2006, he was found guilty under the Arms Act, but absolved of conspiracy and terrorism charges. Bollywood now recoiled from the mafia like a man shrinking from a sore-covered leper on the street. But after two decades of conducting an illicit romance, it was too late to take the moral high ground.

The blasts divided the mafia along religious lines. Dawood's most trusted consigliore, Chhota Rajan, broke away from the group and established himself as a parallel "Hindu" don. Indian authorities put extreme pressure on Dubai to extradite Dawood, so he sought refuge in Pakistan. The nature of his business changed: he became an operative of Pakistan's notorious Inter Services Intelligence agency. Busy with international intrigues, Dawood turned over Mumbai operations to another trusted aide: Abu Salem.

Abu Salem started out as a minor D-Company player, but after the bomb blasts he became a household name. Police investigation revealed that Salem had helped land key arms consignments and had also given weapons to Sanjay Dutt. But, like most of the other big fish in the case, Salem had fled to Dubai much before his nefarious activities were unearthed (he was eventually arrested in Portugal in 2002 and finally extradited to India in 2005). Salem wasn't satisfied with socializing and starlets. He wanted in on the monetary action. Salem introduced extortion to the film industry.

On June 7, 1994, a small-time producer named Javed Riyaz Siddique was shot dead. The murder was allegedly Salem's first Bollywood hit. It was also the first indication that the industry's love affair with criminals had gone horribly wrong. It was believed that Siddique was murdered because he had, against Salem's wishes, tried to change the star cast of a film he was producing called *Tu Vish Main Kanya* (You Are Poison, I Am a Maiden). The actress he was attempting to fire complained to Salem. Three years later, another producer, named Mukesh Duggal, was shot dead. But these were marginal players with shady reputations, and the industry barely registered their absence.

Bollywood only started to pay serious attention on July 31, 1997, when five goons barged into the office of filmmaker Rajiv Rai and opened fire. His father, Gulshan Rai, was a successful and well-known producer. Rajiv's recently released film, *Gupt: The Hidden Truth*, had become a big success. For months before the film's release, Rajiv had been fielding extortion calls from Salem. He had filed a police complaint and had been assigned a bodyguard. Only the timely intervention of the guard and his office staff had saved Rajiv. He immediately shifted base to London. Gulshan Kumar wasn't as lucky.

Extortion was an elegantly simple way of making money. More often than not, it required only a few threat-peppered phone calls—on the street it was called *dum dena*, or giving grief. The modus operandi was this: An underling would call the victim's cell phone, identify himself as "*Bhai ka aadmi*" (Brother's man), and leave a cell number where the target was to call Bhai back. When the victim called, he found himself talking to Salem, who, for reasons never fully fathomed, referred to himself in the third person as "Captain." The Captain demanded cash.

If the victim dithered, Salem reminded him of the mafia's incredibly long reach. Salem assured him that police protection was, at best, a feeble consolation. After all, the D-Company had killed a politician named Ramdas Nayak as he sat next to his bodyguard in his car. Newspapers reported that the bodyguard did not even have time to move, let alone use his gun. After Gulshan Kumar's horrific murder, most victims were happy to buy their lives from Salem. Even some who had filed police complaints and had police protection paid the don. It was widely believed that Salem was running the extortion business quasi-independently, that Dawood was unaware of the hit on Gulshan Kumar. The Mumbai police estimated that Salem built a personal fortune of millions of rupees from Bollywood extortion. Eventually in 1998, Salem broke away from the gang and set himself up as a rival don.

Salem was an equal-opportunity extortionist. He threatened actors, actresses, technicians, event organizers, and even the owner of a film-processing laboratory with equal ferociousness. Sometime in January 1997, he turned his attention to Shah Rukh. One day director Mahesh Bhatt got a call from a senior police officer named Rakesh Maria. "They are going to kill Shah Rukh Khan," Rakesh said. "Find out where he is and immediately stop him from going outdoors." Rakesh, an imposing, taciturn man with an air of understated menace, was known for his web of *khabris* (informers). One of them had tipped him off about a plot to kill Shah Rukh.

Rakesh called Mahesh, who was then making two films with Shah Rukh. Mahesh immediately phoned Shah Rukh. When Mahesh told Shah Rukh that a hired killer was prowling the city and that he should stay indoors until further instructions, Shah Rukh let out a small, sour laugh. Why, he wondered, would anybody want to kill him?

Rakesh was one of the chief investigating officers in the bomb-blast case. He had followed closely Salem's evolution from flunky to feared lieutenant. Rakesh had information that Salem had ordered a hit on Shah Rukh because Shah Rukh had refused to do a film being made by a producer close to Salem. Unlike Salem's other victims, Shah Rukh hadn't received any calls from Salem or his henchmen. In fact, prior to Rakesh's call, Shah Rukh had no inkling that he was on the mafia's radar. Shah Rukh was bewildered and scared. But as Mahesh and he drove to Rakesh's office in south Mumbai, Shah Rukh jokingly asked his director if he was afraid of sitting with him in a car. After all, at any traffic light his alleged assassins could ambush them. Mahesh laughed.

Rakesh, however, was deathly serious. Investigating the blasts had given him an added insight into the upper-level mafiosi. These weren't just run-of-the-mill goons. They were brutal executioners who had remorselessly planned and implemented the destruction of India's financial capital. These were not men to be taken lightly. At the office, Rakesh talked to Shah Rukh about possible motives. Had Shah Rukh had a fight with anyone lately? Was there a conflict of interest with anyone powerful? Was he having an affair? Or had he recently rejected anyone? Some actresses were known for their D-Company connections, and saying no could be as dangerous as saying yes. The discussion yielded nothing. Shah Rukh suggested that perhaps there was a mistake.

Perhaps Salem wanted to kill Shahrukh Mirza, a small-time producer. But Rakesh assured him that the mafia didn't make mistakes. He assigned Shah Rukh a security officer from the Special Operations Squad.

The next month was a suffocating, harrowing waiting game. Shah Rukh tried to keep his movements to a minimum. He changed cars and routes to work every day. Though the mafia rarely targeted wives and children, Gauri was also advised to stay in. Friends came by in the evening to keep the couple company, but little could lighten the tension. Shah Rukh wasn't afraid for himself—"I had this strange misplaced confidence that I will not get shot," he said—but the stress was wearing Gauri down. During this time the two attended the wedding of a famous cricket player. As a fan pulled out a pen to ask for an autograph, Shah Rukh pushed Gauri away, thinking it might be a gun. Each time the car stopped at a traffic light, the guard snapped into alertness, his revolver cocked. He stalked Shah Rukh like a shadow.

Mohan Bhise was a tall, wiry man with a severe gaze that missed little. As a commando in the Special Operations Squad, he had seen a lot of action. He had done security stints with other industry people, but never someone as famous as Shah Rukh. Mohan wore plain clothes and usually kept his revolver hidden. Hindi film sets are crowded with unit men, visitors, family, and friends, and many assumed that he was just another hanger-on of a big star. But Mohan never strayed more than a few feet away from Shah Rukh. He unobtrusively examined each person Shah Rukh interacted with. At first Mohan was shy and a little starstruck. But as days passed uneventfully, he eased into his glamorous job. On the long drives between home and studios, Shah

Rukh and Mohan had extended discussions about education, literature, and the state of the nation.

At the time, Shah Rukh was also shooting for Yash Chopra's *Dil To Pagal Hai*. Part of the film was shot in a nearby tourist town called Khandala. One day, on the drive back, Shah Rukh received his first phone call from Abu Salem. In typical Mumbai street language, Salem asked, *"Haan, kya chal raha hai"* (What's going on?). Shah Rukh asked, "Who's this?" The question prompted a spate of choice Hindi curses. Shah Rukh didn't retaliate. He spoke politely but deliberately in English, situating himself and his caller in separate worlds. Shah Rukh said, "What is the problem, sir?" Salem replied that he was angered by Shah Rukh's refusal to work in a project being made by a Muslim. As a Muslim himself, Salem said, Shah Rukh should give his community some support.

Historically, Bollywood has remained immune to the conspicuous Hindu-Muslim tension that thrives and often erupts in India. From the silent era onward, Hindus and Muslims have worked together without any overt discord or prejudice, perhaps because the only god the film industry really worships is the box office. Fortunately, at the time, Shah Rukh happened to be working with several Muslim directors and pointed this out to Salem: Mansoor Khan, Abbas Mustan, Aziz Mirza. Mahesh's mother was also Muslim. Salem saw Shah Rukh's logic and decided that he would, after all, spare his life. *"Log bolte the tu bahut proudy hai lekin tu bada sharif hai,"* he said. *"Abhi police ki zaroorat nahin tereko. Main nahin maroonga."* (People tell me that you are very proud but you are a decent man. Now you don't need the police. I won't kill you.)

The police, however, weren't relying on Salem keeping his word. Mohan Bhise stayed with Shah Rukh for a little over a month. After him came a series of policemen with automatic weapons. Salem's calls continued. Except now, like an old friend who seldom has time to meet, he was calling to chat and catch up. Salem would make small talk with Shah Rukh. He would try to extract information about other actors and directors. He would also slip in enough details to let Shah Rukh know that at that given moment, Salem knew the actor's whereabouts, whom he was sitting with, and where his security guards were standing. He made fun of the police's attempts to guard Shah Rukh. "He would tell me that he could see me," Shah Rukh said. "It was like living under a telescope. It was very depressing and very scary." Shah Rukh followed Rakesh Maria's dictum: Be polite, don't take information, and don't give any either. But after every conversation Shah Rukh agonized over his words and wondered if he'd managed to say the right things and keep the peace. "I'm not macho enough to turn around and say that I wasn't scared of any of these guys. I was shit scared."

But the grim circumstances of Shah Rukh's life did not impact his work. Many of the scenes of Mahesh's film *Duplicate* were shot on Mumbai streets and several required a slapstick buffoonery. Shah Rukh, Mahesh said, exhibited a "flirting-with-death-attitude. He would do the most hilarious scenes despite the harsh reality knocking at his door." Shah Rukh did not pause before dressing up as a woman with sizeable breasts and makeup, or jumping fully clothed into a sunken bathtub and grabbing at rubber ducks, while a policeman with an assault weapon stood just outside the frame. Shah Rukh said he managed to stay functional because as an actor he was schizophrenic. "Acting is my reality," he said. "Those twenty seconds in front of the camera are the core of my being. Everything else stems from that.

When I'm giving that shot, nothing else exists because everything else is peripheral and unreal."

Salem never asked Shah Rukh for money. A few times he told Shah Rukh to do a particular film, to which Shah Rukh politely replied that since he didn't interfere in Salem's job, Salem should not interfere in his. "I told him, I don't tell you who to shoot so don't tell me which film to do." Incredibly, Salem understood and respected the response. Sometimes Salem boasted about the murders he had orchestrated and the powerful men he had terrorized into giving him money. Shah Rukh would listen politely and simply say "*Jee*" (Yes).

Once, when Shah Rukh was driving to a film industry party, Salem put him on a conference call with two other film people whom Salem was threatening. Shah Rukh could hear Salem abusing both of them. In between the curses, he would pause dramatically and tell Shah Rukh to stay on the phone. Salem made sure that his other victims knew that he had the clout to keep India's biggest star on hold. The call continued for most of the drive. Shah Rukh entered the party to find both of Salem's phone pals present. The three exchanged knowing looks but no one had the nerve to check with the next person whether he had actually been on the other end.

It didn't take long for other gangs to cotton on to Salem's low investment–high yield business tactics. Shah Rukh fielded film offers from the breakaway Chhota Rajan gang. When he refused, they withdrew with surprising decency. Another small-time gangster with a raspy voice and the unfortunate name of Goonga Bhai (Mute Brother) offered Shah Rukh the lead role in a film based on his own life. Shah Rukh believed that the mournful-looking man was trying to go legit, and he didn't want to tell him off rudely. So he tried instead to confuse him with his English. "I'm not able to conceive the kind of emotional graph that I can develop," Shah Rukh told him. "It just doesn't have enough meat." After a year-long pursuit, when Goonga Bhai understood that Shah Rukh just wasn't interested in playing him on-screen, the gangster was wounded. "But I've chosen you because your eyes have the same madness as mine," he said.

The mafia became a Bollywood job hazard. An industry joke went that movie budgets would now have to include the mafia payments. Armed bodyguards became a favored fashion accessory. Of course, some interactions were more frightening than others. In 1998, another Dawood lieutenant, Chhota Shakeel, called Shah Rukh. Like Dawood, Shakeel was one of the key operatives in the bomb blasts and now ran operations from Pakistan. Shakeel was deeply offended by the lyrics of a song in the recently released Shah Rukh film, *Dil Se*. The film was a failure, but the song *Chaiya Chaiya*, which had Shah Rukh dancing on top of a train, had become a national anthem. Shakeel believed that a line in the song said "*Paun jannat tale,*" or Heaven is beneath my feet, a decidedly un-Islamic sentiment. So Shah Rukh found himself in the chillingly comical situation of singing the song to Shakeel over the phone. With both voice and insides shaking, Shah Rukh explained that the words actually were "*Paun jannat chale,*" which is, My feet are going to heaven.

For nearly four years Shah Rukh fielded calls from various factions of the mafia. He bought his peace by having polite and innocuous conversations with killers. His aim was neither to offend them nor succumb to their demands to work in mafia-funded films. He refused their offers, saying that he had no dates, or that he did not find the script compelling enough, but he couched his refusal in respectful terms, addressing them as Mr. Chhota Shakeel and Mr. Abu Salem. He spoke to dangerous mafia dons as he would speak to esteemed filmmakers, and he reported every conversation to the police.

The mafiosi were similarly polite. They sometimes suggested that he meet a particular person or hear a story, but they never threatened Shah Rukh with physical harm. Being a Muslim superstar gave Shah Rukh tremendous leeway with the gangs. Despite their posturing and scare tactics, they were reluctant to kill a Muslim icon (their most high-profile hits were against Hindus: Rajiv Rai, Gulshan Kumar, and, later, Rakesh Roshan). Salem's mother and wife, Salem told Shah Rukh, were big fans. Eventually, when the guns and guards started to grate on his nerves, Shah Rukh ditched them. "I got very disturbed. Our house was small, my son was young, their socks used to smell. It was just claustrophobic." Eventually Shah Rukh hired a private bodyguard and acquired a bulletproof BMW. "Nobody is going to kill me," he joked. "I'm an international treasure now." Unlike many others in Bollywood, Shah Rukh survived the nightmarish years relatively unscathed. But his troubles weren't over yet.

The Fall from Grace

The sadness that envelops a film's failure is singular in its ache. Months of labor, for even the shoddiest films require immense physical work, are blown away in one morning. In India new films are released on Friday, usually with matinee shows. By late afternoon, the industry buzzes with reports. Text messages fly fast and furious: "Washout," "*Pit gayee picture*" (The picture has been pummeled), "*Theater main kauwe bol rahen hain*" (Only crows are cawing in the hall). Meanwhile the film's unit maintains a brave face and assures the press that the word of mouth is positive and the box office will pick up. It rarely does. The Hollywood dictum applies in Bollywood too: A film is like a parachute. If it doesn't open, you're dead.

By Monday, the verdict is clear. Audience curiosity dries up and collections free-fall like a kite with a broken string. For a filmmaker, it's an agonizing collapse of vision, reputation, status, and often finances. People start avoiding his gaze. When they look, it is with an expression of sympathy reserved for someone who has recently had a death in the family. But the compassion contains a barely hidden glee. Success in the movie business is so rare that it inevitably arouses a ravenous envy. Failure is more palatable. When failure becomes chronic, the flashbulbs move away and the flowers stop coming. In January 2000, the flowers stopped coming for Shah Rukh.

It wasn't that he hadn't experienced flops before. By then, he had had twenty-eight releases and many of them were mediocre movies that did mediocre business. Some, like *Trimurti* in 1995 and *Dil Se* in 1998, were the sort of bloated, thunderous flops that have everyone scurrying for cover. But Shah Rukh was Bollywood's Teflon man: Failure did not stick. In fact, after *Trimurti*, Shah Rukh and the film's producer, Subhash Ghai, had decided to defy the fates and celebrate their flop. In New York for the U.S. premiere, they had walked down the streets of Manhattan drunk and laughing, persuading hapless people on the road not to see their film. Besides, every other year Shah Rukh delivered a blockbuster so big that flops seemed like minor aberrations, discordant notes in a grand, soaring theme. Nothing had prepared him for the cacophonous collapse of *Phir Bhi Dil Hai Hindustani* (But the Heart Is Still Indian).

The film was Shah Rukh's first attempt at extending his brand. His romantic-hero image was such a saleable commodity that most producers continued to recycle it for returns. So Shah Rukh attempted to create a signature cinema that had him in a *hatke* (different) role. He was the hero, producer, and propelling engine on *Phir Bhi Dil Hai Hindustani*. Shah Rukh's superstar clout ensured that the industry's best technicians worked on the film. Karan and Aditya were consultants (neither had released a second film yet, but the industry revered them as the boys with the golden guts). So when the film failed, it wasn't just another flop. It was what its heroine and co-producer, Juhi Chawla, called an "*izzat ka sawaal*," or a loss of honor. It was the lowest point of Shah Rukh's career, an inconceivable fall from grace.

In 1999, Shah Rukh, Juhi, and Aziz Mirza created a production company. It seemed, at the time, a great idea. The three had a strong personal and professional bond. Aziz and his wife, Nirmala, had played surrogate parents to Shah Rukh when he had first moved to Mumbai. Aziz was one of Shah Rukh's earliest directors with *Circus*. Both had made their feature-film debuts with *Raju Ban Gaya Gentleman*, in which Juhi was the heroine. In a business where relationships fluctuate with box office receipts, Shah Rukh, Juhi, and Aziz shared an enduring friendship. They also shared a cinematic sensibility. The trio liked to tell clean, simple stories with a social message, a Frank Capra–style cinema, or what Shah Rukh called "the poor man's Raj Kapoor." Their second venture together in 1997 was a small, quirky film called *Yes Boss*, which had Shah Rukh playing an overambitious employee who occasionally scouts women for his boss. It had done only moderate business, leaving all three with a sense that their peculiar brand of cinema was a money-losing proposition and didn't augur well for producers.

The company was born out of a casual conversation. Aziz wanted to make a film with Shah Rukh, but he did not want to exploit their friendship by paying him less. He insisted that Shah Rukh take his market price and a percentage of the profits. Shah Rukh suggested they become partners instead. It was a good time to get into production. The market was buoyant. Apart from theatrical revenues, music, satellite, and overseas markets were bringing in big money.

Other actors were also turning producers. Though Amitabh Bachchan's Amitabh Bachchan Corporation Limited had closed shop, stars such as Ajay Devgan and Aamir Khan were starting their own companies. Shah Rukh, Aziz, and Juhi reasoned that having their own production house would give them creative freedom. They could make their kind of cinema without feeling apologetic about it. They started tossing around names. One idea was Dreams, but to give it a twist, Shah Rukh suggested spelling it with a *z*. The company was called Dreamz Unlimited.

A four-level building was bought and swanky offices created. The nameplate on the door of Shah Rukh's office read: SUPERSTAR. The company had ambitious plans to produce not only movies, but also television and advertising. Shah Rukh, an ardent lover of gadgets and technology, wanted his crew to have the best equipment. He believed that better technique would eventually translate into better movies. So a sister concern called Arclightz and Films Pvt. Ltd. was created and state-of-the-art equipment imported: the latest Arriflex cameras, Kino Flo lenses, Jimmy Jib cranes, and Avid editing suites. In November 2000, yet another subsidiary, named Aryan Informatics (after Shah Rukh's son), launched an entertainment portal called Srkworld.com. The larger dream was that ultimately all these ventures would come together in a mega studio complex that would house post-production facilities, equipment storage, creative offices, and—a typical Shah Rukh touch—a five-star hotel, a multiplex, and a bowling alley. It was the supersized version of the "*Nahin na*" advertising agency fantasy.

This fantasy, much like the one Shah Rukh and Benny shared in their theater days, wasn't rooted in any practical knowledge. None of the partners knew the logistics of starting and running a business. Juhi's husband, Jai Mehta, a corporate man, helped them register the company and put together a blueprint for operations. Yash Johar, who had fifty years of experience in the vagaries of moviemaking, handled production. Juhi's brother Sanjiv was hired as a production executive and sent to apprentice with Yash. Each time Sanjiv called Yash with a problem, Yash replied in a thick Punjabi accent, "Don't worry brather [*sic*]. I'll take care of it." Shah Rukh, Juhi, Aziz, and most of their twenty-odd employees were novices at production, but their inexperience was outweighed by Shah Rukh's star muscle and their collective goodwill within the industry.

Aziz envisioned their first film as being the Indian version of Billy Wilder's classic *The Front Page*. *Phir Bhi Dil Hai Hindustani* is the story of two television journalists who work for rival television channels and stop at nothing to win the ratings war. Both are cynical, ambitious go-getters. But their "anything goes" attitude changes when they become embroiled in a real-life murder. As both become pawns in the hands of their greedy employers, corrupt politicians, and the police, they see the error of their desire for money and power and use the media to reveal the truth. Through the 1990s, satellite had changed the Indian television landscape. By 1999, viewers, who were once bored by two numbingly dull channels, had more than fifty tempting choices. Aziz believed that a movie on the commercialization of the media would be an insightful comment on the increasingly materialistic post-liberalization India.

Karan and Aditya weren't as convinced. Their cinematic instincts were far more commercially attuned. Both understood the benefits of working with a universal subject and were flummoxed by the theme of *Phir Bhi Dil Hai Hindustani*.

They pointed out to Shah Rukh that Sooraj Barjatya, the other poster-boy director of the 1990s, was then making *Hum Saath-Saath Hain* (We Stand United), a modern-day *Ramayana* story. This could be understood by anyone, even Gauri's grandmother, who happened to be visiting Mumbai at the time. But would she get "commercialization of the media"?

The partners strode on unperturbed. Aziz and Juhi were cautious spenders but Shah Rukh was an indulgent producer. His main concern was that the film shouldn't have the slightly cheesy, tawdry look that so many Hindi films did. The first film with his name as producer must have panache. So he instructed Sanjiv to make "anything anybody required available." The budget was set at a steep 150 million rupees ($3 million). Top-notch technicians were hired. Leading cinematographer Santosh Sivan came on board. So did Shah Rukh's close friend and favorite choreographer, Farah Khan (Farah had worked with Shah Rukh since his early films and even designed the signature Shah Rukh Khan move—sweeping his hand through his hair—which had the ladies swooning in the aisles). Twenty-four sets were created for the film. One, the interior of Shah Rukh's house, was not utilized.

Phir Bhi Dil Hai Hindustani was released on January 21, 2000. The premiere was attended by Bollywood's biggest names. Even the old guard—Dilip Kumar, Rekha, and Jaya Bachchan—showed up to see what Shah Rukh Khan had created. The after-party was held at a trendy nightclub called Fire & Ice. The newspaper *Indian Express* reported that Shah Rukh "swung into action on the dance floor with his very pregnant wife Gauri" and Juhi Chawla said "hello to every guest," which left "director Aziz Mirza to bear the brunt of irate viewers who hadn't recovered from the movie!"

Over the years, Gauri's uncle Tejinder had become Shah Rukh's in-house box office pundit. After every release, he would call Shah Rukh to discuss the film, its merits and box office potential. But after watching *Phir Bhi Dil Hai Hindustani*, Tejinder went underground. He refused to take Shah Rukh's calls. Finally Gauri reached him at home and asked why he was avoiding Shah Rukh. Tejinder replied, "What can I tell him? This movie is not good."

The critics made up for Tejinder's reticence. They tore into the film's exhaustingly convoluted plot and its frequent jumps in tone from satire to political statement to emotional drama. The *Times of India* review was headlined: GOOF UPS UNLIMITED. Critic Nikhat Kazmi, who had heralded Shah Rukh as "a new talent" in *Deewana*, now sliced with a sharp knife: "You can dream unlimited. No problem with that. But when you try and articulate those dreams on celluloid, you can't goof up unlimited. Lots of problems with that." The hype and Shah Rukh's star power ensured that cinema halls were full on the first day, but by Monday collections were floundering. In smaller towns such as Vadodra and Ahmedabad, halls emptied out in the first week itself.

On January 14, 2000, exactly one week before *Phir Bhi Dil Hai Hindustani*, a smaller, less-hyped film was released. It was called *Kaho Naa . . . Pyaar Hai* (Say You Love Me). The film was a traditional launch vehicle for a new actor and actress. It was extensively shot on exotic foreign locations and had a foot-thumping sound track and a plot that required the hero to emote, dance, and fight. The film itself was formulaic, but the hero was spectacular. He had fair skin, light eyes, a finely chiseled face, and a V-shaped body painstakingly sculpted in the gym. But he was more than just eye candy. Hrithik Roshan could act. As a performer, he was refreshingly earnest but not clumsy or theatrical as debutants often are. His impressive dance moves—one song had him moving sinuously wearing a see-through figure-hugging black top—were greeted by orgiastic shrieks.

Hrithik hit the audience like a tsunami; everything in his path was reduced to debris, including Aamir Khan's new film *Mela* (Carnival), which released one week before, and *Phir Bhi Dil Hai Hindustani*, which released one week after. The collections for *Kaho Naa . . . Pyaar Hai* refused to drop—in week three, theaters were as full as they had been in week one. Scalpers made a killing as girls screamed Hrithik's name and boys danced in the aisles. Even middle-aged women were reduced to hyperventilating pulp. By March, Hrithik was on the cover of *India Today* magazine with the headline: HEARTTHROB HRITHIK. The magazine stated that with the arrival of Hrithik, all the other actors were looking "a little more tired, a little more jaded." One section was titled "Vs. the Khans." It weighed Hrithik against the Khan triumvirate—and all were declared inferior. For Shah Rukh, the article said, "Great energy and sheer mannerism with flashes of histrionic ability but Hrithik is more sophisticated. Finally you have an actor who is also a star."

Shah Rukh was in London for knee surgery when the *India Today* cover was published. Gauri actually tried to hide the magazine from him. "It was so wrong," he said. "You can't take away ten years of work. You can't suddenly tell me one morning, 'Hey you're displaced. You are too old, you are not good enough.' I couldn't go out of the house without someone asking me what I thought of Hrithik Roshan. It became shameless." Shah Rukh internalized his anger and disappointment. He became uncharacteristically quiet. He hunkered down at home, playing out comforting rituals in his garden with Aryan. "Who is the best?" Shah Rukh would ask. "Papa, you are the best," Aryan would reply. He was only three and did not understand what his father was asking or why he needed the encouragement. But Shah Rukh clung to the reassuring knowledge that at least one person, without reservation or hesitation, still thought that Shah Rukh Khan was unsurpassed.

Although Aamir's film had collapsed with a din equal to Shah Rukh's, Aamir didn't become a target. Hrithik was specifically positioned as the first star in a decade to edge Shah Rukh unceremoniously off his King Khan throne. The backlash against Shah Rukh, compounded by his own criticism of the media after the release of *Phir Bhi Dil Hai Hindustani*, became venomous. The film press, especially *Stardust*, devoted reams of newsprint to downsizing Shah Rukh. The chorus reached such a crescendo that Gauri, who had stopped giving press interviews, agreed to be the cover girl for a women's magazine called *Savvy*. She lashed out at her husband's critics: "The reason people are pulling you down is because they are fed up with your success. But ultimately your fate and future cannot be determined by the press. People who are writing all this are non-achievers compared to Shah Rukh." Gauri's mother, Savita, was especially traumatized by the King Khan obituaries. Shah Rukh assured her that this was just a passing phase and he was, as his character in *Phir Bhi Dil Hai Hindustani* sings, "the best."

The media-stirred storm got a further fillip in May, when Shah Rukh acted in a cheeky Pepsi commercial. In the television ad, a pretty girl playing a game of spin-the-bottle spurns a nerdy Hrithik look-alike with braces and prefers to kiss Shah Rukh instead. Hrithik had recently signed up with

Coca-Cola. The rivalry between two actors became part of the ongoing battle between two multinationals over India's $1 billion soft-drink business. Hrithik and his father, filmmaker Rakesh Roshan, were disappointed with Shah Rukh's participation in this public mockery. Pepsi denied that the model in the commercial even looked like Hrithik, and Prahlad Kakkar, who directed the ad, advised the Roshans to stop throwing tantrums over such trivial issues. By late June, the discord had taken a surreal turn. *Panchjanya*, the mouthpiece magazine of the right-wing Hindu organization Rashtriya Swayamsevak Sangh, ran a cover story that insisted that Hrithik was the Hindu answer to the Muslim Khan supremacy in Bollywood. The article declared that the Pepsi ad was an ugly attempt to destroy Hrithik's popularity because he was challenging the Khans.

Through the sound and fury, one fact remained irrefutable: that *Phir Bhi Dil Hai Hindustani* was a flop. In the weeks after release, the three partners tried their best to salvage their film. They encouraged their contacts in the press to put a positive spin on it. One night they sat in the office till 3 A.M. drafting a six-page letter to Delhi Chief Minister Sheila Dixit requesting that the film be granted tax exemption. That would considerably lower ticket prices and perhaps bring in more viewers. Juhi recalled that Shah Rukh "smoked and typed using his typical confuse-or-convince logic" to plead their case, but it didn't work.

Business deals made on the assumption that the film would be a money spinner went awry. Payments that had been promised never came in. At least one distributor suggested to Shah Rukh that perhaps he could compensate for the distributor's financial loss by dancing at his friend's wedding. For a month, the three took daily stock of their film. They sat in the first-floor conference room taking in the sinking box office reports and negative reviews. On most days at least one person and sometimes all three would be reduced to tears. They took turns crying and consoling each other. Aziz felt especially responsible for the debacle. Shah Rukh and Juhi were like his children. He had nurtured them professionally and personally. For the first time in their long association he felt he had let them down. When the unrelenting gloom became unbearable, all three left Mumbai. "We failed," Shah Rukh said. "Perhaps we can rationalize it by saying that the film was ahead of its times or the issue wasn't universal, but maybe it was just a rank bad film. We are not so stupid that we can't accept that."

This setback did not push Shah Rukh, Juhi, and Aziz into seeking comfort in a safe project (that is, a romantic drama that had Shah Rukh wearing a brand-name sweater and wooing the heroine). The partners sat down together and decided that they had two choices: close shop or make another film they believed in. So instead of a high-glam romance, the follow-up was an impressively handsome period film about a fabled third-century B.C. pacifist emperor. It was called *Asoka*.

Asoka was directed by Santosh Sivan, the cinematographer of *Phir Bhi Dil Hai Hindustani*. Santosh was a smiling man with a shock of unruly hair and a booming laugh. Shah Rukh called him Santa. Santosh had been fascinated by the legend of Emperor Ashoka since his school days and had long nurtured the idea of making a film about him. Santosh and Shah Rukh had become friends in 1997, during the making of *Dil Se*, which was also photographed by Santosh. A part of the film was shot in the beautiful but brutally barren landscape of Ladakh in the Himalayas. While most of the unit suffered from altitude sickness, Santosh and Shah Rukh, the two heaviest smokers, remained defiantly healthy. Both were also ardent hockey players.

Santosh was impressed by Shah Rukh's energy and his enthusiasm for taking risks, creative and physical. Other actors might have balked at dancing on top of a moving train, but Shah Rukh jumped into the "*Chaiya Chaiya*" song without a second's hesitation. He was willing to try the most precarious steps and even offered to dance on top of the train's chimney—Farah, who choreographed the song, said Shah Rukh wanted to make sure that "*Chaiya Chaiya*" was so spectacular that no actor after would attempt a train dance (nobody has). Shah Rukh had never done a period film before, but Santosh believed that the actor could convincingly play Ashoka. As they sat on top of the train, Santosh asked Shah Rukh, "Will you do Ashoka?" Shah Rukh replied, "Why me? Do I look like him?" There are few historical records that authentically establish what Ashoka looked like, but Santosh's script, part history, part legend, part fiction, was compelling enough for Shah Rukh to sign on as hero and producer.

Asoka is about the futility of war. Santosh's script followed the dramatic evolution of Ashoka's life: He starts out as a romantic hero, frolicking in the fields with a beautiful princess, but the bucolic idyll is soon replaced by violence. Ashoka murders his wily half-brothers to become the emperor and then embarks on a ruthless territorial expansion across India. His quest for power becomes so bloody and bitter that his wife abandons him. The film climaxes in an orgy of broken bodies. As the emperor walks through the battlefield stumbling over corpses, he realizes that his is a Pyrrhic victory. There are no winners in a war. Ashoka renounces his kingdom and devotes the rest of his life to spreading the Buddhist message of peace.

Santosh wasn't sure how receptive the audience would be to a film without any winners, so he had planned *Asoka* as a small, spare, minimalist movie. Santosh was a master at telling taut tales with low budgets without compromising on quality. His second film, *The Terrorist*, was made with only $25,000 but was forceful enough to have actor John Malkovich championing it for a U.S. release. But Shah Rukh's spirit, both as actor and star, was intrinsically flamboyant. The drubbing of *Phir Bhi Dil Hai Hindustani* had not altered his basic filmmaking philosophy that style is all. So *Asoka*'s budget and dazzle doubled.

Despite its somber theme, *Asoka* was a visually sensual film. Sivan shot long stretches against languorously green forests and waterfalls. Kareena Kapoor, wearing strategically draped bits of cloth and tattoos, added glamour. In much of the first half, Shah Rukh reprised his romantic persona, only this time in flowing, draped *dhotis* and jewelry. For one fight sequence Shah Rukh learned *Kalaripayattu*, an ancient martial art form from Kerala. For the climactic battle sequence, all stops were pulled out. The scene was shot at a riverbed twenty-four miles outside of Jaipur. The setup required six cameras, 8,000 men, 500 horses, and a crew of 728 people. The final battle of the emperor's life was choreographed, staged, and shot over four days. It was one of the biggest war sequences done in a Hindi film.

Asoka released on October 26, 2001. Three months earlier, another film called *Lagaan* (Land Tax) had been released. Like *Asoka*, *Lagaan* was also a period film. It was also the first film produced by Aamir Khan. Ironically, the lead role played by Aamir had earlier been offered to Shah Rukh. *Lagaan*'s director, Ashutosh Gowariker, had worked with Shah Rukh in *Circus*. Aamir was Ashutosh's first choice, but when he refused the director took his idea to Shah Rukh, who loved it. For six months, Shah Rukh and Ashutosh tried to entice producers. *DDLJ* had just exploded and Shah Rukh was hot property, but Ashutosh's two previous films, both commercial and critical disasters, hung like an albatross around his neck. When no producer came forth, Shah Rukh passed on the project. Ashutosh honed his script further and returned to his original choice, Aamir. This time, Aamir agreed. He wanted to both act and produce.

Lagaan is the story of a ragtag band of villagers in colonial India who attempt to have the land tax abolished by taking on the local British army officers in a game of cricket. It had little to recommend it. Aamir was the only star. Even by Hindi film standards, *Lagaan*, clocking in at three hours and forty-four minutes, was inordinately long. In an era ruled by designer labels and foreign locations, it was also, with its village backdrop and *dhoti-kurtas*, dangerously untrendy. But the film, which ingeniously wove patriotism and the Indian passion for cricket into a riveting narrative, was a Bollywood watershed. It went on to become only the third Indian film ever to win an Oscar nomination for Best Foreign Language Film. Shah Rukh hoped that *Asoka*, equally unconventional, exotic, and ambitious, would find similar success.

The initial signs were encouraging. *Asoka* was invited to the prestigious Venice and Toronto Film Festivals. In a bold but risky move, Shah Rukh, Aziz, and Juhi had decided to become distributors and release the film overseas through their own offices. *Asoka* was the first Hindi film to be promoted abroad as a mainstream release; in the U.K., there were posters in tube stations. The film was widely covered in the mainstream press, with Shah Rukh being dubbed the "Tom Cruise of Hindi films." Many of the reviews were positive. James Christopher of the *Times* wrote, "In terms of color, length and gaudy bravura, there is nothing in British cinema to touch it. What makes it such a generous spectacle is that it works like an old fashioned musical. America lost the knack when cowboys went out of fashion."

But the box office didn't match the hype. In the U.K., *Asoka* hit the top-ten charts but slipped down rapidly. The domestic audience also preferred Shah Rukh in his patented Raj-Rahul roles. *Asoka* did reasonably well in Mumbai and south India, but the rest of the country—Delhi, Rajasthan, Uttar Pradesh—did not bite. *Asoka* was sold at a lower rate than a regular Shah Rukh Khan film so the distributors did not suffer losses. But the company absorbed a hit of over 40 million rupees ($890,000). The decision to become overseas distributors was especially crippling. Shah Rukh, Aziz, and Juhi sat down in the conference room and cried again.

Ironically, Dreamz Unlimited had its first hit when the partners finally decided to play safe. In 2003, the company co-produced *Chalte Chalte* (While We Were Walking), which was directed by Aziz and had Shah Rukh doing the things he does best: romancing a lissome heroine, losing her after some stylized dramatic scenes, weeping, and finally winning her back. The loosely scripted story of an estranged husband and wife wasn't the ambitious cinema the partners had once dreamed of creating (Shah Rukh, hesitant to label it a compromise, said it was a "once-bitten-twice-shy kind of film"), but it was a success. However, the film created dissonance in the company. By now, Juhi was on the matrimony and motherhood track and the lead in *Chalte Chalte* was played by a younger, more commercially viable heroine named Rani

Mukherjee. Juhi was upset that she was being "disregarded as an actor" and decided to "step back." Dreamz Unlimited did not make a film again.

"We enjoyed our failure more than our success," Shah Rukh said, "because I think in our success we hurt each other a lot." The company remained alive on paper, and Shah Rukh maintained that when the three partners were sufficiently excited by an idea, they would regroup. The offices were unchanged except that the nameplate now read Red Chillies Entertainment, the name of Shah Rukh's new production house. Shah Rukh continued his effort to create a distinctive cinema. His enduring success in the films of Aditya and Karan gave him the lease to be more experimental on his home turf. Some of his productions, like Farah's directorial debut, *Main Hoon Na* (I Am Here for You: 2004), were successes, while others, like *Paheli* (Riddle: 2005), which cast him as a village bumpkin, were abject failures. Shah Rukh said, "I have never done a film with the market in mind. Cinema is a *mishran* [mixture] of Lakshmi [the goddess of wealth] and Saraswati [the goddess of knowledge]. I've always gone for Saraswati and Lakshmi has followed. I may be stubborn and an idiot, but it works for me. I know this is a business but I will always dole out art."

Devdas

French critic Michel Mourlet famously remarked that "Charlton Heston is an axiom. By himself alone, he constitutes a tragedy and his presence in any films whatsoever suffices to create beauty." Dilip Kumar, Bollywood's favored leading man through the 1950s and 1960s, inspired a similar rapture. For a generation of viewers, reviewers, actors, and filmmakers, Dilip Kumar's brooding presence was proof that Hindi films were a class act. He refined the frame by appearing in it. Dilip Kumar was the pure, distilled essence of cinema.

Shah Rukh had little resonance of the senior superstar. His agitated energy was in direct contrast to Dilip Kumar's graceful gravitas. Filmmakers saw Shah Rukh more as a throwback to Rajesh Khanna, who created hysteria with his stylized mannerisms, or the manically energetic Shammi Kapoor, who romanced heroines by rolling down hills with them, or even the eccentric genius Kishore Kumar, whose madcap vitality elevated the most mundane plots. Fatima was perhaps the only one who had seriously considered Shah Rukh's resemblance to Dilip Kumar. Her overpowering maternal affection allowed her to see, in her scruffy, hyper son, shades of the great tragic hero.

So when filmmaker Sanjay Leela Bhansali suggested that Shah Rukh reprise Dilip Kumar's role in a remake of the classic tragedy *Devdas*, Bollywood considered it blasphemy. Shah Rukh had a concrete connect with the audience, but as an actor he was deemed a lightweight. He was an indefatigable romantic hero whose beguiling charm promised love without strain. He was a star without a subtext. But Sanjay's view of Shah Rukh was more layered. He saw, he said, "a man with the saddest eyes" who camouflaged his innate gloom with furious energy and incessant conversation. For Sanjay, the dominant note in Shah Rukh's personality was an enduring, unhealed hurt. He believed that only Shah Rukh could be Devdas.

This perception was perhaps as much a function of Sanjay's own nature as an insight into Shah Rukh. Sanjay was a brilliant, tempestuous loner who had come up the hard way. Like Karan and Aditya, Sanjay came from a film family, but his father, unlike theirs, never made it to the A-list. Navin Bhansali was a small-time filmmaker who died an alcoholic, leaving the family in such penury that Sanjay's mother, Leela, whose name Sanjay took as a middle name, was forced to sell soap door to door. One of the lasting memories Sanjay had of his troubled childhood was hiding under the bed while creditors angrily banged on the door. Sanjay had studied editing at the Film and Television Institute of India, but he wasn't given to art house minimalism. He was a connoisseur of song-and-dance sequences, of operatic emotions and colors. Though his first film in 1996, *Khamoshi*—

The Musical (Silence—The Musical), was an unqualified disaster, he had followed it up in 1999 with a successful romantic drama named *Hum Dil De Chuke Sanam* (Straight from the Heart). For his third film, Sanjay wanted to remake *Devdas*.

It was an appropriate fit. Devdas is Indian literature's iconic tragic hero. The novel was first published in 1917. It is widely believed that it was written earlier, in 1901, but its author, Sarat Chandra Chatterjee, was reluctant to have it published, dismissing it as a work written when his mind "was completely befuddled by drink." Alcohol fueled the writer and the character he created. *Devdas* is the story of a proud but indecisive man who is unable to summon the will to oppose parental disapproval and marry his childhood sweetheart, Paro. She is married off to an elder widower. Devdas wallows in his own ineptitude and heartache, corroding slowly in the company of a golden-hearted prostitute named Chandramukhi. Finally, riddled with drink and disease, Devdas dies at Paro's doorstep. Devdas is a tremulous, vacillating man who curiously doesn't have the courage to live his love but has the strength to die for it. This tormented love triangle wasn't an instant hit when it was published, but cinema elevated *Devdas* from melodrama to myth.

The novel was first filmed in 1928. Subsequently ten more versions were made in several languages before Sanjay took the bait. In 1935, director P. C. Barua cast the singing star K. L. Saigal as Devdas and made the dying alcoholic lover a household name. Twenty years later, Bimal Roy, who was the cinematographer on Barua's *Devdas,* remade the film. Though this *Devdas* was unsuccessful at the box office, it was considered to be the definitive cinematic version. Dilip Kumar's understated, controlled performance was a Hindi film landmark. The name passed into local idiom. The character became a state of being. Indians everywhere recognized that when somebody pined, longed, and raged for someone else, they were "doing a Devdas."

The film industry was understandably perplexed by Sanjay's decision to tamper with a classic. Bimal Roy and Dilip Kumar had set the bar so high that failure was foretold for any version thereafter. Besides, *Devdas* seemed irrelevant in a fast-paced, modern India where lovers were more likely to find new passions than drink themselves mournfully to death over lost ones. A multiplex audience, pundits argued, could hardly relate to this archetypal loser from another century. But Sanjay, who had first read the novel as a teenager, wanted to re-interpret *Devdas* for his generation. Bimal Roy's signature was an austere naturalism. His *Devdas* captured the rhythms of rural Bengal in elegant black-and-white compositions. Sanjay's vision was emotionally and visually opulent. He wanted to create a feast for the senses. His heart said: Go Grand.

So Sanjay created the blueprint for the most expensive Indian film made until then. *Devdas* would be shot on sprawling sets. Chandramukhi's *kotha*, where she dances and nurses Devdas through his drunken bouts, was an ornate palace, budgeted at 120 million rupees ($2.6 million). Paro's house, which shimmered with 157,000 pieces of stained glass, a metaphor for her fragile beauty, cost 30 million rupees ($650,000). Costumes, weighed down by pounds of elaborate embroidery, cost hundreds of thousands of rupees each. Every song in the film was a dazzling set piece requiring extensive rehearsals and dozens of dancers. The final budget reached 500 million rupees ($11 million).

This ambitious epic was being bankrolled by one of

Bollywood's most powerful players, Bharat Shah. His clout came from cash. Bharat *bhai*, as he was called, was said to be worth 20 billion rupees ($445 million), with business interests in diamonds, construction, and films. Fond of kitschy shirts and diamond-studded Piaget watches, Bharat lived in a palatial home in south Mumbai and often made the society pages for his flashy lifestyle. Films were a childhood passion. More than anything, he relished playing sugar daddy to Bollywood—in 1995, Bharat had used his contacts in the construction business to help Shah Rukh buy his home. Bharat's family had started a film distribution concern in 1968 and over the decades had distributed, financed, and produced 200-odd films. Bharat had worked with all the big names and helped several small ones complete projects that had been stuck for years. He had the industry on speed dial.

Sanjay met Shah Rukh in February 2000, when he was still smarting from the drubbing of *Phir Bhi Dil Hai Hindustani*. The odds that he could pull off *Devdas* weren't high. Over the years, Shah Rukh had become embalmed in the persona created by the Yash Raj School. His most successful roles seem to blur into one. His attempts at de-mythifying himself were usually undistinguished or unsuccessful. Until then Shah Rukh hadn't done a period film, nor attempted a character as complex and tortured as Devdas. Shah Rukh wasn't particularly enthusiastic about the project, but when Sanjay told him that he would make the film only if Shah Rukh played Devdas, he agreed to do it.

Shah Rukh's face rarely revealed emotions during script narrations. He selected roles by instinct, often because one scene made an impact on him. When he had heard *DDLJ*, Shah Rukh hadn't been convinced of its emotional wallop, but he loved the last scene in which Simran's father lets go of her hand and allows her to go with Raj. *Devdas* interested him because the romance was streaked with a possessive cruelty—in one scene Devdas crushes a bee hovering around Paro because he cannot tolerate anyone else touching her. Shah Rukh couldn't connect with Devdas' self-destructive pining, so he interpreted the character with a more contemporary logic: as a man who cannot make a commitment. He decided that he would play Devdas as a defiant, petulant child who, when his mother takes away his candy, insists on having it. "Devdas is applicable to ninety percent of men," he said. "Men are afraid of commitment. They want to hurt the woman they love. It's a male thing. I am also Devdas without the alcohol."

Paro and Chandramukhi formed the classic virgin/whore dichotomy in the film. One was a pristine, proud, unsullied beauty and the other a loving, sensual companion bereft of conventional morality. Shah Rukh wanted to bring into his portrayal the idea that "a man is never in love with one woman. Men are confused about what they want. They want ownership of a woman but they get bored of her also." Shah Rukh's Devdas was meaner and more modern than the earlier versions. His ardor had a sleek viciousness. Shah Rukh did not see Dilip Kumar's *Devdas*. He went into shooting with the serene awareness that he was not taking on one of India's greatest actors. "If you are running with Carl Lewis, you are relaxed because you are not going to beat him. There is no competition."

Filming started on November 7, 2000. The media buzz had built into a fever pitch. The cast was megawatt: Aishwarya Rai was Paro, Madhuri Dixit was Chandramukhi, and Jackie Shroff was Chunnilal, Devdas' debauched friend, the Pied

Piper who leads Devdas to brothels and alcohol. The gargantuan sets erected at Film City Studio had already filled up reams of newsprint. Problems, which started almost immediately, generated more. On December 8, while shooting an elaborate song sequence in Paro's *haveli*, a technician was killed in a gruesome accident with a storm fan. A month later, *Devdas* suffered a body blow. Bharat Shah was arrested by the Mumbai police and charged under the Maharashtra Control of Organized Crime Act (MCOCA) for abetting mafia don Chhota Shakeel.

One of the films Bharat was financing at the time was the romantic drama *Chori Chori Chupke Chupke* (Stealthily, Silently). The film was being produced by a man named Nazim Rizvi. Nazim had been exposed as a front man for Dawood and arrested on December 13, 2000. He led the police to Bharat. The police had tape recordings of a man discussing business with Dawood's lieutenant, Chhota Shakeel. They believed the man was Bharat Shah. When he was arrested, Bharat had over 1.25 billion rupees ($28 million) invested in eleven films—the biggest was *Devdas*.

The daily shooting expenses on *Devdas* were upward of 700,000 rupees ($15,500). At times, as many as forty-two generators were required to light up the sets. The technical crew swelled into hundreds. Bharat's arrest threatened to sink this *Titanic* even before it had set sail. A fifteen-day schedule was immediately cancelled. The easier option would have been to cut losses and shelve the project, but both Bharat and Sanjay were determined to see it through. Bharat, fiercely protesting his innocence and struggling to survive the horrors of a Mumbai jail, instructed his children that *Devdas* must be made.

The incongruity of the situation was as dramatic as the

film itself. While Bharat languished in a cell, shooting continued in fits and starts. Sanjay canned spectacular dance sequences (in one Madhuri Dixit wore a *ghagra* that weighed over sixty-five pounds—the skirt would keep swirling even after she had stopped), poetic love scenes, and thunderous confrontations. Bharat's son Rashesh shuttled between Delhi, where he was pursuing bail applications for his incarcerated father, and the sets in Mumbai. He tried to impose on Sanjay the importance of running a tight ship but Sanjay was unwilling to compromise on his artistic vision. He was, as Rashesh said, "a different type of person, very emotional, without much idea of budget restraint."

So *Devdas* progressed at a languorous pace. Most of the film was shot at night and lighting the vast sets took several hours. The heroines, swathed in layers of fine textiles, jewelry, and makeup, also took inordinately long to ready themselves—Aishwarya's beautification sometimes lasted six to seven hours. There were days when the technicians switched off the lights and refused to work until they were paid. Sanjay, with hands folded in supplication, would request them to keep working, assuring them that Bharat would soon be released and take care of their dues. But the courts repeatedly continued to reject Bharat's appeals for bail. In August 2001, another technician fell from a height and died. The shooting was fraught with anxiety. A gloom befitting the subject prevailed.

The tone of the film matched the tenor of Shah Rukh's life. These were, he said, his "sad years." Professionally, he regained some of the ground lost to Hrithik Roshan with Aditya's second film, *Mohabbatein* (Loves). The film, about the conflict between a patriarchal school principal and a music teacher, had Shah Rukh reviving his Raj persona with a somber undertone. This Raj's girlfriend commits suicide, so he encourages his young pupils to seize the day and fall in love, annoying the principal who—for reasons never fully explained—is virulently anti-romance. *Mohabbatein*'s script was threadbare, but the performances propped up the film. It was the first time Shah Rukh was pitted against the actor he most worshipped, Amitabh Bachchan. The film climaxes in a confrontation between the two. Shah Rukh admirably held his own against the actor he had grown up imitating.

Shah Rukh did much of *Mohabbatein* and *Devdas* in debilitating pain. A career of convoluted dance steps, risky action sequences, and unhealthy food habits—he survived on caffeine, chicken, and cigarettes—was wearing down his body. Over the next two years, the pain in his back and neck would surge up in varying degrees (in 2004, he had to have surgery for a prolapsed disc). Shah Rukh was also struggling to hold on to his house. Though Shah Rukh and Gauri had moved into *Mannat*, their home was ensnared in a Kafkaesque maze of legal loopholes. Municipal taxes hadn't been paid for years, and there was a strong possibility that the government would repossess and auction the bungalow. But Shah Rukh, who had grown up shuffling from one rented apartment to another, was determined to hold on to his most cherished possession. *Mannat* was his legacy to his children. Even when the cost of retaining it overshot the original price by hundreds of millions of rupees, he refused to let go of it. He worked himself to the bone, doing commercials and even dancing at private functions to pay off the bills.

But perhaps the unkindest cut was the closure of Shah Rukh's dot-com venture. Srkworld.com was launched in November 2000 as an antidote to the depression of *Phir Bhi Dil Hai Hindustani*. Technology fascinated Shah Rukh, and the office, situated in Shah Rukh's old apartment, brimmed with energetic young people and ambitious ideas. Shah Rukh wanted to create a platform for the industry where leading stars would have home pages, films would be Webcast, and merchandise sold (initial offerings included Shah Rukh and Juhi T-shirts). But Srkworld.com was partly owned by a company called B4U, which in turn was partly owned by Bharat Shah. After his arrest, funds dried up. By March 2001, the losses piled into millions and Shah Rukh had to shut shop. He broke the news to his thirty-two employees and wept. He said, "Some of them hadn't even been introduced to me properly. They started crying too. I've never broken down in front of so many people." The specially made merchandise—T-shirts, files, posters, pens—was put into storage.

These laments, large and small, were fodder for the actor. Shah Rukh became Devdas by bringing his underlying sadness—the core that Sanjay had so keenly observed—to the forefront. In some scenes, he saw a residue of his father. One sequence in the film has Devdas lying drunk in a boat. Scattered *diyas* (lamps) light the night sky. His servant, the only one who remains loyal to him till the end, is rowing and begging Devdas to stop the self-destruction. Meer did not drink, but for Shah Rukh, the image of a broken man in a boat on a dark lake recalled perfectly his father, who had also died lonely and sad.

When Shah Rukh first started out in television, director Lekh Tandon had instructed him in playing a tragic character and the art of dying memorably on-screen. The key was not being pitiful. A character, even one in the throes of death, must not beg the audience for sympathy. Shah Rukh remembered this and laced Devdas' most pathetic moments with an anger. In the climax of the film, Devdas inches toward death as his carriage races to Paro's house. He had promised her that he would come before dying. In the last scene, he lies in front of her gate, barely breathing. His ravaged face is almost ugly. But even here, Shah Rukh preserved Devdas' intrinsic pride. He stares at death unafraid. Finally his eyes, taking in a blurred vision of Paro running toward him, harden.

Much of the film's second half narrates Devdas' descent into an inebriated hell. Shah Rukh decided to add authenticity to his performance by actually drinking. On most evenings, Shah Rukh would come in and memorize his lines. He would rehearse the scenes until he had the movements down pat and then he would start to drink Bacardi. Shah Rukh drank just enough so that his eyes glazed over, but not so much that he forgot the lines or fumbled his movements. At dawn, Shah Rukh would go home, exhausted and hungover. The process sapped him. His friends worried that a year of playing Devdas would turn him into an alcoholic.

Meanwhile, Aishwarya Rai was grappling with her personal demons. Aishwarya, a former Miss World, had worked in Sanjay's second film, *Hum Dil De Chuke Sanam*. During the making, she had fallen in love with her co-star, Salman Khan. For two years, Aishwarya and Salman had conducted a tempestuous affair in a fish bowl (there were rumors of parental disapproval, physical abuse, intimidation), and by the time *Devdas* was shot the relationship had disintegrated into an unpleasant, incoherent mess. Salman had become a real-life Devdas, simultaneously self-destructing and attempting to salvage his romance. He was as much a part of the *Devdas* shoot as the crew.

Salman would spend nights lying intoxicated on the floor of Aishwarya's trailer. One night, Shah Rukh and Aishwarya were doing a romantic scene that required Shah Rukh to extricate a thorn from her foot. Salman was on the set, and he volunteered to demonstrate how this should be done. Shah Rukh agreed and as Salman did the shot, Sanjay rolled the cameras. It was a poignant moment: a spent, tragic lover enacting his own life for film. Aishwarya cried. It was the last time the two were captured on film together. Finally on April 29, 2002, after 260 shooting shifts, at five in the morning, Sanjay announced that the film was wrapped. The hum of the generators fell silent. Sanjay told his crew to leave but no one moved. They could hardly believe that *Devdas* was over.

Three weeks earlier, on April 3, the division bench of the Supreme Court of India had upheld Bharat Shah's ninth appeal for bail. Bharat had developed various ailments in jail and had, under court orders, been shifted to a posh Mumbai hospital. After fifteen months of arrest, he was gaunt, sunken-cheeked, lighter by twenty-two pounds, and suffering from cardiac and neurological problems. When his wife broke the news to him that he had been granted bail, Bharat wept. Meanwhile the Cannes Film Festival had selected *Devdas* to be screened out of competition. It was almost as if the gods of cinema, impressed by the crew's determination to see the project through, had decided to smile again.

Until *Devdas*, mainstream Hindi films were largely film-festival untouchables. The cinema of song and dance did not fit into a Western aesthetic. Hindi films were considered loud and melodramatic, and were rarely shown at international platforms. This wasn't the case in the early 1950s, when films such as Raj Kapoor's *Awara* (Vagabond) and Bimal Roy's classic *Do Bigha Zameen* (Two Acres of Land) were screened at Cannes. But in 1956 Satyajit Ray's *Pather Panchali* redefined Indian film for the West. Western critics henceforth deemed art house, songless, "realistic" Indian cinema to be more worthy, and popular cinema slipped into oblivion.

For decades, Bollywood had remained an uncelebrated, "Third World" cinema. But at the fifty-fifth festival in Cannes, the Hindi film industry took a bow on a global stage. Earlier that year, Aamir Khan's *Lagaan* had won an Oscar nomination. It didn't win the award, but *Lagaan* started a certain momentum for popular Hindi film, which *Devdas* furthered. On May 23, *Devdas* had its world premiere at the *Salle Lumiere*. Shah Rukh, Aishwarya, and Sanjay provided the requisite theatrics by coming to the venue in a horse-drawn carriage, with the men in traditional Nehru jackets and Aishwarya in a sari. They did photo-ops on the beach and the gardens of the Savoy. Aishwarya was a media magnet. The Indian delegation, made up of over 100-odd bureaucrats, filmmakers, and businessmen, amplified the Hindi film presence. There were glitzy parties, posh lunches, and a strong buzz that Bollywood had arrived. Shah Rukh recalled, "It may not have been, but it seemed to us that Cannes was about *Devdas*."

Devdas clocked in at 165 minutes. Though the Cannes audience gave the film a standing ovation, most of the international critics left well before the three hours of swirling colors and melodrama were over. The reviews ranged from rapture to disdain. Derek Malcom drubbed it in the *Guardian* as "a pretty silly three hours worth of romance, song and dance, and utterly tasteless—if luxuriant—production design." But *Time* magazine's Richard Corliss, a Bollywood buff, was bowled over. He called Sanjay a "young master of the medium." At year end, *Devdas* ranked number four on his top-ten movie list, above *Minority Report* and *Lord of the Rings: The Two Towers*. Corliss wrote: "*Devdas* is a visual ravishment with huge sets, fabulous frocks and beautiful people to fill them; it has a grandeur that old Hollywood moguls would have loved."

The Indian contingent at the Cannes screening wasn't as enamored. Their response was decidedly muted. Shah Rukh was complimented on his acting, but the film felt too long and overdecorated. The only person who was convinced that it would work was Gauri. She was right. *Devdas* was released on July 12. Indian critics censured Sanjay for emphasizing grandeur over story and taking too many cinematic liberties with Sarat Chandra's original story (Sanjay's version has Paro and Chandramukhi meeting, discussing their love for Devdas, and improbably doing a dance number together, while in the book they cross paths but never meet). But the audience, both in India and overseas, embraced the film. The sets and costumes weren't distractions but attractions. The saris worn in *Devdas* got as much attention as the script. *Devdas* notched up big numbers, eventually grossing over $12 million worldwide. The film was India's official entry for the Oscars and won a BAFTA nomination for the best foreign film.

On December 3, 2002, Shah Rukh was called in to a special court as a witness in the ongoing Bharat Shah case. The police alleged that Shah Rukh was one of the many stars threatened by Nazim Rizvi. The prosecutor said that Shah Rukh was asked by Nazim to act in a mafia-funded film and also forced to speak with Shakeel. Shah Rukh denied the charges, as did most of the other actors who were questioned in the case. Like most of the other industry witnesses, he was declared hostile. Rohini Salian, the public prosecutor in the case, accused the industry of cowardice. She believed that they had, perhaps under pressure, taken the easier route. She said, "Shah Rukh had to turn hostile because he is obligated to Bharat Shah. He was Devdas. But by not telling the truth in court, the film industry indirectly supported the underworld." Shah Rukh maintained that he had not compromised. "Those people had never threatened or behaved badly with me, so I'm not sure what the cops expected me to say."

On September 30, 2003, Bharat Shah was given "the benefit of the doubt" and acquitted of "aiding and abetting" charges, but he was found guilty on lesser charges of deliberately concealing information about Nazim Rizvi and Shakeel's business and extortion plans. He was sentenced to one year in prison but was let off as he had already spent fifteen months in jail. The buzz in legal corridors was that Bharat had spent an astounding 500 million rupees ($11 million) on the country's best defense lawyers—enough to fund another *Devdas*. Nazim Rizvi, presumably with much less money at his disposal, was sentenced to six years in jail. He appealed his conviction and was granted bail in December 2003. He had already spent three years in prison.

In 2003, Shah Rukh monopolized several award ceremonies. He won all the leading Best Actor awards: Filmfare, Screen, and Zee Cine Awards. Even the Disney Kids Channel Awards judged him the best actor for *Devdas*. Devdas was a difficult role exacerbated by difficult circumstances. Shah Rukh's performance was measured against Dilip Kumar's quietly searing intensity and deemed compelling. Shah Rukh had raced against Indian cinema's Carl Lewis and acquitted himself honorably. With *Devdas*, Shah Rukh reconstructed his own myth. He expanded his vocabulary as a romantic hero and proved that he could be more than just Rahul or Raj. Despite the Herculean hurdles, he had successfully created a new-millennium *Devdas*. All was finally well with the world. Shah Rukh was King Khan again.

King of Bollywood

King Khan. Four-foot-high letters, festooned with sparkling lightbulbs, spelled out Shah Rukh's moniker like a halo around the red-cushioned throne. The audience first heard strains of the theme song, "*Tujhe Dekha Toh Yeh Jana Sanam*" (Only After Seeing You Did I Know), from his most successful film, *DDLJ*. Then, sitting on this throne, Shah Rukh descended, god-like, from the ceiling to the stage, rousing a crescendo of screams and applause from the 3,000-odd people who had gathered at the Swami Vivekananda Convention Centre in Mauritius on March 4, 2006, for the Zee Cine Awards.

The event was a typically Bollywood mix of stars, songs, and dances, interspersed with dozens of awards and just as many gushing acceptance speeches. Shah Rukh was the evening's showstopper. In a spectacular climax, he presented a lengthy tribute to Yash Chopra revisiting the movie milestones of his own career—*Darr*, *DDLJ*, *Veer-Zaara*. At the end of the act, Shah Rukh was joined onstage by Yash, a roster of actors who had worked in Yash's films, and the prime minister of Mauritius, Navinchandra Ramgoolam, who, looking slightly dazzled by the high-wattage company, expressed gratitude that his country could host this extravaganza. There wasn't much restraint or subtlety on display that night, but even by Hindi film kitsch standards, the King Khan throne was overblown; Shah Rukh, after getting off, looked at it and remarked, "This is scary." However, the garish accessory underlined an essential truth: that Shah Rukh Khan was King of Bollywood.

The Zee Television channel has a footprint across 130 countries. The awards show was telecast repeatedly, mostly at prime time, and reached, according to channel estimates, approximately 200 million viewers. These numbers were substantial but not startling. By the turn of the century, Shah Rukh and Bollywood were attracting record crowds in the most unlikely places. Fans were dancing in the aisles in Poland, where a subtitled version of *Kabhi Khushi Kabhie Gham* was released in 2005. In neighboring Germany, passion for Hindi film had already reached such a pitch that a local German-language magazine named *Bollywood Rapid Eye Magazine* was launched in 2006. (The first issue had Shah Rukh on the cover.) The same year, the Virgin store on the Champs-Élysées in Paris was overrun by fans thronging to catch a glimpse of Shah Rukh and his co-stars, Preity Zinta and Rani Mukherjee, who were there to attend the premiere of their film *Veer-Zaara*. When the crowd hit 5,000, the doors of the "megastore" had to be shut.

In the U.K., song and dance seduced the last bastion of high brow: the British Academy of Film and Television Arts. In July 2006, the academy celebrated popular Hindi cinema in a weekend event called BAFTA Goes Bollywood.

There were screenings, felicitations, and photo-ops; Shah Rukh, Karan, and Yash Chopra were among those feted. In an amusing reverse-colonization, the David Lean Room, named after the great British filmmaker and the academy's first chairman, was given a "Bollywood makeover." That is, a wedding services company based in Leicester, the Lakhani Group, artfully arranged Indian thrones, carvings, pedestals, and *diyas* (lamps), and draped the walls with lights.

Bollywood's visibility on the world stage as a vibrant and profoundly popular art form was part of a larger Indian economic and cultural renaissance. From 1990 to 2005, India was the second-fastest-growing country in the world after China. The economy averaged a 6 percent growth, accelerating to 7.5 in 2005. It was as though a sluggish, impoverished nation with venal leaders and weary citizens collectively shook off its fetters and decided to take on the world. Decades ago, on August 15, 1947, the first Indian prime minister, Jawaharlal Nehru, had famously proclaimed: "A moment comes, which comes but rarely in history, when we step out from the old to the new, when an age ends and when the soul of a nation, long suppressed, finds utterance." His historic words, which marked the birth of an independent India, had a special resonance through the 1990s as the country reinvented itself. India, in the new millennium, echoed the India of the 1950s: a nation newly born, taking confident strides into a shining future. At least in urban centers, Indians seized the day with a conviction that just as the twentieth century had belonged to America, the twenty-first would be theirs.

This national optimism came from a buoyant economy, which, unlike China's, was driven not by the state but by the entrepreneur sector. Despite hobbling corruption, populist politics, and crumbling infrastructure, resilient Indian businessmen had created world-class private companies and a booming stock market. India emerged as a world leader in information technology and business outsourcing (in 2006, IT was estimated to have generated revenues of $36 billion, nearly 5 percent of the GDP). *Time* magazine, in a June 19, 2006, cover story titled "India's New Dawn," reported that a new word had appeared in watercooler conversations in America: Bangalored. "It means your job just moved to India without you." The same report also stated that India now had more billionaires than China, and that the ten richest Indians were wealthier than their counterparts in Britain.

A widely quoted 2003 study by Goldman Sachs projected that over the next fifty years, India would be the fastest growing of the world economies. The study computed that by 2040, India would overtake Japan to become the third largest economy in the world after China and the United States. The world was bullish on India. The country was, as a March 2006 *Newsweek* magazine article stated, "the hottest of hot markets." Leading multinational companies such as IBM, Nokia, and Hyundai established a presence in India. In a cover story called "The New India," *Newsweek* reported: "The buzz in financial circles a few months ago was that every man and his dog could raise money to invest in India. Now the thinking is that a man is no longer required."

In cities and small towns across India, boom time was writ large. The incessant ring of cell phones (by 2006, 5 million–odd connections were being added each month), the shiny new malls and multiplexes, the Starbucks-style cafés where a cappuccino cost more than a kilo of lentils, and the dozens of new lifestyle magazines promoting deliriously expensive designer labels all underlined India's new avatar. But a country this large and complex could hardly follow a simplistic script of globalization equals prosperity and happiness.

The changing landscape of India camouflaged more complicated truths: of the 550,000 villages where two-thirds of the country's population lived untouched by progress, of the over 300 million Indians who survived on less than a dollar a day, of the centuries-old aggressions between Hindus and Muslims, rich and poor, powerful and powerless, that simmered and routinely erupted in bombs, murders, and riots. This disconnect in the country was made apparent in the 2004 national elections, in which the ruling, BJP-led National Democratic Alliance was unexpectedly defeated by the Indian National Congress. The NDA marketed itself fiercely on slogans such as "India Shining" and the "Feel Good Factor," and was widely predicted to retain its majority. But the ornery electorate proved to be more sophisticated than politicians, political commentators, and numerous exit polls. Their India was less than shining, so they voted the politicians out.

Despite these difficult subtexts, the India story, of a lumbering Third World nation recasting itself as an economic superstar, caught the global imagination. Influential Western media glowingly reported on the transformation. Headlines such as CAN INDIA FLY? (cover story, *The Economist*, June 3–9, 2006), AN ECONOMY UNSHACKLED (*Foreign Affairs*, July/August 2006), and INDIA INC. (cover story, *Time*, June 26, 2006) became routine. At the 2006 World Economic Forum in Davos, India was the uncontested star. An Indian "dream team" of key industrialists and policymakers, led by the finance minister, P. Chidambaram, fiercely marketed brand India using every resource possible, including Bollywood sound tracks, pashmina shawls, the services of a Michelin-star Indian chef, and billboards that read: INDIA EVERYWHERE. It was.

The economic revival prompted a cultural resurgence. The idea of India altered. The country was no longer an alien planet of snake charmers, where widows were burned on their husband's pyre and cows stopped traffic. First-time visitors still worked their way through malaria, Delhi Belly, and the horror of smiling, skeletal children begging for money, but the culture shock was assuaged by five-star conveniences (whole-wheat pasta imported from Italy, raspberry jam from Maine) and comforting familiar names such as McDonald's, Coke, and Subway. Urban India spoke an international language of world-class restaurants, trendy wine bars, deliciously decadent spas, and brand-name shopping; Burberry, Trussardi, Cartier, Versace set up shops in which one handbag cost more than the monthly wage of most Indians. In 2006, India's first Rolls-Royce showroom opened in Mumbai.

India was a hot new destination and exotic muse—designers as varied as Roberto Cavalli and Jean Paul Gaultier sent models down the runway in India-inspired designs. In turn, local designers showed at fashion weeks in Milan, London, and New York. A new generation of Indian writers furthered the buzz with headline-grabbing million-dollar advances and books translated into dozens of languages. Similarly, at auctions, contemporary Indian art prompted frantic bidding even among non-Indian buyers and broke the million-dollar glass ceiling. It was as though a global consensus had decreed that after decades of false starts and fractured promises, India had finally arrived.

Bollywood, the subcontinent's most distinctive cultural marker, spearheaded brand India. Globally, most other film industries had been flattened out, but Hindi cinema remained the lone David that had not buckled under the Hollywood Goliath. In terms of budgets and revenues generated, Bollywood was still very much the poor cousin—the most expensive Hindi film cost as much as a few minutes of visual effects in the most expensive Hollywood ones—but the sheer number of films produced and the worldwide passion they generated forced the West to pay attention. Though Hindi films were largely unable to penetrate mainstream Western markets—audiences were highly reluctant to sit through three hours of subtitles and songs—critical opinion about Hindi cinema shifted. Once dismissed as gaudy melodrama, Bollywood was now regarded as a unique, substantial, and viable cinematic form.

Leading film festivals courted Bollywood. Programmers from Cannes, Berlin, Toronto, and Venice trawled through film offices in Mumbai looking for the appropriate Hindi film to showcase. Earlier, directors had attempted to tailor their films to Western tastes by sending songless versions, but now the more urbane and gritty Hindi films were rejected by festival scouts for not being "Bollywood enough." Important actors and directors were invited to sit on festival juries. Hindi cinema also came into academic focus. In prestigious British and American universities, anthropologists, scholars, and historians pondered the form and its larger context. The Hindi film industry attained a measure of what New York University anthropologist Dr. Tejaswini Ganti called "cultural legitimacy." That is, "an acceptance from sectors of society, which haven't been their traditional audience base."

Filmmakers toiling in Mumbai's sweltering studios understood that they were now prominent players in a global cultural exchange. Many nursed dreams of creating crossover cinema—a film like Taiwanese director Ang Lee's *Crouching Tiger, Hidden Dragon*, which retained a unique ethnic sensibility but still managed to gross $128 million in the U.S.

However, few were willing to dilute the popular form to reach Western audiences. Bollywood wanted to connect with Hollywood, but only on its own terms. In 2004, Harvey Weinstein, then head of Miramax Films, visited Mumbai and spent an evening chatting with select A-list names, including Shah Rukh, Aditya, and Karan. But the interaction didn't go beyond polite networking. Karan said, "Harvey Weinstein came and went. He didn't call us and we didn't call him. We are the only film country in the world which functions so independently. We don't need foreign studios." But by 2005, the studios had decided that they needed Bollywood. In October that year, Sony Pictures Entertainment announced its first Hindi language film, *Saawariya* (Beloved), a musical romance, with debutant actors, to be directed by Sanjay Bhansali.

This conversation with Hollywood and the world at large was possible because Bollywood no longer functioned like the Wild West. The mafia menace was under control. The major figures were either detained (Abu Salem was arrested in 2002) or had gone underground in the Middle East and Pakistan (in 2003, the U.S. identified Dawood as a "specially designated global terrorist" and froze his assets). The old bazaar-style working had been jettisoned by publicly traded production companies and multiplexes, which delivered computerized collection reports, check payments, and bound scripts.

Of course it was corporatization with a quintessentially Bollywood twist. The industry remained a large joint family with powerful cinematic dynasties like Yash and Aditya firmly entrenched. Some areas defied evolution—hinterland collections were still impossible to monitor, and personal relationships were still far more important than legally binding contracts—but largely, Bollywood bloomed and boomed.

In 2006, a PricewaterhouseCoopers report, *The Indian Entertainment and Media Industry*, estimated that the Indian film industry had grown at an incredible 20 percent in the previous year and predicted similar growth for the next five years. The industry, estimated at 68 billion rupees ($1.5 billion) in 2005, was projected to reach 153 billion rupees ($3.4 billion) by 2010.

Shah Rukh was at the forefront of the Bollywood explosion. Over the years, the hits piled up but Shah Rukh was no longer just an incredibly successful, money-generating actor. He was the emblem of a new India, the repository of 1.1 billion fantasies. In 2005, the Indian government officially conferred on him the status of model citizen. Shah Rukh was given the Padma Shri, the country's fourth-highest civilian award, as recognition of his distinguished service in the arts. In January 2007, it was announced that Shah Rakh would be immortalized in wax at the Madame Tussauds museum in London. He was the third Bollywood actor re-created in wax, after Amitabh Bachchan and Aishwarya Rai.

After fifteen years in the business, Shah Rukh said that he had reached a stage where he recognized his limitations and worked with them. "There is not going to be some new revelation, another layer when this layer is over." But he chose roles that determinedly destroyed the Raj/Rahul construct. In Karan's third film, the 2006 *Kabhi Alvida Naa Kehna* (Never Say Goodbye), a treatise on the modern Indian marriage and infidelity, Shah Rukh played a footballer whose soaring career is cut short by a car accident that leaves him with a limp. He becomes an embittered, grouchy man so seething with resentment, especially at his wife's high-flying career at a fashion magazine, that he's mean even to his six-year-old son. He finally finds laughter and a semblance of peace in the arms of another woman who is also married. Shah Rukh, the iconic Indian romantic hero, Bollywood's ideal husband, is shown having an extramarital affair and even sleeping with another man's wife.

Two months later, he followed up with *Don*. The film was a remake of a 1978 Amitabh Bachchan film, in which Amitabh plays two roles—that of a dreaded don and that of a street performer who happens to resemble the don and is recruited by the police to penetrate the gang. The 2006 version was a *Mission: Impossible*–style thriller in which Shah Rukh plays an international criminal draped in guns, gadgets, drugs, and blondes. The earlier *Don* is essentially the simpleton street performer's story but in Shah Rukh's film, the criminal is king. He wears fabulous clothes and kills with panache. He delivers his signature dialogue—"*Don ka intezaar toh gyaara mulkon ki police kar rahi hai, lekin ek baat samajhlo, don ko pakadna mushkil hi nahin, namumkin hai.*" (Cops from eleven countries are waiting for Don, but understand one thing; to catch Don isn't just difficult, it's impossible.)—with great style and positively revels in his sleek malice. It was almost as if Shah Rukh's career had come full circle and he was doing an upgraded haute couture version of the lethal Ajay from *Baazigar*. Once again, even as Shah Rukh broke necks, murdered informers with carefully aimed golf balls, and generally spread mayhem, the audience stayed connected with him. Both *Kabhi Alvida Naa Kehna* and *Don* were big successes. In January 2007, Shah Rukh went back to television, hosting *Kaun Banega Crorepati*, the Indian version of *Who Wants to Be a Millionaire*. Here, too, he was stepping into the shoes of Amitabh Bachchan, who had earlier hosted two seasons of the show.

As producer, Shah Rukh wanted to push the envelope

even further. He dreamed of creating films as varied as the finely layered drama *Crash* to special effects extravaganzas such as *Superman* and *Batman*. In April 2006, he started a special effects division called Red Chillies VFX. Shah Rukh's ambition was to produce and perhaps even direct a Hindi film that the world would embrace. "I will make a film and the world will know it. From the guy in a cinema hall in Ghatkopar to Steven Spielberg, everyone will watch it."

Shah Rukh was the ultimate brand ambassador for Bollywood and India. He extended the reach of Hindi films, seducing improbable viewers in distant spaces. So in Australia, a fifty-plus housewife named Sandi Mann, who said that Shah Rukh put "passion, magic and delight" in her life, devoted her days to running six Shah Rukh online fan clubs (she belonged to over a hundred), collecting memorabilia, magazines, DVDs, and communing with other fans on the Internet. In 2002, to celebrate Shah Rukh's birthday, Sandi had a star in the Scorpius constellation named Shah Rukh Khan. The following year, she bought him a block of land on the moon. Sandi believed that Shah Rukh had "some kind of grace within him, like he's been touched by God."

These stories of worship were repeated with varying intensity around the globe. Women showed up at Shah Rukh's door, requesting that they be allowed to wash his feet and drink the water. Others wrote him letters in blood (presumably their own). One fan, a young man named Vishal, living in Lucknow, re-christened himself Vishahrukh and believed that he had beat the cancer gnawing at his kidneys because Shah Rukh was on his side.

Shah Rukh's life was now so fantastic that he could no longer tell the difference between acting and reality. He said his life resembled a PS2 game. "I live in an unreal world, my persona is unreal, I myself am unreal." But Shah Rukh had endured both tremendous personal tragedy and overwhelming professional success, and the extremes of this experience gave him the wisdom to stay grounded even as he was venerated and serenaded around the world.

Shah Rukh did not, in the old-fashioned way of superstars, become a delusional megalomaniac. He acknowledged and savored the surreal space he was in but he also remained detached and keenly aware that one day, these intense passions, frenzied screams, and the manic dance of flashbulbs would be silent. Shah Rukh understood well that his deification came with an expiration date. He knew that when viewers tired of his charm, they would subscribe to a new myth.

Shah Rukh said: "I know it's going nowhere. At the end of all the awards, rewards, and adulation, I'll be an old man coming to a function and people will patronizingly call me onstage. I'm saying this because I'm thinking I will be as great as Dilip Kumar or Amitabh Bachchan. Maybe it won't even be that. Maybe I will be a small dusty man in a small dusty town. But that doesn't take away from me entertaining everyone and living each moment with gusto."

It also didn't stop him from nurturing the impossible dream: eternal stardom. Shah Rukh said: "My grandmother used to tell me, '*Zyada photo mat keecho. Har photo ke saath three seconds life ke kam ho jatein hain.*' (Don't have too many pictures taken. Each photograph robs you of three seconds of your life.) I want so many cameras taking pictures of me at the same time that I live only for a moment. The cameras go *khachak!* And somebody asks, 'What happened?' And they say, 'He got photographed to death. He got shot.' I think that would be the nicest way to go."

Sources

This book includes material taken from original interviews that I conducted with the following individuals:

Nikhil Advani
Shaad Ali
Kajal Anand
Harry Baweja
Sanjay Leela Bhansali
Mahesh Bhatt
Mohan Bhise
Raju Bulchandani
Abbas Burmawalla
Mustan Burmawalla
Bala Chandra
Juhi Chawla
Sanjiv Chawla
Ramesh Chibba
Savita Chibba
Vikrant Chibba
Aditya Chopra
Keith D'Costa
Eric D'Souza
Rachel Dwyer
Tejaswani Ganti
Subhash Ghai
Ashutosh Gowariker
Karan Johar
Barry John
Prasoon Joshi
Kwanghuyun Jung
Nasreen Munni Kabir
Prahlad Kakkar
Raj Kanwar

Raj (Colonel) Kapoor
Surinder Kapoor
Mani Kaul
Renuka Keron
Ahsan Khan
Farah Khan
Gauri Khan
Laila Raza Khan
Mansoor Khan
Shah Rukh Khan
Vivek Khushalani
Pradip Krishen
Snehal Lakhani
Sandi Mann
Rakesh Maria
Bhavanimal Mathur
Sushila Mathur
Rajiv Mehra
Ashok Mehta
Ketan Mehta
Mansoor Khan Mir
Aziz Mirza
Haroon Mirza
Devyani Ogale
Chikki Pandey
Avtar Panesar
Renu Poswal
Gyan Prakash
Vipul Prakash
Nishi Prem
Savita Raisingh
Gita Ram
D. Ranganathan
Deejay Rekha
Rituraj
Arnab Roy
Sanjoy Roy
Rohini Salian
Santaram
Divya Seth
Bharat Shah
Kundan Shah
Rashesh Shah
Raman Sharma
Bhavesh Sheth
Amrita Singh
Gopal Singh
Tirlochan Singh
Santosh Sivan
D. Sivanandhan
Lekh Tandon
Benny Thomas
Neeru Tiwari
Tejinder Tiwari
Ram Gopal Varma
Viveck Vaswani
Seetha Venkateshwaran
Vishahrukh

References

1. Bollywood Dreams

Banker, Ashok. *Bollywood*. New Delhi: Penguin Books India, 2001.

Das, Gurcharan. *India Unbound*. New Delhi: Penguin Books India, 2002.

Dyer, Richard. *Stars*. London: British Film Institute, 1998.

Ganti, Tejaswini. *Bollywood: A Guidebook to Popular Indian Cinema*. New York: Routledge, 2004.

Hansen, Kathryn. "The Indar Sabha Phenomenon: Public Theatre and Consumption in Greater India (1853–1956)." In *Pleasure and the Nation, The History, Politics and Consumption of Public Culture in India,* edited by Rachel Dwyer and Christopher Pinney, 76–114. New Delhi: Oxford University Press, 2001.

Joshi, Lalit Mohan, ed. *Bollywood: Popular Indian Cinema*. London: Dakini Ltd., 2001.

Kabir, Nasreen Munni. "The Outer World of Shah Rukh Khan," Chapter 7. *The Inner/Outer World of Shah Rukh Khan,* DVD. Produced by Hyphen Films for Channel 4 and Red Chillies International. U.K. and Mumbai: Eros International, 2005.

Kaur, Raminder, and Ajay J. Sinha. *Bollyworld: Popular Indian Cinema Through a Transnational Lens*. New Delhi: Sage Publications, 2005.

Khosla, Mukesh. "Prime Time for Couch Potatoes." Tribuneindia .com, December 19, 1999, http://www.tribuneindia.com/1999/99dec19/sundayhead2.htm.

Larkin, Brian. "Indian Films and Nigerian Lovers: Media and the Creation of Parallel Modernities." *Africa: Journal of the International African Institute*, vol. 67, no. 3 (1997): http://www.jstor.org.

Perry, Alex. "Shah Rukh Khan Bollywood's Brightest Star." *Time Asia*, October 4, 2004.

PricewaterhouseCoopers. *The Indian Entertainment and Media Industry Unravelling the Potential*. Report presented at FICCI-FRAMES Convention on Entertainment and Media, Mumbai, March 22–24, 2006.

Raheja, Dinesh, and Jitendra Kothari. *Indian Cinema: The Bollywood Saga*. New Delhi: Roli & Janssen, 2004.

Rangoonwalla, Firoze. "The Emergence of Talkies." In *Encyclopaedia of Hindi Cinema*, editorial board Gulzar and Govind Nihalani, Saibal Chatterjee, 43–59. New Delhi: Encyclopaedia Britannica, Inc. Mumbai: Popular Prakashan Pvt. Ltd., 2003.

Safire, William. *On Language*: "The New Black." *New York Times*, May 30, 2004, http://select.nytimes.com/search/restricted/article.

Sarma, Nirupama. The Communication Initiative—The Changing Face of Indian Media (Fall 1998). Comminit.com: http://www.comminit.com/strategicthinking/streview/sld-2120.html.

Shahane, Girish. "Ham and Eggs." *Time Out Mumbai*, December 31, 2004–January 13, 2005.

Swaminathan, Roopa. *Stardust*. New Delhi: Penguin Books India, 2004.

Tharoor, Shashi. *India: From Midnight to the Millennium*. New Delhi: Penguin Books India, 2000.

Thomas, Rosie. *Melodrama and the Negotiation of Morality in Mainstream Hindi Film*. The British Library, www.bl.uk.

2. Peshawar: The Street of the Storytellers

Awasthi, Kavita. "Fathers and Sons." *Movie*, December 1997.

Bacher, John. "Islamic Nonviolent Resistance in the Struggle for Indian Independence." *Peace Magazine*, December 1988/January 1989, www.peacemagazine.org/archive/v04n6p19a.htm.

Banerji, Rahul. "In Pathan Country, Shah Rukh Is King." *Asian Age,* March 19, 2004, http://www.asianage.com.

Chatterjee, Gayatri. *Mother India*. London: British Film Institute, 2002.

Cities of Pakistan Information Portal, http://www.muskurahat.com/pakistan/cities/Peshawar.asp.

Dalrymple, William. *City of Djinns*. Middlesex: Penguin Books, 2003.

Das, Gurcharan. *India Unbound*. New Delhi: Penguin Books India, 2002.

Desai, Meghnad. *Nehru's Hero Dilip Kumar in the Life of India*. New Delhi: The Lotus Collection, 2004.

Guha, Ramachandra. "They Too Wrote Our History." *Outlook*, August 22, 2005.

Jain, Madhu. *The Kapoors: The First Family of Indian Cinema*. New Delhi: Penguin Books India, 2005.

Joshi, Lalit Mohan. "Bollywood 100 Years." In *Bollywood Popular Indian Cinema,* edited by Lalit Mohan Joshi, 12–55. London: Dakini Ltd., 2001.

Malik, Amita. "The Golden Age." In *Encyclopaedia of Hindi Cinema,* editorial board Gulzar and Govind Nihalani, Saibal Chatterjee, 61–74. New Delhi: Encyclopaedia Britannica, Inc. Mumbai: Popular Prakashan Pvt. Ltd., 2003.

Manto, Saadat Hassan. *Stars from Another Sky: The Bombay Film World of the 1940s*. Translated by Khalid Hasan. New Delhi: Penguin Books India, 1998.

Prakash, Shruti. "When Shahrukh's Uncle Outfoxed Jinnah." *Hindustan Times*, August 18, 1997.

Raheja, Dinesh, and Jitendra Kothari. *Indian Cinema: The Bollywood Saga*. New Delhi: Roli & Janssen, 2004.

Seth, Jayesh. *Ek Aitihasik Karishma*. Documentary produced by Sterling Investments Pvt. Ltd. Mumbai: Shemaroo Video, 2004.

Shariff, Faisal. "Peshawar: The Shah Rukh Connection." Rediff.com, May 2004, http://specials.rediff.com/news/2004/may/31s101.htm.

Spear, Percival. *A History of India* 2. Middlesex: Penguin Books, 1970.

3. A "Lady-Killer" Is Born

Chaudhuri, Shantanu Ray. *Icons from Bollywood*. New Delhi: Penguin Books India, 2005.

Dalrymple, William. *City of Djinns*. Middlesex: Penguin Books, 2003.

Haham, Connie. *Enchantment of the Mind: Manmohan Desai's Films*. New Delhi: The Lotus Collection, 2006.

Kabir, Nasreen Munni. *Talking Films: Conversations on Hindi Cinema with Javed Akhtar*. New Delhi: Oxford University Press, 1999.

Mohamed, Khalid. *To Be or Not to Be: Amitabh Bachchan*. Mumbai: Saraswati Creations, 2002.

Raheja, Dinesh, and Jitendra Kothari. *Indian Cinema: The Bollywood Saga*. New Delhi: Roli & Janssen, 2004.

Rao, Maithili. "Rebels Without a Cause." In *Encyclopaedia of Hindi Cinema,* editorial board Gulzar and Govind Nihalani, Saibal Chatterjee, 93–116. New Delhi: Encyclopaedia Britannica, Inc. Mumbai: Popular Prakashan Pvt. Ltd., 2003.

Somaaya, Bhawana. *Amitabh Bachchan: The Legend*. New Delhi: Macmillan India Ltd., 1999.

Tharoor, Shashi. *India: From Midnight to the Millennium*. New Delhi: Penguin Books India, 2000.

4. No-Man's-Land

Ghosh, Biswadeep. *Hall of Fame: Shah Rukh Khan*. Mumbai: Magna Publishing Co. Ltd., 2004.

St. Columbas.net. The official Web site of St. Columba's School, New Delhi, http://www.stcolumbas.net.

5. You Should Be in the Movies

Joshi, Lalit Mohan. "India's Art House Cinema." *Imagine Asia: A Celebration of South Asian Film*, 2005, http://www.bfi.org.uk/Features/imagineasia/guide/contemporary/India-arthouse.html.

Rao, Maithili. "Rebels Without a Cause." In *Encyclopaedia of Hindi Cinema*, editorial board Gulzar and Govind Nihalani, Saibal Chatterjee, 93–116. New Delhi: Encyclopaedia Britannica, Inc. Mumbai: Popular Prakashan Pvt. Ltd., 2003.

Roy, Arundhati. *In Which Annie Gives It Those Ones: The Original Screenplay*. New Delhi: Penguin Books India, 2003.

Saha, Atanu. "English Theater: New Directions." *The Tribune*, June 29, 2001, http://www.tribuneindia.com/2001/20010629/art-trib.htm#1.

6. Scandal in Panscheel Park

Das, Mahua. "The Faujis Are Here!" *Showtime*, 1989.

Indiatelevision.com. "A Snapshot of Indian Television History," http://www.indiantelevision.com/indianbroadcast/history/historyoftele.htm.

Jain, Madhu. "Going to the Movies." *India Today*, August 11, 1989.

Mathai, Palakunnathu, G. "Doordarshan: A Sponsored Success." *India Today*, June 30, 1984.

Mitra, Sumit. "Television: The Spreading Screen." *India Today*, December 31, 1985.

7. The Television Years

Mohamed, Khalid. "A Garden, a Director & The Idiot." *The Times of India Sunday Review*, December 16, 1990.

8. Life After Death

Raheja, Dinesh, and Jitendra Kothari. *Indian Cinema: The Bollywood Saga*. New Delhi: Roli & Janssen, 2004.

Somaaya, Bhawana. *Salaam Bollywood: The Pain and the Passion*. Surrey: Spantech & Lancer, 1999.

9. Super Brat

Analysis. Wikipedia. http://en.wikipedia.org/wiki/The_Idiot_(novel).

Aura of the Stars, June 1994.

Cine Blitz, "Shah Rukh and Deepa's Steamy Scenes Revealed!" September 1992.

Dwyer, Rachel. "Shooting Stars: The Indian Film Magazine." In *Pleasure and the Nation, The History, Politics and Consumption of Public Culture in India,* edited by Rachel Dwyer and Christopher Pinney, 247–285. New Delhi: Oxford University Press, 2001.

Gonsalves, Stardust. "A Bonfire of Vanities." *Screen*, September 4, 1992.

Katiyar, Arun. "Shah Rukh Khan on the Road to Stardom." *India Today*, August 15, 1992.

Kazmi, Nikhat. Review of *Deewana. Times of India*, June 28, 1992.

Khan, Shah Rukh, in conversation with Nasreen Munni Kabir. Outtakes for *The Inner/Outer World of Shah Rukh Khan,* DVD. Produced by Hyphen Films for Channel 4 and Red Chillies International. U.K. and Mumbai: Eros International, 2005.

Prem, Nishi. "Will Shah Rukh's Intensity Burn Him Out!?" *Stardust*, September 1991.

———. "Can the Industry Digest Shah Rukh Khan's Arrogance?" *Stardust*, September 1992.

———. "Mrs. Shah Rukh Khan: I Am No Longer Insecure." *Stardust*, February 1993.

Raheja, Dinesh, and Jitendra Kothari. *Indian Cinema: The Bollywood Saga*. New Delhi: Roli & Janssen, 2004.

Rahman, M. "A Film Cause Celebre." *India Today*, July 15, 1992.

Zankar, Anil. "Heroes and Villains: Good versus Evil." In *Encyclopaedia of Hindi Cinema,* editorial board Gulzar and Govind Nihalani, Saibal Chatterjee, 355–366. New Delhi: Encyclopaedia Britannica, Inc. Mumbai: Popular Prakashan Pvt. Ltd., 2003.

10. Murder, He Wrote

Dwyer, Rachel. *Yash Chopra*. London: British Film Institute, 2002.

Filmfare. "Best Actor: Shah Rukh Khan, Baazigar. Critics's Best Performance: SRK, Kabhi Haan Kabhi Naa," March 1994.

Yash Raj Films. http://yashrajfilms.com/profile/yash1.htm.

11. The Brave-Hearted Takes the Box Office

Brijnath, Rohit, and Anupama Chopra. "Lord of All He Surveys." *India Today*, March 23, 1998.

Chandra, Anupama. "Goodbye to Formula?" *India Today*, November 30, 1995.

Chatterjee, Saibal. "Back to the Movies." *Outlook*, January 17, 1996.

Chopra, Anupama. "Ready for the Raunchy." *India Today*, January 8, 2001.

———. *Dilwale Dulhania Le Jayenge*. London: British Film Institute, 2002.

Deshpande, Satish. *Contemporary India: A Sociological View*. New Delhi: Penguin Books India, 2003.

Dwyer, Rachel. *All You Want Is Money, All You Need Is Love, Sex and Romance in Modern India*. London: Cassell, 2000.

Kapoor, Sanjay. "Liberal Face, Hot Heads." *Asiaweek*, March 17, 2000, http://www.asiaweek.com/asiaweek/magazine/2000/1317/viewpoint.

Kazmi, Nikhat. *Ire in the Soul: Bollywood's Angry Years*. New Delhi: HarperCollins Publishers, 1996.

Masand, Rajeev. "Look Now, He's Changing." *Indian Express*, August 22, 2000.

Pillai, Jitesh. "Best Actor Shah Rukh Khan." *Filmfare*, April 1996.

Rajshri Web site. *Sooraj Barjatya: The Man with the Midas Touch*, http://www.rajshri.com/sooraj.html.

Rao, Maithili. "Between Rebellion and Submission." *Himalmag*, vol. 12 (9), 1999, http://himalmag.com/99Sep/between.htm.

Swami, Praveen. "Furore Over a Film." *Frontline*, December 19, 1998–January 01, 1999, http://www.flonnet.com/Fl1526/15260430/htm.

Tharoor, Shashi. *India: From Midnight to the Millennium*. New Delhi: Penguin Books India, 2000.

Uberoi, Patricia. "The Diaspora Comes Home: Disciplining Desire in *DDLJ*." *Contributions to Indian Sociology*, vol. 32: no. 2, July–December 1988.

Varma, Pavan K. *The Great Indian Middle Class*. New Delhi: Penguin Books India, 1999.

12. A Global Icon

Aiyar, Shankar V., and Anupama Chopra. "Boy Meets Girl." *India Today*, January 31, 2000.

Chopra, Anupama. "Bye-bye Bharat." *India Today*, December 1, 1997.

———. "Candy Floss Films." *India Today*, February 9, 1998.

———. "Golden Goose." *India Today*, November 1, 1999.

———. "Cry Baby." *India Today*, December 3, 2001.

Choudhary, Anuradha. "Smile, Karan Johar Has the Last Laugh." *Filmfare*, February 2002.

Film Source. "UK Films Opening for: 1989 . . . 2006 GBP." *Nielsen EDI,* March 3, 2006.

Dharma Productions Web site. http://www1.dharma-production.com.

Joshi, Namrata. "The K. Jo Effect." *Outlook*, December 22, 2003.

Khatib, Shabana. "KG3: What Makes Karan So Garam?" *Stardust*, December 2001.

Pathak, Rahul. "The New Generation." *India Today*, January 31, 1994.

Pendakur, Manjunath, and Radha Subramanyam. "India Part I: Indian Cinema Beyond National Borders." In *New Patterns in Global Television*, edited by John Sinclair, Elizabeth Jacka, and Stuart Cunningham, 67–82. New Delhi: Oxford University Press, 1996.

Pillai, Jitesh. "The Method to His Madness." *Times of India*, May 7, 1998.

"Tuning In to the Indian Youth." *Sources of Cool: India Study 2001*. MTV Asia LDC.

13. Brand SRK

Aiyar, Shankar V., and Anupama Chopra. "Waiting for Action." *India Today*, May 25, 1998.

Bamzai, Kaveree, and Sandeep Unnithan. "Show Business." *India Today*, February 21, 2003.

Bogdanovich, Peter. *Who the Hell's in It*. New York: Alfred A. Knopf, 2004.

Bollywood: Emerging Business Trends & Growth Drivers. YES Bank Ltd., Film & Television Producers' Guild of India, 2005.

Chopra, Anupama, and Nandita Chowdhury. "The New Bollywood Brigade." *India Today*, June 28, 1999.

Gahlaut, Kanika. "Salebrity." *India Today*, December 20, 2004.

Indiatelevision.com, "Ads with Celebrities Draw High Recall—Study," December 27, 2002, http://www.indiantelevision.com/mam/headlines/y2k2/dec/decmam43.htm.

Kabir, Nasreen Munni. *Bollywood: The Indian Cinema Story*. London: Channel 4 Books, 2001.

Mahurkar, Uday, and Anna M.M. Vetticad. "Leisure Storeys." *India Today*, September 24, 2001.

Nazareth, Marianne de. "If It's Jeans, I Want John's." *Deccan Herald*. August 26, 2005, http://www.deccanherald/deccanherald/Aug262005/living83232005825.asp.

Pillai, Jitesh. "One on One." *Filmfare,* May 1998.

———. "Urban Legend. The Final Cut: Shah Rukh Khan." Indiatimes.com, August 2001, http://downloads.movies.indiatimes.com/site/august2001/infocus.html.

Rabo India. *The Indian Motion Picture Industry: A Structural and Financial Perspective*. Report presented at the FICCI-FRAMES Convention on Entertainment and Media, Mumbai, March 14–16, 2003.

Sehgal, Rashme. "Mad, Bad and Successful." *Times of India*, May 24, 1999.

Sharma, Aparna. "India's Experience with the Multiplex." Seminar Web Edition, June 5, 2003, http://www.india-seminar.com/2003/525/525aparnasharma.htm.

Somaaya, Bhawana. *The Story So Far*. Mumbai: Indian Express Newspapers (Bom) Ltd., 2003.

Suresh, K. "The Evergreen Celebrity." *The Hindu Business Online*. March 17, 2005, http://www.thehindubusinessonline.com/Catalyst/2005/03/17/stories/2005031700100200.htm.

14. Mobsters and Movies

Ashraf, Firdaus Syed, and Suparn Verma. "Gulshan Kumar Shot Dead!" 1997, Rediff.com. http://rediff.com/news/aug/12super.htm.

Bhatnagar, Rakesh. "Abu Salem Will Find It Tough in Courts." *DNA*, November 12, 2005.

Bhatt, Mahesh. "We're Still Scared after All These Years." *DNA. Sunday*, November 13, 2005.

Bhuse, Nishant. "Kya Apna Bombay Aa Gaya?" *MidDay*, November 12, 2005.

Bobb, Dilip, and Coomi Kapoor. "Crackdown in Bombay." *India Today*, May 15, 1985.

Chandra, Anupama. "Into Production." *Sunday*, January 1993.

Chopra, Anupama. "Panic Sets In." *India Today*, September 8, 1997.

Joshi, Charu Lata. "Rolls Royce in Dawoodland." *Outlook*, August 25, 1997.

Kapoor, Coomi. "The Gang Bang." *India Today*, October 31, 1983.

Ketkar, Prafulla. "The Changing Character of the Mumbai Mafia." *Institute of Peace & Conflict Studies*. Article 972, February 28, 2003, http://www.ipcs.org/newkashmirlevel2.jsp?Action=showView 2kValue=928subcatid=null8mod=null.

Koppikar, Smruti. "Murder in Mumbai." *India Today*, August 25, 1997.

Koppikar, Smruti, Anupama Chopra, and Anita Anand. "Suspect No. 1." *India Today*, September 29, 1992.

Najmi, Quaied, and Dnyanesh Jathar. "Don in Twilight Zone." *The Week*, March 9, 2003.

Pillai, Ajith. "The Mafia Calls the Shots." Outlook-India.com, August 25, 1997, http://outlookindia.com.

Pradhan, Bharathi S. *Colas, Cars & Communal Harmony*. Bombay: India Book Distributors (Bombay) Ltd., 2003.

Raval, Sheela. "In Don's Company." *India Today*, April 22, 2002.

Sanghvi, Vir. "Godfather III: The Terrorist." *Sunday Hindustan Times*, November 13, 2005.

Sivanandhan, D. *Organized Crime Gangs in Mumbai City.* 1999–2000. Reference report used by Mumbai Police Crime Branch.

Swami, Praveen. "The Stars and the Dons." *Frontline,* August 17–30, 2002.

Vasuki, S. N. "Gang Wars Battle for Supremacy." *India Today,* December 11, 1988.

Zaidi, S. Hussain. *Black Friday: The True Story of the Bombay Bomb Blasts.* New Delhi: Penguin Books India, 2002.

———. "Salem's List." *Mumbai Mirror,* November 13, 2005.

———. "Godfathers No More." *Mumbai Mirror,* November 20, 2005.

15. The Fall from Grace

Akhtar, Shameem. "Kaho Na Star Hai." Outlookindia.com, February 21, 2000. http://www.outlookinida.com/full.asp?fname=profilesFodname=20002214&sid=1.

Bhatkal, Satyajit. *The Spirit of Lagaan.* Mumbai: Popular Prakashan Pvt. Ltd., 2002.

Bhatti, Meeta. "Out and About." *Indian Express,* January 28, 2000, http://www.indianexpress.com/ie/daily/20000128/ien28005.html.

Chopra, Anupama. Review of *Phir Bhi Dil Hai Hindustani. India Today,* January 31, 2000, http://www.indiatoday.com/itoday/20000131/cinema.html.

———. "Dreams Limited." *India Today,* November 26, 2001.

Christopher, James. Review of *Asoka, The Times,* quoted in "Conqueror Cornered: *Asoka* Abroad" by Ishara Bhasi, *India Today,* November 26, 2001.

Deb, Sandipan. "Raju Ban Gaya Businessman." Outlookindia.com, December 25, 2000, http://outlookindia.com/fullprint.asp?choice=2&fodname=20001225&fname=Cover+Story.

Desai, MSM. "Box Office." *Screen India,* February 4, 2000, http://www.screenindia.com/feb04/film5.htm.

Fernandes, Vivek. "Now, It's H for Hrithik!" Rediff.com, May 29, 2000, http://www.rediff.com/entertai/2000/may/29book.htm.

Indiafm.com. "The Coke-Pepsi War: Hrithik in Crossfire." 2000, http://www.indiafm.com/scoop/may/1205coke/index.shtml.

Jain, Madhu. "Mister Sexy." *India Today on the Net,* March 20, 2000, http://www.indiatoday.com/itoday/20000320/cover.html.

Kazmi, Nikhat. Review of *Phir Bhi Dil Hai Hindustani*. *Sunday Times*, January 23, 2000.

Khambatta, Lara. "Phir Bhi Aziz Sticks to His Guns." *Stardust*, February 2000.

Khan, Gauri. "I Believe." *Savvy*, May 20, 2000.

Masand, Rajeev. "Phirbhi, phir bhi . . . SRK Debates the Fate of His Film." *MidDay*, January 29, 2000.

Mohamed, Khalid. "Shahnama." *The Sunday Times of India*, September 23, 2001.

Pillai, Jitesh. "I Object to Personalised Criticism." *Times of India*, January 30, 2000.

Rahman, Maseeh. "A Cola War Gets Personal." TIMEasia.com, June 12, 2000, http://www.time.com/time/asia/magazine/2000/0612/india.html.

Shiekh, Mushtaq. *The Making of Asoka*. New Delhi: HarperCollins Publishers India, 2001.

Stardust, "Fracas Over a Flop: Why Is Shah Rukh Blaming the Media for His Film's Failure?" March 2000.

Stardust International. "Shocking Details!" May 2000.

16. Devdas

Bamzai, Kaveree, Manish Dubey, and Aditi Arora. "India's Cannes Party." *India Today on the Net*, June 3, 2002, http://www.indiatoday.com/Itoday/20020-603/cinema.shtml&SET=T.

Bhatt, Arunkumar. "Bharat Shah Convicted." *The Hindu*, October 1, 2003, http://www.thehindu.com/2003/10/01/stories/2003100102501200.htm.

Chopra, Anupama. "Shah Rukh Khan Star Stuck." *India Today*, March 24, 2003.

Corliss, Richard. "Cannes Kiss Off." *Time*, June 3, 2002, http://www.time.com/time/asia/magazine/article/0,13673,501020610-257165,00.html.

Dwyer, Rachel. *100 Bollywood Films*. New Delhi: The Lotus Collection, 2005.

Dyer, Richard. *Stars*. London: British Film Institute, 1998.

Filmfare, "The Filmfare Power List." December 2003.

The Free Press Journal. "After Big B Temple, It's Shah Rukh's Museum in Kolkota," January 30, 2002.

———. "Shah Rukh Fans Line Up for 'Devdas' Carnival." July 24, 2002.

Malcom, Derek. Review of *Devdas*. *The Guardian*, May 28, 2002, http://film.guardian.co.uk/cannes2002/story/0,723658,00.html.

Patil, Prasad. "Salem Never Called Me: Shah Rukh." *MidDay*, December 4, 2002, http://web.mid-day.com/1news/city/2002/december/38071.htm.

Pearson, Bryan. "Bollywood's Shah Guilty in Mob Case." Variety.com, September 30, 2003, http://www.variety.com/article/VR1117893245?categoryid=19&cs=1.

Raval, Sheela. "'Hostile' Stars Change the Script." *India Today*, December 6, 2002.

Raval, Sheela, and Anupama Chopra. "Slow Motion." *India Today*. April 15, 2002.

———. "Devdas: Bollywood's Gamble." *India Today*, May 20, 2002.

Reynolds, Nigel, and Amit Roy. "Bollywood Looks the Part in Cannes." *Telegraph*, May 24, 2002, http://www.telegraph.co.uk/news/main.

Shiekh, Mushtaq. *Devdas: The Indian Hamlet*. Mumbai: Mega Bollywood Pvt. Ltd., 2002.

Somaaya, Bhawana. *The Story So Far*. Mumbai: Indian Express Newspapers (Bom) Ltd., 2003.

17. King of Bollywood

Bafta.com, "BAFTA Goes Bollywood." 2006, http://bafta.com/site/Page375.html.

Baker, Aryn. "Bangalore Goes Global." *Time Asia*, June 19, 2006.

Baliga, Shashi. "I Don't Live in La La Land." *Filmfare*, September 2004.

Bhutani, Surender. "Shah-Rukh Polish Fans Clap, Dance Away." Hindustantimes.com, July 26, 2005, http://www.hindustantimes.com/news/181_1441967,00110003.htm.

Das, Gurcharan. "The India Model." *Foreign Affairs*, July/August

2006, http://www.foreignaffairs.org/20060701faessay85401/gurcharan-das/the-india-model.html.

"India, Darling of Davos, Seeks Investment." *ABC News*, January 28, 2006, http://abcnews.go.com/Business/wireStory?id=1553154&ad=true.

Indiatimes.com, "Bollywood Going Global: Shah Rukh." June 13, 2006, http://timesofindia.com/articleshow/1641907.cms.

Landler, Mark. "'India Everywhere' in the Alps." NYTimes.com, January 26, 2006, http://select.nytimes.com/.

Long, Simon. "Now for the Hard Part: A Survey of Business in India." *The Economist*, June 3, 2006.

Mehta, Suketu. "Welcome to Bollywood." *National Geographic*, February 2005.

Mishra, Pankaj. "The Myth of the New India." NYTimes.com, July 6, 2006, http://www.nytimes.com/2006/07/06/opinion/06mishra.html.

Mohan, C. Raja. "India and the Balance of Power." *Foreign Affairs*, July/August 2006, http://www.foreignaffairs.org/20060701.

PricewaterhouseCoopers. *The Indian Entertainment and Media Industry Unravelling the Potential*. Report presented at FICCI-FRAMES Convention on Entertainment and Media, Mumbai, March 22–24, 2006.

Purie, Aroon. "Hype & Hardsell." *India Today* on the Net, February 13, 2006, http://www.indiatoday.com/itoday/20060213/cover.html&SET=T.

Sangghvi, Malavika. "Even When I'm in Bed, I'm On Stage." *Sunday Times of India,* January 2, 2005.

Sharma, Ruchir. "Taking It Easy." MSNBC.com, March 6, 2006, http://www.msnbc.msn.com/id/11568880/site/newsweek/print/1.

Tejpal, Tarun. "The New Masters." *Asiaweek*, August 8, 1997, http://www.pathfinder.com/asiaweek/97/0808/cs10.html.

Wilson, Dominic, and Roopa Purushothaman. "Dreaming with BRICs: The Path to 2050 Global Economics Paper No. 99." GS Global Economics Web site, October 1, 2003, http://www.gs.com/insight/research/reports/99.pdf.

Yash Raj Films official Web site. http://yashrajfilms.com/.

Zakaria, Fareed. "India Rising." MSNBC.com, March 6, 2006, http://www.msnbc.msn.com/id/11571348/site/newsweek/print/1/.
Zee Telefilms Ltd. *LIC Zee Cine Awards.* Television program, Mumbai: Zee Television, March 4, 2005.

Index